TikTok

Digital Media and Society Series

TikTok

Creativity and Culture in Short Video

D. BONDY VALDOVINOS KAYE
JING ZENG
PATRIK WIKSTRÖM

polity

First published in 2022 by Polity Press

Polity Press
65 Bridge Street
Cambridge CB2 1UR, UK

Polity Press
101 Station Landing
Suite 300
Medford, MA 02155, USA

ISBN-13: 978-1-5095-4892-7
ISBN-13: 978-1-5095-4893-4(pb)

A catalogue record for this book is available from the British Library.

Library of Congress Control Number: 2021950725

Typeset in 10.25 on 13pt Scala
by Fakenham Prepress Solutions, Fakenham, Norfolk NR21 8NL
Printed and bound in Great Britain by CPI Group (UK) Ltd, Croydon

The publisher has used its best endeavours to ensure that the URLs for external websites referred to in this book are correct and active at the time of going to press. However, the publisher has no responsibility for the websites and can make no guarantee that a site will remain live or that the content is or will remain appropriate.

Every effort has been made to trace all copyright holders, but if any have been overlooked the publisher will be pleased to include any necessary credits in any subsequent reprint or edition.

For further information on Polity, visit our website:
politybooks.com

Contents

Acknowledgements

This book is the product of an unexpected collaboration that has given the three of us an opportunity to work closely together, share ideas, and grow as scholars. There are several individuals without whom this project would not have been possible, above all the many informants who gave us the precious gift of their time and insights. Thank you to the members of JazzTok and their friends who generously and enthusiastically took part in distance interviews via Zoom in early 2021.

We value our many incredible colleagues at LabEx Industries Culturelles & Création Artistique at the Sorbonne University, Paris Nord, at the Institut für Kommunikationswissenschaft und Medienforschung at the University of Zurich, and at the Digital Media Research Centre at Queensland University of Technology and greatly appreciate their insightful critiques, stimulating conversations, and enduring friendship. We thank the TikTok Cultures Research Network for creating a space for us to develop ideas and to learn from the continuously emerging voices.

We are deeply grateful to Mary Savigar and Stephanie Homer at Polity for their guidance, encouragement, and kindness throughout this process. Thanks also to our two anonymous reviewers for providing instructive feedback that has strengthened this book. Special thanks to River Juno for the beautiful illustrations featured throughout this book.

Finally, thank you to our family members and close friends for giving us their love and support, offering thoughts and suggestions for this book, and putting up for so many months with our incessant talk about the latest TikTok trends.

Figures

Tables

Introduction
Creativity and Culture in Short Video

On 13 April 2021, a video[1] was uploaded to the short video platform TikTok in which a pair of hands are shown holding a butcher's knife, a banana, and a cutting board. The video is polished and of professional quality, presenting the aesthetic of a do-it-yourself (DIY) life hack video. The disembodied hands begin to use the massive knife to peel a banana, cutting out large chunks of the fruit with each blade stroke. The song playing in the background is 'Chug Jug with You',[2] recorded in late 2018 by YouTuber Leviathan.

After about 15 seconds, just as the disembodied chef presents the boxy, mangled, albeit peeled banana,[3] the video abruptly cuts to a young man in a sparse room sitting motionless and expressionless in front of a banana on his desk. Wordlessly, he picks up the banana and peels it with his hands. Without changing his expression, he presents the peeled banana to the camera, gestures to it with his hand (see Figure 0.1), and leans forward to end the recording while shaking his head in disbelief, as if to say, 'are you serious?' The second part of the video appears to be completely unedited and has no music at all. The only sounds that can be heard are the peeling of the banana and the faint voices and noises from the room where the young man is sitting.

The video was created by @Khaby.Lame (Khabane Lame), a Senegalese Italian man, who was 21 at the time. Khaby began posting videos in mid-2020 after losing his job in a factory in Chivasso, a commune in Turin, during the 2020 coronavirus pandemic. His early TikTok videos were either silent or in Italian, aimed at local audiences, but upon discovering that

Figure 0.1. A 'Stitch' of @khaby.lame demonstrating how to peel a banana in a video shared in April 2021.

his life hack reaction videos could go viral he stopped posting in Italian and kept going with the recipe that seemed to work (Horowitz & Lorenz, 2021).

Life hack videos, where creators demonstrate novel or creative solutions to minor everyday problems, and their parody counterparts, where creators perform a simple task in a ridiculous and impractical manner, portrayed as a life hack, translate well into the short format of TikTok. Unlike videos shared on platforms such as YouTube or Facebook, TikTok videos generally do not include a title that might differentiate between the serious and the silly. Users also encounter videos by scrolling through an endlessly refreshed feed, as opposed to selecting videos to watch from a homepage or menu. Therefore, when users scroll through a new 30-second life hack video, it can be difficult to spot from the start whether it is serious or a parody.

The video is using a TikTok feature called Stitch, which allows users to clip a section of the video they were just watching and to stitch their own content at the end of it, so as to create a new video. Khaby is skilfully using the Stitch feature to create an ironic juxtaposition between the first and the second video – a comedic device frequently used in short-format videos. As the video begins, the viewer is watching what appears to be an earnest life hack for bananas. Moments pass and the viewer starts to wonder: 'Wait... Why are they performing surgery on a banana? Why don't they just peel it?' Right at the point where viewers realize they are being trolled and are about to scroll away, the video cuts to Khaby. As a surrogate for the viewer, Khaby is silent, raw, and dominated by his facial expressions, which speak volumes as to what he thinks about the life hack video. Khaby reflects on his talent and technique simply by noting that 'it's [his] face and [...] expressions which make people laugh' (Horowitz & Lorenz, 2021).

During the three months immediately after being uploaded, Khaby's 30-second banana-peeling video attracted 255 million views and 36 million likes. Khaby continued posting videos by following this successful recipe and, combined, his videos have attracted billions of views and likes and have expanded Khaby's fanbase from basically zero to 70 million in only three months. As of mid-2021, his account is the third most followed account on TikTok, and his globally diverse following outnumbers the population of Italy, millions of users viewing, engaging, and creating their own videos on the basis of his content.

Khaby's simple banana-peeling video is a powerful example of how the short-video format is used to weave a complex tapestry of internet practices and memes and how it encapsulates many of the practices, phenomena, and challenges of creativity and culture that we are exploring in this volume. We will return to Khaby's career in later chapters; but before that we introduce our excursion in the next section by conceptualizing TikTok as a platform. This section discusses what we consider to be a short video trend in digital media culture. We then acknowledge the transformational impact of the COVID-19 pandemic on digital media and the rapid growth of TikTok's user base. Before finishing the chapter by outlining the structure of the book, we discuss the emergent field of TikTok scholarship and four perspectives we employ in our study of creativity and culture in short video.

TikTok as a 'platform'

TikTok can be explored as a *product* launched and operated by the Chinese company ByteDance, and it can be analysed as a *business* that generates most of its revenues from advertising. TikTok can also be understood as an *app* employed by its users to create and share short videos, or as a *tool* used for entertainment, marketing, or education. In this book, however, we conceptualize and discuss TikTok as a *platform*.

Platforms are, in a generic sense, online software infrastructure in the form of apps or web interfaces that allow users to share, interact, and develop new forms of use and utility. But the concept of platform also has a rhetorical function. Given the ontological nature of what this concept stands for, the fact that a platform lets actors stand upon it and 'gives leverage, durability, and visibility' (Schwarz, 2017, p. 377), the term 'platform' has been employed by digital companies to promote certain discourses.

As Gillespie (2010) points out, companies strategically refer to their technologies as 'platforms', as a way 'not only to sell, convince, persuade, protect, triumph or condemn, but to make claims about what these technologies are and are not' (p. 359). For example, by describing itself as a 'platform for creative self-expression', a 'global entertainment platform' (TikTok, 2020a, 2020f), TikTok sells the image of a space for joy and creativity to its users and advertisers and at the same time distances itself from the serious allegations it has been facing in some of the markets where it operates (more discussion on TikTok controversies in chapter 6).

To think of TikTok as a platform also requires us to investigate how its technological features, functions, and logic interplay with, and respond to, different social and cultural practices. This process of mutual shaping between digital platforms and entities that deploy the infrastructure can be described as *platformization* (Helmond, 2015; Van Dijck, Poell, & de Waal, 2018).

As oligopolies are dominated by big technology companies such as Facebook, Google, and Amazon, our sociopolitical life and cultural activities are becoming increasingly dependent on a small number of dominant platforms. In such a 'platform-centred situation', as Jean Burgess (2021, p. 21) described it, platformization serves as a useful theoretical construct to problematize the power of technology companies. An overarching objective of this book is to discuss the implication and problems of TikTok's platformization of creative culture, social activities, and information governance.

One factor that makes TikTok a particularly interesting case for the study of platformization is its unique location in the global platform system. TikTok is not born out of Silicon Valley, as most other international digital media platforms. TikTok has its heritage from China, and the mature short-video industry in the Chinese market has benefited the platform's development overseas. At home, TikTok's mother company ByteDance operates a 'sibling' short-video platform called Douyin, which shares most of its features and functions with TikTok. Douyin's triumphs and struggles at home, as we will discuss throughout this book, have been crucial to the success of TikTok's global development. However, as a response to international suspicion about its Chinese roots, TikTok works hard to distance itself from its Chinese mother company and sibling platform.

In the fast-growing scholarship on platform studies, platformization and platform systems in China have often been discussed as atypical and different from the western norm, due to that country's particular technological and governing conditions.[4] For instance, Wang and Lobato (2019) showed that platformization processes in China are distinct from similar processes in other markets and that the difference involves both macro-level factors such as market regulation and micro-level factors such as platforms' affordances. They argued that these distinctive characteristics call for a 'spatialized platform theory that is sensitive to the historical origins of particular platforms' and for the need to 'de-Westernize' platform studies (p. 367).

The conditions that govern platformization processes in the Chinese markets are indeed embedded in the development trajectory of most technology companies in China. This means that ByteDance's two sibling platforms, Douyin and TikTok, offer a unique opportunity for us to study how almost identical platforms operate in very different markets and regulatory environments while they mirror and influence each other. This process has been conceptualized by Kaye, Chen, and Zeng (2021) as *parallel platformization*. This concept expands on the logic of platform localization or regionalization – processes in which developers adapt platforms to new markets (IndiaSA Comms Team, 2019; Perez, 2019) – by considering how firms iterate platform infrastructures and adapt (or not) to different modes of governance.

We are using this concept in our interrogation of the TikTok's platform specifics. However, it is necessary to note that our parallel approach does not promote the binary dichotomization of China versus 'the West' (de Kloet et al., 2019), or a sensationalist notion that Chinese digital markets are vast and unique (Herold & de Seta, 2015). Rather, through engaging examples from Douyin and the Chinese short-video industry throughout this book, we aim to illuminate the intersections, interdependence, and conflict between the two platform ecologies.

The short video turn

TikTok is not the world's first short-video platform. In Europe, in the United States, and across Asia, there have been several popular short-video platforms before TikTok such as Vine, Dubsmash, and Kuaishou (see the review of short-video platforms in chapter 1). However, TikTok is the first short-video platform that succeeded in growing into an international mainstream operation and whose influence has been able to rival that of major Silicon Valley technology companies such as Instagram, Facebook, and YouTube. As a response to the new competition from TikTok, these Silicon Valley platforms have launched their own short-video services, including Instagram Reels and YouTube Shorts.

We argue that the fast growth of TikTok and other similar short-video services heralds the rise of a *short-video turn*. This phenomenon should be seen as the continuation of the 'visual turn' in social media (Gibbs et al., 2015) that was signified by the proliferation of visually rich platforms (e.g. Instagram) and communication (e.g. selfies, GIF, vlogs). The short-video format has been employed to communicate funny memes, social campaigns, educational tutorials, and investigative news. But, unlike their longer-format cousins such as YouTube videos, bite-size videos on TikTok are characterized by a higher degree of sociality, immediacy, and playfulness.

The availability of fast internet (e.g. 5G) and smartphones has facilitated the prevalence of audiovisuality-dominated mobile communication. However, besides the technological advance, an arguably more important factor that contributes to the short-video turn is the rise of a youthful and creative generation, generation Z (Gen Z).[5] The rise of TikTok coincides with the maturing of Gen Z as members of the society with a desire to create, connect, and make themselves heard. Facebook, Instagram, and Twitter are often perceived by Gen Z as 'uncool' and full of 'nosy' family members, while emerging short-video platforms that cater for youth (e.g. Muscial.ly and Dubsmash) already became an important social space for many members of the Gen Z cohort.

On these platforms, the video challenges evolved into the new meme, dances and lip-sync performance became the new selfie, and body gestures serve as the new emojis (Rettberg, 2017). By incorporating modalities of videos, teens and pre-teens cultivate their own vernacular and create their visual grammar. The youth creative culture continues to influence the platform, even with an increasingly diversified user base on these platforms.

TikTok and the pandemic

Since its launch in 2018, TikTok has become one of the fastest growing digital media platforms in the world. As of mid-2020, TikTok reported almost 700 million monthly active users outside China and 600 million daily active users of the sibling platform Douyin in the Chinese market (Iqbal, 2021). Even though TikTok has been banned from some of its largest markets (e.g. India), the number of users has likely continued to grow after this data was reported.

As shown in Figure 0.2, the worldwide downloads of TikTok reached their peak during the 2020 COVID-19 outbreak, partially as a result of extensive lockdowns around the world. As Wells, Li, and Lin (2020) put it, 'TikTok has been one of the world's biggest distractions during the pandemic'. With orders for school closures and home offices rolled out in different parts of the world, the short-video platform came to be used by many to pass the time, socialize, or learn new skills. To a large extent, the pandemic could be instrumentally

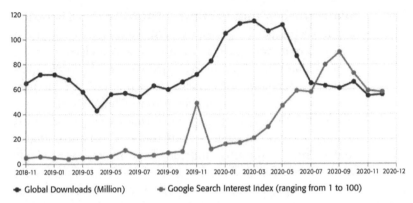

Figure 0.2. TikTok's worldwide download and Google's Search Interest Index, *s.v.* 'TikTok'. Figure created by Jing Zeng, Crystal Abidin, and Mike Schäfer.

considered the tipping point of the TikTok platform, in terms of both its user base and the public discussions about it.

First, before the COVID-19 outbreak, the dominance of Gen Z TikTokers was very prominent. As pointed out by Milovan Savic (2021), TikTok's predecessor Musical.ly was intentionally designed to appeal to the teenage and pre-teen markets and at the same time rhetorically positioned to circumvent moral panic around kids' usage of technology. Since the start of the pandemic in 2020, users from much more diverse age groups have joined the platform. For instance, TikTokers have seen the emergence of #over30, #over40, and #over50 clubs on the platform where older creators were able to socialize and share relatable stories and jokes with their peers on topics such as parenting, married life, or their struggles to execute TikTok dance routines. At the same time, older family members who were once simply the target of Gen Z's TikTok pranks have become active and engaging creators themselves, as several videos with hashtags such as #DadsOfTikTok and #MomsOfTikTok went viral.

Second, the public sentiment towards TikTok shifted significantly around 2020. On the one hand, the platform's Chinese roots raised concern over issues such as data safety and censorship (Kuo, 2019; M. Singh, 2020). Discussion about TikTok has been heavily politicized on account of the Sino-US trade war and the 2020 presidential election in the United States. In response to allegations, the platform's international operations self-imposed a 'whitewashing' strategy designed to distance the platform from China. On the other hand, as TikTok's popularity and media coverage continued to grow, the general public's indifference turned into curiosity and eventually scrutiny, and the platform has increasingly been surrounded by criticism. One of the main controversies has been around TikTok's perceived lack of protection for children. As mentioned earlier, as Musical.ly evolved into TikTok, it passed on its popularity among youngsters as a legacy; but the existence of a young user base has gradually turned from a blessing into a curse. The platform's failure in handling children's data has led to lawsuits filed in Europe and the United States. Additionally, concerns over illicit content, including pornography and violence, are also rising, and have even resulted in the platform's permanent shutdown in some markets, for example Pakistan.

In response, as we will discuss at some length in chapters 4 and 6, TikTok launched a wide variety of campaigns to improve its image. For instance, after the COVID-19 outbreak, TikTok organized a high-profile collaboration with the World Health Organization (WHO), in order to offer health information to the youth. This initiative was followed by public health workers as well as by school teachers, who turned the platform into a learning channel during COVID-19 lockdowns. The agenda item of selling TikTok's educational potential existed before the pandemic, but was catalysed by the health crisis.

If TikTok's popularity grows, public attention to its impact, and especially to potential threats, will grow as well. This mainstreaming drives the need for scholarly attention to be dedicated to the platform. TikTok research is still in its infancy, and in the next section we provide a brief overview of this emerging field.

TikTok scholarship

The rapid rise of TikTok and media interest in this phenomenon have attracted the attention of a wide range of scholars around the world. In April 2021, 122 publications related to TikTok have been recorded in the Scopus database.[6] As Zeng, Abidin, and Schäfer's (2021) review of these publications indicates, studies of TikTok started to appear in academic journals in 2019 and took off during the COVID-19 pandemic, which saw a surge of research interest in the platform's potential to disseminate health information. Researchers from the fields of computer science and social science took the lead in researching TikTok; their focus was on the technological architecture, user behaviours, and content characteristics. In mid-2021, a range of studies have been devoted to conducting in-depth investigations into the platform's sociopolitical and cultural profile.

In the early stages of this scholarship, TikTok was discussed as a 'bite-size YouTube', and TikTok videos were considered to be 'another form of vlog'. As more cultural and media studies scholars began to contribute to this reasearch, the focus shifted and TikTok – together with the short-video format – was recognized as a separate category, distinct from its long-form ancestors. The most relevant studies from this emerging body of scholarship will be discussed throughout the present book.

As TikTok gradually becomes an established part of mainstream media culture, we are expecting to see the scholarship on TikTok, as well as on short videos in general, rapidly grow and diversify. The platform's features, user dynamics, and regulations are changing fast; this opens new opportunities for academic research, but also brings challenges to it. By the time you are reading this book, TikTok may have already evolved and changed, or even may no longer exist. However, in terms of media political economy, the story of the bumpy rise (or rise and fall) of Chinese social media in the global market is itself significant. By focusing on the early years of TikTok, this book documents the challenges that the platform faces to fit into the international contexts. Moreover, our discussion of the mutual shaping between short videos and the creative culture of a new 'media generation' (Bolin, 2017) is relevant to many other platforms. In the next section we elaborate on four theoretical approaches to creativity that we use in our analysis.

Perspectives on creativity

In our examination of creativity and culture in short video, we focus on four ways to conceptualize creative practices: vernacular, social, distributed, and circumscribed creativity. These four perspectives are introduced in what follows.

Vernacular creativity. We use Burgess' (2006) concept of 'vernacular creativity' to describe TikTokers' affective and platform-specific communicative styles. In her original work, Burgess used this term to conceptualize creative communicative practices in digital storytelling that emerge from an everyday and mundane context. As we will argue throughout this book, short videos are a form of digital storytelling, and the vernacular creativity embedded in the platforms is closely intertwined with digital youth culture and platform affordance. Furthermore, drawing on Burgess and Green's (2018) foundational work on YouTube, we will explore areas of tension between open vernacular creativity and commercial interests on TikTok.

Social creativity. Our approach to creativity in the context of TikTok's platform infrastructures is inspired by Glăveanu's (2020) work, which emphasizes a sociocultural theory of perspectives and affordances. Glăveanu's 'perspective-affordance' theory of creativity foregrounds the 'social, material, and cultural ecology of positions, perspectives, actions, and affordances that make up creative processes above and beyond isolated people and products' (p. 350). This approach advocates study of the processes that mutually shape creativity between social, material, and cultural assemblages. In this regard, the approach complements theories of platformization that identify similar mutually shaping sociotechnical processes between people, platforms, and corporations (van Dijck et al., 2018). We refer to Glăveanu's approach simply as 'social creativity' in this book. We apply social creativity to our discussion of four specific platform features on TikTok that we argue are designed to facilitate creative interactions on the platform.

Distributed creativity. In discussing TikTok communities' participatory production of creative work, we employ the concept of 'distributed creativity'. The term was coined by Sawyer and DeZutter (2009) distributed and refers to activity among groups of individuals that results in a product that no one person is responsible for creating. Distributed creativity can be unrestrained and unpredictable, as in spontaneous improvisational performances by thespians or musicians. Using the example of a group of jazz musicians, we examine how distributed creativity contributes to building tight-knit communities on TikTok through the practice of virtually simulating musical jamming.

Circumscribed creativity. Finally, through the case study of how social activism takes place on TikTok, we introduce Kaye, Chen, and Zeng's (2021) concept of 'circumscribed creativity' to describe how the creative potential of TikTok is both stimulated and constrained by short-video features and platform policies. Circumscribed creativity is theoretically grounded in circumscribed agency, a concept that refers to the autonomy afforded to individuals in normally rigid organizations to facilitate creative cultural production (Lotz, 2014; Havens, 2014). We expand this concept by connecting it to research on templatability (Leaver, Highfield, & Abidin, 2019) and imitation publics (Zulli & Zulli, 2020) on social media. In the context of TikTok, circumscribed creativity underlines how the platform introduces features and functions designed to encourage creation and re-creation of memetic content and at the same time actively sets boundaries on its users' creativity through regulatory and algorithmic mechanisms. Before moving on, we want to acknowledge that this book is focused on the creativity and culture of users who *visibly* participate on TikTok by creating their own videos, by using socially creative features such as Stitch, and by posting public comments. The practices of *non-creating users* (see e.g. Preece, Nonnecke, & Andrews, 2004; Velasquez et al., 2014; Light, 2014; Sakariassen & Meijer, 2021) are indeed an essential part of a platform's community, and in chapter 2 we recognize that non-creating users participate actively in shaping their own algorithmic feed and the recommendations shown to others, despite having never posted a video or a comment on TikTok. However, the formal interrogation of non-creating users' practices on TikTok is beyond the scope of this book and remains a productive avenue for future research.

Outline of this book

In this book we advance an argument about the creativity and culture of short video; and we do this through an in-depth case study of TikTok.

Chapter 1 presents an evolutionary history of short video. There we contextualize the short-video format and distinguish four defining features of short-video platforms: length of content, endless scroll, native video production, and replicability. We demonstrate how the development of short-video platforms in China progressed relatively smoothly, by comparison with the chaotic and interrupted development of short-video platforms from Silicon Valley. We review four short-video platforms that preceded TikTok and that each added and solidified certain features and affordances that would come to define the platform genre. We conclude with an extensive account of TikTok's parent company ByteDance, charting its rise from a bedroom start-up to an international media titan.

In chapter 2 we begin our analysis of platformization at the platform infrastructure level, looking at affordances and features. We begin by considering the platform affordances that make TikTok an inherently mobile and music-centric platform. We divide TikTok's platform features into four broad categories. First we discuss the 'For You' page, the main page for viewing content, and the algorithmic recommender system that powers it. Next we identify and define the platform's primary socially creative features and discuss how they encourage active and creative participation on TikTok. The third and fourth sections are a review of the video creation features and social media features that are not unique to TikTok but are useful for illustrating how familiar features are integrated, contested, iterated, and appropriated on a short-video platform.

After laying out the various features that facilitate social creativity on TikTok, we explore how they influence cultures of community building and activism. In chapter 3 we examine community formation on TikTok. The chapter is informed by Tönnies' (1965 [1887]) concepts of *Gesellschaft* ('society', calculating and impersonal) and *Gemeinschaft* ('community', intimate and interpersonal), also employed by Ling (2012) in the study of mobile technologies and community building. We illustrate *Gesellschaft* on TikTok through a case study of 'mainstream TikTok', which is composed of the most globally popular TikTokers and determined via follower count. We profile some of these mainstream TikTokers as 'nomads', who have migrated to TikTok from other short-video platforms that were shuttered (e.g. Vine, Musical.ly), and as 'natives', who started on TikTok and became famous there. We illustrate

Gemeinschaft on TikTok through an in-depth qualitative case study of JazzTok, a niche community of musicians who developed an intimate community by engaging in distributed creativity: they played music on TikTok together using socially creative features.

Chapter 4 presents two case studies of activism on TikTok: #forClimate and #saveTikTok. There we explore examples of how Gen Z TikTokers strategically use the platform's socially creative features and vernacular cultures to inform, educate, and mobilize others. The first case study reviews 'green memes' and TikTok challenges that raise awareness and initiate action to combat the ongoing climate crisis. The second case study involves the collective effort to save TikTok in 2020, when the platform was facing the threat of being banned in the United States. We conclude this chapter by revisiting the role of circumscribed creativity in promoting TikTok activism.

Chapter 5 returns to our platformization analysis of TikTok by moving on to the market level. There we consider platform economies on TikTok. We first discuss the various advertising strategies that generate revenues on and for the platform. Next, we consider how practices of e-commerce such as *daihuo* ('influencing someone's decision to purchase') are indicative of the challenges of parallel platformization. *Daihuo* is an example of a business model brought over from Douyin that for various reasons has not been as effective on TikTok as on its platform sibling. We also discuss live streaming as another example of a market mismatch between TikTok and Douyin. We then move on to business models that generate revenue for TikTok creators – including revenue in the form of virtual currency, influencer sponsorships, and the TikTok Creator Fund. We critique the precarity of platform labour on TikTok, exacerbated as it is by limited avenues of monetization and a general lack of transparency. We conclude this chapter by returning to our earlier argument that TikTok is a music-centric platform – which we do with the help of an illustrative case study of TikTok's influence and impact on the music industry.

Chapter 6 takes our platformization analysis of TikTok to the level of governance. There we present additional struggles of parallel platformization, as evidenced by geopolitical skirmishes that resulted in TikTok's being banned in some countries and threatened to be banned in others. We then discuss two forms of governance – *of* and *by* TikTok. First we focus on the copyright governance of TikTok; this is followed by an analysis of the governance of user visibility as managed by TikTok. Then we identify the contours of a strategic pattern, one of cultivating *positive content*, which is used by ByteDance repeatedly to respond to controversies that emerge at the platform governance level.

We end in chapter 7 with a summary of our main arguments and directions for future research. We argue that the development of TikTok has been shaped by geopolitical contestation and has given the direction of competition in the international short-video industry. Further, we point to tensions between automated curation and user control that can contribute, simultaneously, to a sense of agency and to a sense of powerlessness. We then restate our core arguments that TikTok represents an evolutionary step in short video, that audio is a central pillar in TikTok's evolution, and that this evolution has opened the door to a more direct competition between two globally dominant platform ecosystems: Silicon Valley and China. We conclude this book with final thoughts about the future of TikTok and of the short-video format.

I

A Brief History of the Short
Video Industry

In this chapter we define and historicize the short-video format and short-video platforms. We start by arguing that short video is an evolutionary step in vernacular creative content, and we do so by defining the format and presenting four characteristics of short-video platforms: video duration, endless scroll, integrated content creation features, and replicability. We then illustrate these characteristics by reviewing the comparatively more mature Chinese short-video industry that influenced international short video platforms.

The second section traces the evolution of international short-video platforms through four examples: Vine, Snapchat, Flipagram, and Musical.ly. We argue that each of these platforms contributed to establishing specific norms and practices of the short video industry.

In the third section we review the origins and development of ByteDance's actual core product: its algorithmic technology. We also note the competitive aspirations of ByteDance's founder, who had his eyes on international markets from a very early stage. We discuss the elements of the competitive strategy that enabled ByteDance to establish a dominant position in the international short-video industry. Lastly, we discuss the implications, advantages, and challenges that arose from the parallel development of ByteDance's two sibling platforms, Douyin for the Chinese market and TikTok for international markets.

The short-video format

One way to define the short-video format is simply to acknowledge that these videos are indeed short – generally shorter than one minute (Kaye, Chen, & Zeng, 2021). Short-video content has existed in various forms for decades, but it is through the emergence of dedicated short-video online platforms that the format has come to signify much more than just a recording of a very short video. An illustrative parallel to the evolution of the short-video format is how microblogging constituted an evolutionary step for blogging. Blogging or weblogging had become widely popular in the early noughties, as several online websites hosted bloggers' postings about a vast spectrum of topics, genres, and content (Rettberg, 2014). In 2006, Twitter launched as a site to host microblogging, placing emphasis on character limits and brevity of expression (Burgess & Baym, 2020). On Twitter, users were prompted to share short, succinct updates on what they were doing and, later, on what was happening around them – in no more than 140 characters. This limit would later be expanded to 280 characters but microblogging on Twitter still required bloggers to adopt a different platform logic or to shift their understanding of blogging. There was notable ambivalence and confusion as to the role and function of Twitter in its early years (Burgess & Baym, 2020), but gradually users developed strategies and norms for the shorter format. Encouraging feedback from the audience regarding creative and adept postings showed users which strategies worked and which ones did not.

Similarly, by the time short-video platforms began to grow, first in China and later internationally, the format of vlogging – video blogging – was well established and massively popular. Vloggers had established conventions for how to shoot and share video content: conventions regarding length, editing, and detail, all of which were disrupted by the advent of short-video vlogging. Yet to claim that short video is merely a condensation of 'vlogging' is an oversimplification. Short-video vlogs were indeed popularized by so-called Story features (Newton, 2017) that were introduced by several platforms such as Snapchat and Facebook, but the format of short video extends far beyond vlogging content.

Twitter is an example of the shift in platform vernacular that occurred between blogging and microblogging, and it constitutes an illustrative parallel to what has also happened between digital video content and short-video content. The parallel shows how the short-video format is inherently connected with the dedicated platform used for producing, editing, sharing, viewing, and engaging with short videos and communities.

In the next section we explore a number of common features of these dedicated short-video platforms that make them distinct from other digital media platforms.

Short-video platforms

Short-video platforms are apps developed for, and primarily used on, mobile devices such as smartphones or tablets (Kong, 2018). We identify four characteristics of short-video platforms: video duration, endless scroll, integrated content creation features, and replicability.

First, as already mentioned, short-video platforms prioritize content that is short in duration, often ranging between 15 and 60 seconds. Short-video length or duration can vary between platforms. For instance, the early international short-video platform Vine allowed creators to upload videos of maximum six seconds at launch. Kuaishou, an early short-video platform in China, allowed two maximum lengths for videos: 11 seconds and 57 seconds (Lin & de Kloet, 2019) and later on Douyin, developed by ByteDance, extended these two lengths slightly – to 15 and 60 seconds respectively. Of note here is the fact that the length of videos is enforced by the platforms themselves, not normatively imposed by users.

Second, short-video platforms use an endless scroll feature to curate, discover, and consume content. Endless scroll means that users can swipe through new content from the creators they follow, or find new content recommended by algorithmic recommender systems (see Figure 1.1; also chapter 2). Endless scroll makes content on these platforms ephemeral and adds the potential for virality or spreadability. TikTok has never included a View History feature whereby one could go back and seek out short videos that appeared in one's feed. Therefore, if a user does not interact with the video in some way, for instance by liking or commenting on the video, saving the video link, or following the creator, it can be difficult to find that particular video or its creator again. This also means that content that receives high levels of engagement may find its way to users' endless scroll feeds, even when it is only tangentially related to their interests.

Figure 1.1. TikTok main viewing interface.

Third, short-video platforms make videos easy to film, edit, add effects to, and post using the same platform. Mobile cameras, particularly those attached to smartphones, have dramatically lowered entry barriers for amateur photographers and videographers. While it is relatively straightforward to point and shoot videos, editing and, to a lesser extent, sharing videos still require additional technical skills. Short-video platforms bundle shooting, editing, and sharing seamlessly into one (Figure 1.2), placing a clear emphasis on video creation, in much the same way as image-sharing platforms such as Instagram. The relative ease with which videos can be created and distributed encourages participation among users who might not usually engage in content creation.

Finally, short-video platforms make content easy to replicate. Shifman (2013) explains that turning everyday digital artefacts

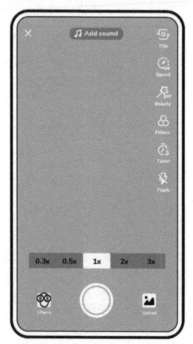

Figure 1.2. TikTok video creation interface.

into memes involves imitation and replication. Memetic short videos, which tap into deeper cultural meaning, are easy to replicate for several of the reasons listed here (Zulli & Zulli, 2020). They are short, which means that they do not require too much time to re-create, they can find their way to wider audiences through endless scrolling, and they can be created by using the short-video platform's internal interface. As we discuss in chapter 2, TikTok includes features that further facilitate replication through social participation, such as the Use This Sound and Duet features (see Figure 1.3 and Figure 2.1). These features allow viewers to create a new video on the basis of the one they were just watching, and only with a few taps of the finger. Alongside the ability to shoot, edit, and upload videos in one place, short-video platforms seamlessly push viewers to replicate content or participate in trends.

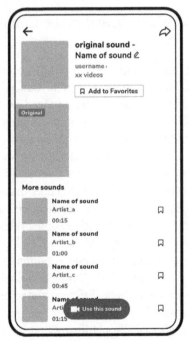

Figure 1.3. Use This Sound interface.

The short-video format and the features just discussed predate TikTok and, as we noted in the introduction, TikTok was certainly not the first short-video platform to find mainstream international popularity. As a growing number of platforms have entered the international short-video market, the common features that define these platforms and make them distinct from other types of digital media platforms have become more pronounced. What is interesting to note is that many of these features have not been invented by the dominant media and technology companies based in Silicon Valley. Rather, most of the short-video platform features that distinguish these platforms from other digital media ones have emerged in the self-sustained digital media ecosystem of China. In the next section we turn our attention to the evolution of the short-video format in this market.

The short-video format in the Chinese media market

McLelland, Yu, and Goggin (2017, p. 59) describe mainland China's digital landscape as a 'self-sustained social media ecosystem' due to the restrictions imposed by the infamous 'Great Firewall' that stymies the flow of international web content and limits the use of international internet services. McClelland et al. further note that China's 'local dynamics, individual agency, and indigenous innovation in domesticating Western technologies and concepts' have also pushed the Chinese digital landscape on a distinctive path.

By 'domesticating' western technologies (McLelland et al., 2017), Chinese media companies have developed a range of highly successful copycat (*shanzhai*) versions of international digital media platforms.[1] The Chinese *shanzhai* platforms have gradually evolved along different trajectories and have become increasingly localized and increasingly distinct from the western versions of the platforms that were their source of inspiration.

China's digital tech sector was initially focused solely on the massive domestic market. This complacency about not exploring overseas opportunities, combined with a lack of understanding and experience of foreign markets, contributed to several high-profile failures of Chinese digital companies in their attempts at internationalization.

However, the growing experience and sophistication of China's digital technology sectors have turned some Chinese media companies into innovation leaders in their areas and have enabled Chinese internet products to make successful inroads into the global market. This business strategy is further supported by a government policy known as the Digital Silk Road initiative, which encourages and incentivizes Chinese digital companies to expand overseas (Fung et al., 2018; Seoane, 2020).

Chinese digital products' path to 'going out' (*zou chuqu*) is, however, full of obstacles (Keane & Wu, 2018). Political factors such as the US–China trade war have led to heightened scrutiny from international onlookers who impose barriers to prevent Chinese digital platforms such as WeChat, and even hardware manufacturers such as Huawei, from gaining a footing outside China (Murphy, 2020). As we discuss in chapter 6, Chinese short-video platforms have become the target of governmental sanctions in different regions. After the geopolitical contestations of mid-2020, India banned TikTok, together with a number of other Chinese platforms and internet services. Later that year, both the Australian and the US governments also threatened to block TikTok (Kaye, Rodriguez et al., 2021).

Notwithstanding these challenges, China's short-video platforms have become a pin-up for Chinese internet products that aim to go international. Between 2012 and 2014, several competing short-video products have been launched in China, including Kuaishou, Weishi (by Tencent), Meipai, Miaopai, and Musical.ly. Musical.ly's success, unlike that of other platforms that targeted the Chinese market, started (and ended) in the American and European market, as we will see later. In 2014, the Shanghai-based company launched a lip-syncing app named Musical.ly, which quickly became popular in North America and Europe (Robinson, 2016). When ByteDance introduced its short-video app Douyin in 2016, it was a late arrival to the Chinese short-video scene. However, as we are going to show, its successful acquisition of Musical.ly, which later merged into TikTok, constituted the foundation for TikTok's global success.

Musical.ly's and TikTok's success stories have inspired several Chinese companies to enter the international short-video market. For instance, in 2018 the Chinese company JOYY acquired the Singapore-based BIGO, whose short-video app Likee (formerly LIKE) has been TikTok's main competitor in Southeast Asia (Qu, 2020). Two other examples are Vskit, a short-video app developed specifically for African markets by the Chinese company Transsnet (see Transnet About, 2021), and Kwai, the international version of the Beijing-based short-video platform Kuaishou, which set its sights on the Brazilian market (R. Singh, 2020). Both these initiatives are progressing well: in 2019 Vskit and Kwai topped the download charts respectively in Nigeria and Brazil (Tavares, 2019; Emekalam, 2019). Kuaishou continued its aggressive international expansion in 2020 by launching two short-video apps in order to compete with ByteDance and TikTok; these are SnackVideo (April 2020) and Zynn (May 2020). Figure 1.4 shows a timeline of the development of Chinese short-video companies.

How the four short-video platform features were introduced by Kuaishou and Meipai

China's burgeoning short-video industry contains a plethora of platforms dedicated to social entertainment, news and information, and video editing (Kong, 2018). To show how the four features we announced – length, endless scroll, creation

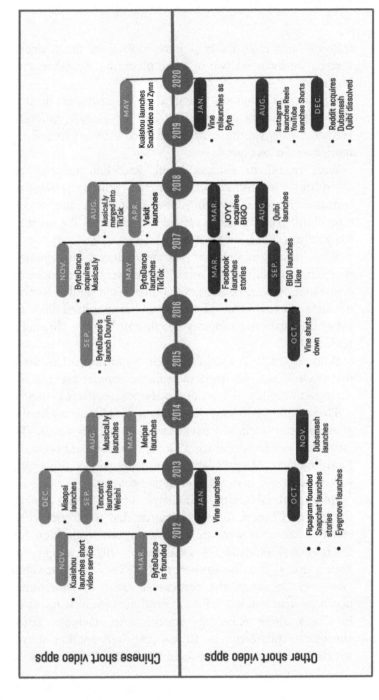

Figure 1.4. Timeline of the short video industry. Created by the authors.

features, and replicability – have evolved in the Chinese market, we focus on two of these platforms: Kuaishou and Meipai.

With regard to length, Kuaishou, as we have seen, limited videos to a duration between 11 and 57 seconds, whereas Meipai initially set the length of a video between 10 and no more than 60 seconds.[2]

With regard to endless scroll, Kuaishou emphasized algorithmic recommendation as the primary mode of consuming and discovering new content. A proprietary algorithmic recommender system was sitting at the heart of the platform (Lin & de Kloet, 2019).

With regard to creation features, Meipai championed recording and editing in order to give users the capacity to create unique video content, which they could send to friends or share publicly. One of its slogans emphasized that, by using this platform, ordinary people can become 'directors' (Cai, 2016).

With regard to replicability, both platforms had features that made it easy for users to replicate popular content, for example the ability to reuse audio and visual effects instantly.

These innovations on Kuaishou and Meipai made the platforms garner massive user bases in China (Su, 2019). The four features were also integral to the establishment of one of Kuaishou's and Meipai's largest competitors, Douyin, which will be examined in detail later in this chapter.

In an annual Chinese internet report, Yeung (2019) found that Chinese digital platforms that were once criticized as *shanzhai* were now becoming an inspiration for international *shanzhai*. A catalyst for this development, Yeung notes, was the growth and success of short-video platforms. In 2017, the forecasted value of short-video platforms had ballooned into a multi billion-dollar industry in China alone (Cheung, 2020). Since October 2018, short-video platforms in China had 648 million users, which accounted for almost 80% of all internet users in the country (China Internet Network Information Center, 2021) and by December 2020 that user base had grown to 873 million, with a staggering 88% penetration rate among Chinese internet users (Thomala, 2021). Cheung (2020) attributes the success of short-video platforms in China to the rapid cycles of content production – their matches the faster pace of life in China's urban centres – as well as to these platforms' appeal to marketers and advertisers in China. E-Commerce has played a significant role in the short-video platform boom in China; this will be discussed in chapter 5.

As Figure 1.4 shows, many Chinese tech companies established a competitive and profitable market for short-video platforms from 2012 onward. Platforms such as Kuaishou, Meipai, and Douyin have been able to develop relatively unobstructed, by comparison with short-video platforms in international markets (Su, 2019). As a result, the international short-video market lagged considerably behind its Chinese counterpart throughout the 2010s. In the next section we return to this international short-video market, to explore its evolution over the past decade.

Silicon Valley-based short video platforms

For the better part of the 2010s, both the format and the platforms of short video were struggling to find a niche and a clear market leader outside China. The format was not as well established as that of other varieties of digital or social media, and major platform companies were reluctant to take big risks on it, much to the chagrin of early short-video adopters. The emerging international market for this new genre was volatile and uncertain, but early iterations of international short-video platforms still throw glimpses into several of the features that made the format so popular in China.

One 'pre-platform' example of online short-video content was based on Flash animations.[3] Animated short videos became popular in the early twenty-first century; they were created by ordinary users with tools such as Adobe Flash, and were shared on personal websites or on early content aggregation websites that predated YouTube (Winkie, 2015). Flash animations allowed users to explore new technical capabilities of creating and sharing video content, engaging in remix cultures, and generating online communities. In the days before the advent of YouTube or other digital platforms (Burgess & Green, 2018; van Dijck et al., 2018), the short-video format was an innate component of the phenomenon of online participatory culture (Jenkins, 2006). Shorter Flash animations could be created with comparatively less effort than longer-format content; they demanded less bandwidth to upload and view; and they could more easily become spreadable viral memes.

Launched in 2005, YouTube quickly took centre stage in matters of online video content – be it short-video content or not. Because of copyright concerns, YouTube began by setting the maximum length of videos at 10 minutes. Users could find workarounds to circumvent the 10-minute length, but some of the most popular videos on the platform were well under that mark. On a list of 12 popular early YouTube viral videos published in 2020, the average length of a piece is 2 minutes and 30 seconds, and this interval covers short skits, viral songs, and clips such as of the dramatic chipmunk, which is only 6 seconds long (Spanos et al., 2020).

Burgess and Green (2018, p. 79) highlight how users pushed the limits of short-video editing through 'frenetic, irreverent, nonsensical' videos remixed in chaotic cycles. The style originated on content-hosting forums and later migrated to YouTube, where it came to be known to its creators as YouTube Poop (Burgess & Green, 2018). YouTubers also found ways to exemplify the potential to communicate ideas, culture, and creativity in the form of short-video poetry. Since 2012, the popular international forum website Reddit has hosted a dedicated short-video forum named r/YouTube Haiku. The YouTube Haiku subreddit (or forum) aggregates links to short videos on YouTube. The instructions for posting on r/YouTubeHaiku state:

> A place to share the best videos UNDER 30 seconds! Videos 14 seconds and under are known as Haiku videos and 15–30 seconds are Poetry! You can also share Meme videos up to 30 seconds long under the appropriate [Meme] tag! (Reddit, 2021)

The guidelines for posting YouTube haikus and poems are reminiscent of the length limitations characteristic of short-video platforms. By imposing these limits, the moderators of r/YouTube Haiku influenced members of that community either to create or to seek out informative, subversive, controversial, or humorous short videos on YouTube (Haberman, 2012).[4] Some YouTubers also experimented with short video by microvlogging – that is, by compressing the established vlog format into a shorter format. To achieve this, some microvloggers used services such as 12seconds.tv, a website designed to work in tandem with Twitter that was launched in 2008 and was shut down in 2010 (Burgess & Green, 2018).

In addition to YouTube, the graphics interchange format (GIF) demonstrated the *memeability* of the short-video format among users in international markets. Animated GIFs were also easily shared online thanks to their smaller file size and lack of audio. GIF creators could capture moments from TV, film, or other videos that circulated on the internet; and they could also build on what other GIF makers had created. Miltner and Highfield (2017) describe GIFs as polysemic, in the sense that they can be symbolically interpreted and recontextualized online, by users and creators, as artefacts designed to communicate affect and to demonstrate cultural knowledge online. Crucially, however, GIFs are only visual; so perhaps they can be considered to represent the silent era of short videos. As we will argue shortly, audio is a major component on TikTok and other short-video platforms, as it adds a layer to the polysemy of GIFs. Even so, the cultural significance of GIFs is evident in their current ubiquity. There are now dedicated GIF-hosting websites such as Giphy and GIF keyboards that have become integrated features on digital platforms such as Facebook and WhatsApp.

Flash animations, YouTube shorts, and GIFs all signal the presence of short-video content in international markets prior to the debut of short-video platforms. But these examples are not compelling evidence for the popularity of the short-video format. Flash animations would frequently exceed 60 seconds; YouTube Poop and Poetry are fairly niche types of content in the broader YouTube ecology; and the fact that GIFs are silent and lack audio means that it would be quite a stretch to include them under the umbrella of the short-video format.

In the next sections we review the fraught developmental path of four international short-video platforms. Despite never finding firm footing, these platforms paved the way for TikTok and its competitors by proving that there was demand for short-video platforms outside China and by establishing the hallmarks of what is today short-video culture.

Templates: Vine

Backed by the Silicon Valley powerhouse Twitter, Vine was the first successful international short-video platform. Vine was acquired by Twitter in October 2012, just three months before its official launch in January 2013 (Isaac, 2016). At launch, it included many characteristic short-video format features. The length of videos on Vine – Vines – was initially capped at just six seconds, which made them exceptionally short even by short-video standards. Additionally, the main way to view Vines was by scrolling through a feed similar to the Twitter feed: it ran endlessly through trending content and allowed users to follow other users and see more of their content.

Users could also create, edit, and share content directly, through the Vine app (see Figure 1.5). A standout quality of Vines was their replicability and potential to go viral. With a maximum length of only six seconds, Vine pushed the limits of creative brevity, a challenge eagerly met by its users.

Vine showcased the power of using templates for video content that were similar to the templates seen on other visual social media platforms. On digital platforms, templatability refers to the ways in which algorithmic systems strive to present to users aesthetically similar content by promoting popular content 'templates' (Leaver et al., 2020). Interactions between people and platforms drive the use of templates. The

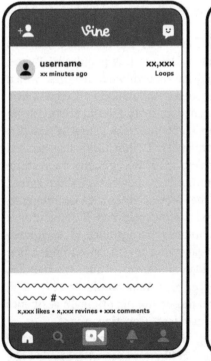
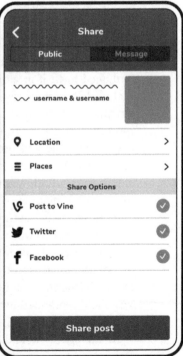

Figure 1.5a and 1.5b. Vine's main viewing page and sharing feature.

platform's recommender system suggests popular content to users, who then internalize the recommendation logic and try to 'please the algorithm' by posting the types of content they expect to become widely popular.

Monetization models also influence templates, for instance by pushing sponsored content that incorporates popular templates expected to increase engagement and click-through rates. Templates allow users a degree of agency: thus users can choose which kinds of templates they wish to incorporate into their own content. At the same time they limit originality, insofar as users can post only something that is based on a template. As we explain in later chapters, TikTok builds on templatability as a design principle by designing platform features that circumscribe creativity to users, nudging them to pick up certain sounds or effects employed in trending templates.

Vine grew to a base of over 200 million active users in three years since its launch. Despite this popularity, Twitter struggled to fit it in alongside its own video features, which included Twitter's native video function and Periscope, a live-streaming platform launched in 2015 (Hern, 2015). Facing mounting pressure from competitors and internal conflict over Vine's role and profitability, Twitter ultimately decided to shutter Vine in December 2016. Recognizing the cultural significance of Vine communities, however, Twitter agreed to create a Vine archive that preserved the videos, moments, and movements captured on the platform (Dalton, 2017). The Vine archive was ultimately discontinued in April 2019 (Twitter, 2021). In later years, after the massive proliferation of international short-video platforms, Vine's co-founder, Dom Hofmann, announced that Vine would be revived in 2020 and rebranded Byte, preserving the original's aesthetics and the six-second limit on videos (Constine, 2020).

In an article heralding the end of Vine, the journalist Robinson Meyer remarks that 'there was nowhere online like Vine' (Meyer, 2016, p. 1). Vine was a space for spontaneous, random, and diverse content. Just like longer-format digital media, Vine demonstrated that short-video platforms, too, were a site for political contestation, identity construction, and profesionalization, compressed into a short-form package. Meyer concludes the article with an elegiac statement: 'And with Vine's death comes the larger passing of an era of the social internet' (ibid.). While this prediction ultimately proved wrong, Vine's passing did mark an important milestone for international short-video platforms. Audiences who loved Vine's frenetic energy and creators who had acquired considerable followings in their three years on Vine were suddenly set adrift, searching for a new space where they might recapture the short-video magic. Vine also demonstrated to Silicon Valley tech companies and investors that the short-video format was popular, albeit risky. When even a company as large and significant as Twitter could not figure out how best to incorporate it, major players began exploring alternative forms of short video.

Stories: Snapchat

While Vine could be considered the first successful short-video platform dedicated to short-form content, other competing platforms began to incorporate Stories, a feature that would become most closely associated with the short-video format on international platforms. In October 2013, ten months after the launch of Vine, Snapchat launched Stories (Parker, 2015). Snapchat was designed to be a messaging platform; users could send and receive Snaps – photos or ten-second videos – that would delete themselves immediately after viewing. Rettberg (2018, p. 188) describes Snapchat as 'the antithesis of the web' at launch in 2011, because there were no URLs, back buttons, or archives; in short, it was ephemeral. The ephemeral nature of the Snaps feature popularized Snapchat as an alternative to other messaging platforms, particularly for private or intimate communication between users. The

Stories feature transformed Snapchat into a quasi-short-video platform, allowing users to tap into the creativity and community afforded by the format.

Stories allowed users to record ten-seconds videos or ten-seconds photo compilations that would be visible to one's mutual friends and, later, to all followers (see Figure 1.6). As on Vine, users and creators were now faced with the creative challenge to communicate ideas, information, and memes in a limited time frame. Snapchat Stories were slightly longer than Vines and users could string together a series of stories to post longer content or updates. Like the eponymous Snaps, however, Snapchat Stories deleted themselves after

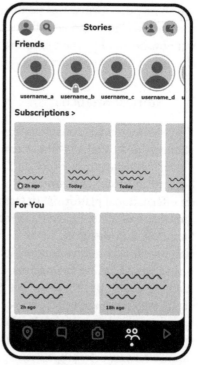

Figure 1.6a and 1.6b. Snapchat video creation interface and Stories feature.

24 hours, unless they were saved by users. The addition of Stories enabled users to post short daily vlogs to update friends on what they were doing, make and display creative content, and engage with other users in new and meaningful ways.

The popularity of Stories as short-form daily vlogs did not elude Snapchat's Silicon Valley competitors. Instagram and, later, Facebook launched their own story features, in a move that was framed as an 'all-out assault on Snapchat' (Newton, 2017). Instagram launched a Stories feature in August 2016, and its growth was touted as 'the biggest driver for Instagram's overall success' (Leaver et al., 2019, p. 31). In just over six months, the number of users of Instagram Stories surpassed Snapchat's 166 million daily active users. In August 2018, two years after the launch of Stories, Instagram reported 400 million daily active users, more than doubling Snapchat's at the time (Wagner, 2018).

Despite being videos that are short, Stories are distinct from the short-video format we defined so far. Stories were designed and marketed to be video-centric status updates – short vlogs. This is not to say that creators did not create and share episodic, narrative, or other forms of content through this feature, but Stories provided less incentive to do so by virtue of their ephemerality. Stories were not intended to become digital artefacts. Stories on Snapchat deleted themselves automatically after 24 hours and were gone forever unless users chose to download them, at the cost of losing data storage space on their personal devices. By contrast, Vine compilations uploaded to YouTube have millions of views and are still attracting nostalgic viewers half a decade after Vine was shut down. Stories represented a step towards integrating short-video features on international platforms but still failed to reproduce Vine's cultural impact. Stories lacked the algorithmic features of discoverability and replicability that characterize other spiritual successors to Vine, up to and including TikTok.

Music: Flipagram

Around the time when Snapchat introduced Stories, another dedicated short-video platform debuted to piggyback on Vine's growing success. Flipagram launched in October 2013 and allowed users to create 30-second digital slideshows set to music. Like Stories, Flips were not exactly short videos per se. They could be viewed as videos, but consisted of static images from a user's camera roll or from another visual social media platform such as Instagram. Also, just as with Stories, users could showcase personal moments through photo collages on Flipagram; but they could also create humorous mash-ups of images or remixes of others' photos, for creative effect. Flipagram capitalized on the cross-platform promotion of short-video content. Even before the official launch of Instagram Stories, Flipagram gave users an option to share their creations on Instagram as a video, in addition to posting on Flipagram; in this way the platform was nodding to the fact that many popular users would probably have established a larger following elsewhere. Two years after the launch, *Forbes* proclaimed that 'Flipagram could be bigger than Instagram' for two main reasons: the platform made it easier to create videos than did YouTube, and at the same time it offered more options for creativity than did Vine or Instagram (Chaykowski, 2015).

Flipagram's main contribution to the evolution of short-video platforms was the centralization of audio as a key component (see Figure 1.7). Flipagram claimed that it was the first platform, short-video or otherwise, to have music as a core component (Ingham, 2015). Despite the CEO Farah Mohit's initially cavalier attitude to music licensing (Ingham, 2016), Flipagram managed to secure licensing deals with Universal Music Group, Sony Music Entertainment, Warner Music, Merlin, and the Orchard and with music publishers such as Sony/ATV Music Publishing, Universal Music Publishing Group and BMG, as well as smaller publishers

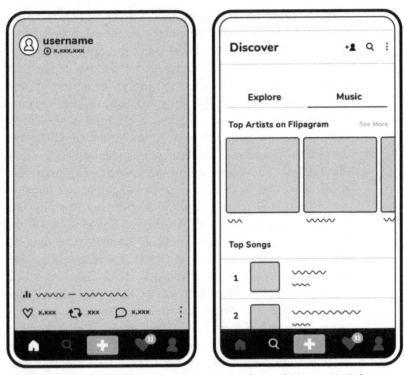

Figure 1.7a and 1.7b. Flipagram's main viewing interface and Discover Music feature.

via the National Music Publishers' Association (Ingham, 2016). With these licensing agreements in place, Flipagram could provide copyright-protected music for creative reuse, and also offer an internal music store. The developers seemingly took cues from the copyright wars that plagued YouTube in the mid-to-late noughties (Burgess & Green, 2018) by prioritizing licensed content hosted on their platform and courting positive relationships with artists and labels. Users could legally use songs from their favourite artists. They could also follow their favourites artists on Flipagram, as the platform added hundreds of verified artists as users around the time when it secured agreements with major music companies (Ross, 2016).

In the same article that claimed that Flipagram could be Instagram's killer, Mohit noted that he intended to 'build a relevance algorithm that shows users the right Flips at the right time' (Chaykowski, 2015). As we discuss in the next chapter, TikTok's algorithmic recommender system is one of the most important distinguishing features that separate it from other digital media, and even from other short-video platforms. Rather than build one in house, Flipagram decided to outsource its recommender system, a decision that ultimately led to its demise. In February 2017, Flipagram was acquired by an unknown 'Chinese news aggregator company' called Toutiao (Wagner, 2017). A Vox article documenting the sale notes that the two companies were linked via a Silicon Valley venture capital firm, Sequoia Capital. According to Mohit, Flipagram's founder and CEO, the rationale for the sale was to improve the platform's social features, which he described as being inferior to those of competitors like Facebook and Snapchat, by using Toutiao's powerful 'personalization content feeds'. The article fails to mention that Toutiao was actually the name of a subsidiary; in reality, the algorithmic technology for which Mohit was willing to sell his company was developed by Toutiao's parent, a company called ByteDance.

Community: Musical.ly

The last short-video platform in our evolutionary chart is not exactly international. Born in Shanghai and later based in California, Musical.ly (see Figure 1.8) became heir apparent to the short-video throne abdicated by the Vine closure. Although Musical.ly was created by Chinese developers, we place it in the ranks of international short-video platforms, as its founders explicitly targeted the US market when the platform launched officially in August 2014 (Spangler, 2016). Musical.ly began as a short-video platform aimed specifically at hosting educational content, and it was positioned

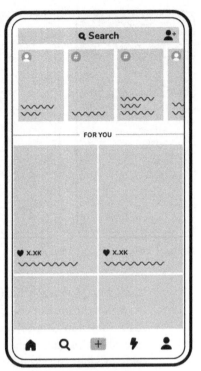

Figure 1.8a and 1.8b. Musical.ly's main viewing interface and Search feature.

as a short-form massive open online course (MOOC). While laudable in theory, in practice a short-form MOOC was 'doomed to be a failure' even by the founders' admission, and they soon pivoted to a music creation app that was more accessible to wider user bases (Carson, 2016, p. 1).

Musical.ly featured an endless scroll feed; it also had a Stories feature and further emphasized the interconnectivity between social media and digital content creation features (see Figure 1.9). Even from Musical.ly's early days as a short-MOOC platform, its founders placed social networking and community building at the heart of their product, through features designed to encourage 'Musers' to connect and interact with one another (Newlands, 2016). Such features

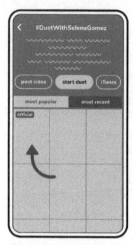  

Figure 1.9a–c. Musical.ly's Duet feature.

included Q&A, a specific feed for audiences to raise questions to which the creator could respond in subsequent videos; and BFF (best fan forever), which allowed spotlighted audience members to direct message platform creators and create side-by-side Duet videos together – a feature that would become a staple of the short-video genre (see Figure 1.9). These features were designed to foster the kind of 'social creation' that encouraged users to draw inspiration from, or build upon, the creativity of others (Dwyer, 2016; see also chapter 3). As the name implies, Musical.ly also prioritized audio, just like its competitor Flipagram. And in order to enhance its creative audio features, Musical.ly took further cues from another nascent competitor in the short-video space.

Lip-syncing and remixing audio clips, two main features on Musical.ly, were the main focus of a German-engineered short-video platform called Dubsmash, which launched in November 2014, six months after Musical.ly. As with Musical.ly, Dubsmash users had access to a wide array of internal audio and visual clips, as well as to audio recording features designed to facilitate lip-syncing and remixing. Lip-syncing on Musical.ly and Dubsmash inspired competitors to develop similar features. One example is Facebook's ill-fated Lip Sync Live feature, which was put in place after securing licensing deals with major music labels (Deahl, 2018). Dubsmash was unable to compete with the combined powers of incumbent Facebook and Instagram as well as with the rapid growth of Musical.ly (Kircher, 2015). Despite its dwindling user base, Dubsmash managed to stave off being acquired and integrated into larger platforms until December 2020 when it was acquired by Reddit (Shu, 2020).

Another area in which Musical.ly succeeded while many of its short video competitors failed was the monetization of infrastructures. Making money from a short-video platform was not as straightforward as it was from platforms such as YouTube or Instagram. Vine's extremely short format posed a challenge for advertisers, and Flipagram's use of licensed music restricted options for monetization. Musical.ly featured an in-app monetization system, built around virtual gifting (see chapter 5), and also leaned heavily towards 'influencer' marketing and paid promotional deals for creators who sought to professionalize their cultural labour on the platform (Robehmed, 2017). 'Influencer' is a term used 'to describe a model of marketing and advertising that targets key individuals who exert influence over a large pool of potential customers' (Abidin, 2018, p. 72). As we discuss in chapter 5, the monetization models on Musical.ly clearly reflect the logic of platform economies in China. These additional avenues for monetization on Musical.ly appealed to established short-video stars who had gained massive followings on Vine in the years before the platform was shuttered in 2016.

Like Flipagram, Musical.ly was acquired by ByteDance in 2017. Unlike Flipagram, Musical.ly continued to operate as an independent platform after its acquisition, as ByteDance announced. Coincidentally, ByteDance had launched its own international short-video platform, TikTok, five months earlier.

Once again, millions of short-video users and creators were faced with the precarious possibility that Musical.ly would be shut down. Indeed, ByteDance did eventually dissolve and absorb Musical.ly into its TikTok platform in August 2018 (Chen, 2019). Whereas in the aftermath of Vine's closure users had scrambled for a suitable substitute, Musical.ly's user base could find familiar surroundings on TikTok (Dwyer, 2016). Many of the most popular features were preserved, and new features were introduced that enhanced the short-video experience, building on several years of evolution of the genre.

*

Each of these four platforms sheds light on different aspects of the evolution of the format and the platforms of short video outside the Chinese market. Vine popularized templatability and demonstrated the format's potential for creative and cultural expression. Snapchat Stories made the concept of recording and sharing more accessible and commonplace on digital platforms, but were too ephemeral and lacked the creative muscle of Vine. Flipagram highlighted the importance of audio, while also foreshadowing the importance of algorithmic recommender systems for short video. Musical.ly added features for social creativity and community, as well as more support for professionalization through monetization models. At the same time, the impermanence of international short-video platforms left users, creators, tech companies, and investors to wonder whether the format would ever find its niche. Vine was a runaway success before Twitter suddenly and unexpectedly pulled the plug; Snapchat never fully implemented the shift to become a short-video platform; and Flipagram and Musical.ly were both acquired by the same company while they were gaining traction. But when western investors and entrepreneurs questioned the viability of the short-video format, it was time for ByteDance to make its move. In the next section we examine the development of

ByteDance and its evolution towards becoming the world's leading short-video company.

ByteDance

The ByteDance headquarters is a multi-storey compound in an industrial park of Beijing's Haidian District. The ByteDance office appears unassuming from the outside: a white-brick building emblazoned with a logo in both Chinese and English. The doors of a small waiting room open into a massive open-plan office floor and a sea of computer terminals and programmers. Just to the side of the main floor is a corridor that features an elaborate timeline celebrating the history of the company and its growth from a bedroom start-up into one of the most successful tech companies in China and around the world. The timeline charts collaborations with leading researchers in China, the launches of each product, and performance benchmarks.

Many of the milestones in the corporate timeline highlight various stages of development of ByteDance's algorithmic and artificial intelligence (AI) technologies. ByteDance takes immense pride in its technologies, and many of the conversations with community managers during a company visit focus on their various applications in ByteDance's core product lines.

Perhaps no example of the significance of this area to the company is more illuminating than the lengths it was willing to go to protect its algorithmic technology in 2020. In chapter 6 we discuss the geopolitical contestation that nearly saw TikTok banned in the United States. Of note here is that, when the US government attempted to force a sale or a divestment of TikTok to US tech companies in 2020, the TikTok algorithmic recommender system was resoundingly removed from the negotiating table. A representative of ByteDance stated: 'The car can be sold, but not the engine' (Xin and Qu, 2020, p. 1); and the Chinese government even passed new export laws designed to specifically restrict 'computing and data processing technologies', including 'content recommendation' systems (Feng, Qu, & Lee, 2020, p. 1). We preface our analysis of ByteDance's corporate history with these vignettes to underscore that ByteDance's core product is its recommender systems and a range of other AI innovations and that short video and TikTok is merely one of several products where this foundational technology has been applied.

The algorithm above all else

ByteDance's corporate creation myth tells us a story of how, when the company was founded in 2012 by the computer scientist Yiming Zhang, the priority was to develop its recommender system (Yang and Wang, 2020). ByteDance partnered with researchers from Beijing University to build the foundational technology that would eventually be put to commercial use in a range of online platforms such as Toutiao, Xigua, and Douyin. The company has remained focused on its recommender system and other AI-related technologies. In 2016 it opened its AI Labs, a research facility focused on the research and development of a broad range of AI technologies, where developers and computer science students were promised that their 'ideas can be practically tested and fast-tracked for product development' (AI Lab, 2021).

The first commercial application of the company's core technologies was Jinri Toutiao (Toutiao), an algorithmically driven news aggregation platform. Many of the features initially tested via Toutiao would earn ByteDance international acclaim later on, when deployed on its short-video platforms (Kaye, Chen, & Zeng, 2021). Toutiao, whose name literally means 'headlines', is a multifunctional platform with news creation and distribution functions that enable journalists, users, and algorithms to produce and consume multimedia news content directly through the platform. The news production features of Toutiao gained worldwide attention in 2016, when the news coverage of the Rio Olympics was written by Toutiao, being automatically produced by ByteDance's algorithms. This coverage was shown to be faster to print and more frequently published in other media outlets than coverage written by humans (Hariharan, 2017). Toutiao also hosts other functions, such as a monetization system designed to support journalism, short video sections, games, social networking, and location-based services (Jing, 2018). The flagship feature of Toutiao is its algorithmic recommender system, which learns users' preferences through interactions and engagement with content and recommends content accordingly. The algorithmic recommender system was cited as a key factor that contributed to ByteDance's early success with Toutiao (Knight, 2018); later on the company would magnify this success by packaging the same technology into its other platforms.

Two aspects of ByteDance's approach to Toutiao are relevant to understanding its approach to Douyin and TikTok. First, ByteDance continues the tradition whereby tech and digital media companies insist that they are not media companies (Napoli & Caplan, 2017). ByteDance did not employ any journalists when it launched Toutiao, and the founder himself, Yiming Zhang, has been quoted in order to avoid positioning the company in the journalism industry: 'The most important thing is that we are not a news business... We are more like a search business or a social media platform. We are doing very innovative work. We are not a copycat of a US company, both in product and technology' (Chen & Bergen, 2018). In that statement, Zhang not only admits that the company is larger than the specific commercial functions of Toutiao, but distances and dissociates the company from news. The latter half of the statement highlights the second insight from Toutiao that is relevant to TikTok: ByteDance is not a copycat (*shanzhai*). To demonstrate that what they were doing was unique and innovative, ByteDance made

Toutiao's product and business its first foray into international markets.

Already in ByteDance's early days, Yiming Zhang held an ambition to expand his company beyond the Chinese borders. Zhang is quoted saying that he wanted his company to be 'as borderless as Google' (Rogers, 2019, p. 1). In a 2014 visit to Silicon Valley, he expressed frustration with Chinese tech companies for not expanding beyond their insular national market, and in a public address he called on them to engage with international competitors in Silicon Valley (Minxi, 2020).

In 2015, as Toutiao was rising to be a market leader in China, ByteDance launched Top Buzz, an international version of Toutiao aimed at English-speaking audiences (Yang & Goh, 2020). Top Buzz was designed to parallel Toutiao's features and their crown jewel: the algorithmically curated news feed that would recommend stories to readers on the basis of their own inputs (Smolentceva, 2019). ByteDance also launched other international versions of Toutiao aimed at different markets; Helo, for example, was marketed in India (Ahuja & Dalal, 2018). While Top Buzz was initially popular, its user statistics began to decline steadily, until the platform was eventually shut down by ByteDance in 2020 (Yang and Goh, 2020). Toutiao, however, remains the dominant news aggregation platform in China.

ByteDance enters the short-video market

ByteDance launched Douyin in September 2016, originally under the name A.me, and this new platform was able to expand its user base to 100 million within a year (Graziani, 2018), even though it faced steep competition from the three major platform companies nicknamed the 'prophets of mass innovation' – Baidu, Alibaba, and Tencent (BAT) – which collectively control more than 70% of the Chinese internet market (Access to China, 2020; see Figure 1.10). The

Figure 1.10a and 1.10b. Douyin's main viewing interface and Discover page.

concept of mass innovation (万众创新) refers to a national strategy that seeks to promote prosperity and flourishing through processes of innovation (Keane and Su, 2018). BAT exemplifies the mantra of mass innovation through their market dominance in China and gradual diffusion to other neighbours in East and Southeast Asia (Leong, 2018). Competing in the short-video market in China meant direct competition between ByteDance and BAT short-video platforms such the Tencent-backed Weishi (微视) and the Baidu-backed Haokan Video (好看视频) and Quanmin Video (全民小视频), as well as other rising start-ups, for instance Meipai and Kuaishou (Graziani, 2018; Chen, 2019). In 2019 short-video competition intensified when Tencent reportedly invested over US$ 2bn in Douyin's largest competitor, Kuaishou (Deng & Hu, 2019).

ByteDance decided at an early stage that Douyin would be its second prominent attempt at 'going out'. When Top Buzz launched internationally, ByteDance faced an uphill battle to establish a market presence for the news aggregation platform from the ground up. This is a common challenge for firms with ambitions to expand internationally, and for this reason a traditional strategy is to get a foothold in the new market by acquiring 'a small position that a firm intentionally establishes within a market in which it does not yet compete' (Upson et al., 2012, p. 93).

ByteDance's acquisitions of Flipagram and Musical.ly can be considered two such 'foothold moves', made respectively in February and November of 2017. The exact value of these sales is not publicly available, but the Flipagram deal is estimated to have sat around the US$ 70 million mark, whereas the Musical.ly deal is estimated to have been significantly higher, between US$ 800 million and 1 billion (Dave, 2017; 2018).

The acquisitions meant that, when attempting to bring Douyin to international markets, ByteDance had the benefit of leveraging an existing audience by acquiring a competitor rather than starting from scratch. Musical.ly reportedly had over 200 million subscribers in the United States when it was acquired by ByteDance (Dave, 2018). The decision to acquire Musical.ly was a strategic move that 'combined [Douyin's] AI-fed streams and monetization track record with Musical.ly's product innovation and grasp of users' needs and tastes in the West' (Fannin, 2019, p. 1).

Flipagram had a much different platform infrastructure from Douyin's, being primarily used to make photo collages set to music. The Musical.ly platform, by contrast, was much more similar to Douyin's. By integrating features from Douyin and by preserving features from Musical.ly, users coming from Musical.ly could have an easier time adjusting to TikTok (Spangler, 2018). One of the first features that were incorporated from Douyin to Musical.ly was an algorithmically curated For You feed that leveraged ByteDance's recommender system and is still the main feature that sets TikTok apart from many of its competitors (Price, 2018).

In the years after TikTok's international launch, competition in the short-video platform significantly intensified. The most notable contenders were already dominant Silicon Valley-based incumbents such as Instagram with Reels (Figure 1.11) and YouTube with Shorts, both revealed in mid-2020. Instagram Reels is functionally and aesthetically very similar to TikTok: it emphasizes endless scrolling,

Figure 1.11a and 1.11b. Instagram Reels: its main viewing interface and video creation features.

content creation features, and a range of social networking features to connect with and share content (Instagram, 2020; see Figure 1.12). In mid-2021, YouTube Shorts was still available only in the United States and in India and was connected to the main YouTube platform. Shorts is a portal for viewing short videos that mimics TikTok's interfaces, but it limits the ability to create a new Short at any time, urging viewers instead to subscribe to creators (Gartenberg, 2021; see Figure 1.13).

Earlier in 2020, an old competitor re-emerged, to enter the increasingly vibrant short-video market. In January 2020 Vine's founder, Dom Hoffman, announced the launch of

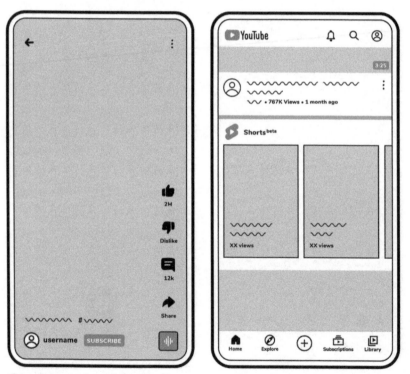

Figure 1.12a and 1.12b. YouTube Shorts' main viewing interface and positioning on the main YouTube mobile platform.

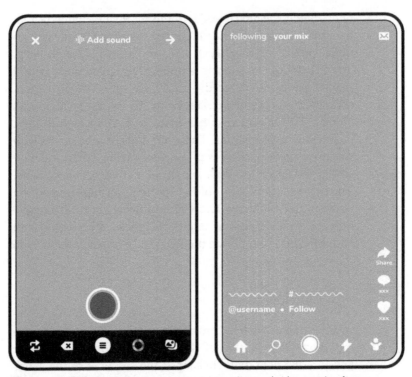

Figure 1.13a and 1.13b. Byte's main viewing interface and video creation feature.

Byte, a rebranded version of its predecessor that preserved the integral feature of allowing only six-second-long videos (Constine, 2020; see Figure 1.14). Even Snapchat has tried to get in on the short-video frenzy, announcing in 2020 that users could now integrate music and audio clips into their Snaps (Durkee, 2020).

The growing interest, from both incumbents and new entrants, and the heightened competition in the short-video market are signs of how the market is evolving and gradually becoming more mature. The look and feel of incumbent short-video platforms demonstrate that Silicon Valley competitors are now producing *shanzhai* or copies of TikTok (see Figures 1.12, 1.13, and 1.14). In mid-2021, ByteDance remains undoubtedly the global leader of the short-video industry and, buoyed by its growth, has indicated that it is considering an initial public offering (IPO) later in the year (Xin & Feng, 2021). ByteDance's success is noteworthy, given the different market pressures it faced – in China with Douyin and in several international markets with TikTok (see chapters 5 and 6). TikTok's success has inspired BAT to expand their businesses outside China. These attempts have been met with various degrees of success in the Asia-Pacific region and with strong resistance in North American and European markets. The expansive ambitions of BAT portend further competition between Silicon Valley and Chinese firms; and this competition will only continue as other Chinese firms follow suit and learn how to replicate the ByteDance expansion model to their businesses.

Conclusion

In this chapter we have provided a historical context to illustrate how the evolution of short-video platforms in Chinese and international markets shaped the contours of the short-video industry as it exists today. These evolutionary processes are well documented on other digital media platforms. Historicizing the development of digital platforms reveals a messy and modular journey, co-constructed by developers, users, and society. In-depth scholarly interrogations of WeChat, Twitter, YouTube, and Instagram offer illustrative examples of how platforms experience significant changes throughout their existence and how they drive or at least influence significant changes in society (Burgess & Green, 2018; Chen, Mao, & Qiu, 2018; Leaver et al., 2019; Murthy, 2013). While the history of TikTok as a solitary platform is brief, the history of the short-video format and of short-video platforms spans a decade and helps to paint a clearer picture of the social and cultural politics that have emerged on these platforms.

Using the framework of parallel platformization, in the following chapters we move on to explore the infrastructures, markets, and governance of TikTok. The next chapter looks at the features, functions, and practices of the TikTok platform. We go into further depth to explain the platform's affordances, to acknowledge the similarities and differences between TikTok and Douyin, and to highlight decisions made by ByteDance at the infrastructure level of platformization.

2

The TikTok Platform Infrastructure

In the previous chapter we presented the history of short-video platforms and identified four characteristics of the format: the duration of videos, the endless scroll, the integrated content creation features, and replicability. In this chapter we take a closer look at the specifics of the TikTok platform and examine the features and functions that constitute the TikTok platform infrastructure (Plantin et al., 2018), understood as the platform's user interfaces, data servers, backend programming, intermediary systems, complementor services, and so on (Nieborg & Poell, 2018).

We begin by recognizing TikTok as an inherently music-centric mobile short-video platform. We then move on to discuss the algorithmic recommender system packaged as the For You page, which sits at the heart of the TikTok experience for both creators and viewers. Next we present a number of TikTok's key platform features and a set of key user-driven practices that have emerged and are now intrinsic parts of TikTok's platform culture.

Inherently mobile and music-centric

TikTok is an inherently music-centric and mobile short-video platform. Digital and social media platforms are increasingly mobile-dependent, which means that they are designed to be used on a mobile device. Some platforms (notably YouTube and Facebook) began as websites and eventually migrated to mobile platforms while maintaining support for browser versions. But short-video platforms such as

Vine were primarily accessed via mobile devices from the beginning and Douyin has never supported a web browser interface. Similarly, while a limited version of the TikTok platform can be accessed via a web browser, most features, and primarily content creation ones, are available only in the mobile app. TikTok's mobile affordances are essential to its functionality, but they do not distinguish TikTok from other short-video platforms.

Yet TikTok does differ from many other competing short-video platforms in the way in which music percolates through the platform's user experience. For example, music centricity is immediately visible in the TikTok video main screen (see Figure 1.1), where an animation designed as a rotating vinyl disc is found in the bottom right corner. Musical notes are floating away from the rotating disc, to indicate that music is playing. This animation serves as a button to access the 'Use This Sound' feature (to be presented later in this section) and is always visible, regardless of whether the audio in the video is indeed music or not.

Another example of TikTok's music centricity is found in its video creation section (see Figure 1.2), where the top icon is a button designed as 'Add-Sound'. This icon leads to the heart of the platform's active music discovery section, which has many parallels to music-streaming platforms such as Apple Music, Deezer, or Spotify. For instance, the top area of this section is a carousel featuring six artists who promote their new releases; the section also sports a range of themed playlists and the ability to add songs to a user's favourites. The main difference between the TikTok music discovery section and the leading music-streaming platforms is that the TikTok experience is focused on finding music to be integrated into the users' short-video productions, not on listening to a list of songs from an album or a playlist. For this reason, songs on the TikTok platform are cut to one minute or less, and a user cannot autoplay a list of songs without interacting with the app.

TikTok's music-centric nature shows in several features and practices that will be discussed later in this chapter. For instance, features such as Duet or Use This Sound and practices such as lip-syncing or attributional practices all have their roots in music. TikTok's music centricity has also guided several aspects of the analysis presented in this volume. For instance, our interviews and the cases we discuss are in different ways related to music, and we also devote a significant section of our examination of the TikTok economy to the interplay between the platform and the recorded music industry.

Next in this chapter we continue the presentation of the platform's infrastructures by turning our attention to the most central component of the TikTok experience: TikTok's recommender system, packaged as the For You page.

The For You algorithm

One of the best-known components of the TikTok platform is the For You page. It is the landing page when one opens the TikTok app, and it features an endless scroll of new videos recommended to users on the basis of a variety of factors determined by ByteDance's highly sophisticated algorithmic recommender system. Here we refer to this algorithm as the For You algorithm.

On the basis of the platform's official explanation of the For You algorithm (TikTok, 2020b), three factors determine which videos are included in a user's For You page: user behaviours, video characteristics, and the device setting (language and location). TikTok tracks and analyses users' engagement metrics, and the more data are generated from a user's activities on the platform, the more accurate do profiling and prediction become, at least in principle. As TikTok puts it, 'the best way to curate your For You feed is to simply use and enjoy the app' (ibid.).

TikTok's addictive algorithm predates the platform; as discussed in the previous chapter, the proprietary algorithm was a fundamental building block for the first services developed by ByteDance. From ByteDance's first news aggregator app – Toutiao – to its current portfolio of more than ten social media platforms, recommendation algorithms are the key differentiator against competitors.

Everyday interactions with the For You algorithm

Algorithms are widely used by digital platforms to organize and personalize information (Gillespie, 2014; Sandvig et al., 2016). The For You algorithm plays a particularly important role in shaping users' everyday experiences on TikTok (Kaye & Burgess, 2021). In what follows we detail three areas of everyday interactions influenced by algorithmic recommendation: content discovery, personalization, and spreadability.

Content discovery. The For You algorithm shapes how content is discovered on the platform. The app's user interface places the For You page front and centre in its design, and the moment users open the app they are instantly taken into the endless scrolling experience. As a result of this way of proceeding, passive exposure to curated content becomes the default mode for content discovery on TikTok. It is worth noting that 'passive exposure' does not mean that users play no role in determining what they watch. As mentioned earlier, the For You page is algorithmically curated on the basis of users' engagement with videos. 'Passiveness' in this context highlights the platform logic that users' initiative in determining what they want to watch is secondary to the recommendation algorithm.

Personalization. The platform logic of content personalization centres on TikTok's algorithmic understanding of what its users enjoy watching. While on social media such as

Instagram, Facebook, and Twitter the users' network serves as a key filter that decides what can in principle become visible on the homepage, the impact of network relationships is less crucial on the For You page. Instead, its personalization is based largely on real-time learning about the users' engagement with different content.

On the one hand, such a system and its addiction-inducing logic serves the purpose of locking users in and generating traffic. On the other hand, however, this form of hyper-personalization comes at a high cost when we consider content diversity. The problem of filter bubbles caused by digital platform usage has been under debate for a decade – in fact ever since Eli Pariser's book *The Filter Bubble* in 2011.

Streaming platforms such as Spotify have been shown to increase the homogenization of listeners' musical experiences (Borreau, Moreau, & Wikström, in press); Facebook and Twitter have been accused of perpetuating 'filter bubbles', which encourage users to consume content that reinforces established opinions and beliefs (Boukes, 2019; Matamoros-Fernández, 2017). Considering the mechanism used to personalize the For You page, the content space of TikTok is arguably more fragmented and polarized than the content space of feeds one may receive from other platforms. As the digital media researcher Axel Bruns (2019) points out, the so-called filter bubble is easy to burst on social media, because even people from the same network regularly share diverse topics for varied purposes. This makes it a regular experience on Twitter or Facebook to encounter content that is perceived as different, irrelevant, and boring.

However, on TikTok, the For You page's primary mission is to keep users interested so they go on scrolling and engaging with the content for as long as possible. This limited mission leaves a narrow margin where the platform risks confronting users with content they do not like. TikTok presents itself as an entertainment platform that 'brings joy',[1] but, as more users employ the platform for propagating political and sometimes controversial messages, the consequence of hyper-personalization complemented by its For You algorithm will continue to grow.

Spreadability. The dependence of content discovery and personalization on For You algorithms also has great implications for how videos can achieve spreadability on the platform. In their 2013 book *Spreadable Media*, Henry Jenkins, Sam Ford, and Joshua Green (2013) introduced the concept of spreadability, to which they referred as 'the potential – both technical and cultural – for audiences to share content for their own purposes, sometimes with the permission of right holders, sometimes against their wishes' (p. 3). As indicated by this definition as well as implicit in its wide application, a participatory culture of content sharing and remixing is a key characteristic of digital communication.

On Facebook and Twitter, the spreadability of posts can be repost-based, which means that tweets become more visible when shared by other accounts, which can be either of humans or of bots. In the case of TikTok videos, by contrast, spreadability is (re-)creation-based. TikTok users cannot directly repost a video clip to their followers, but they can create new videos through socially creative features such as Duet or Stitch, discussed later in this chapter. These features and the logic of (re-)creation-based spreadability have a direct impact on the formation of connections between TikTok users. Despite the lack of networks with strong personal ties on TikTok, communities there are formed around content creation, for example by inviting other TikTokers to take on challenges and to participate in meme (re-)creation. In chapter 3 we will discuss how this form of creativity-driven sociality fosters the emergence of communities on TikTok.

Algorithmic folklore

Given the importance of the For You page in TikTok's ecosystem, it is unsurprising that the question of 'how to get the For You algorithm to pick your content' is regularly discussed among TikTokers. Like any other platform, TikTok does not offer real insights through which users may manipulate the system and optimize their visibility. As a result of this algorithmic opacity, TikTokers share their theories of how the recommendation system works, along with tips about how to get content featured on other users' For You page.

In the absence of an authoritative explanation, users often develop their own 'folk' theories of how social media's content governance works (Myers West, 2018). For instance, Sophie Bishop's (2019) research on YouTube discusses how knowledge of the platform's algorithms is collaboratively and informally developed by vloggers in the form of *algorithmic gossip*. According to Bishop's definition, algorithmic gossip refers to 'communally and socially informed theories and strategies pertaining to recommender algorithms, shared and implemented to engender financial consistency and visibility on algorithmically structured social media platforms' (2019, p. 2589). TikTok-specific algorithmic gossip is widely available on the platform itself and on other platforms. From early YouTube videos on 'how to become Musical.ly famous' made by teens to today's mentoring channels dedicated to propelling TikTokers on the path to visibility, the opacity of the algorithm is itself capitalized by content creators.

One commonly shared, but also rebutted, piece of algorithmic gossip is the claim that including hashtags such as #fyp, #foryou, #foryoupage, and #xyzcba[2] will boost a video's chances of being recommended by the For You algorithm. Despite the lack of evidence to support this theory, and although some TikTokers point out that these hashtags can be countereffective, as they may attract the suspicion that the video is spam, the hashtags in question are still commonly used in videos today.

In our interviews,[3] Shout (@vocaloutburst) explained, for example, that they would often conduct tests to experiment with different hashtags in order to see which tags and trends would most improve the visibility of their videos. As another example, Damoyee (@damoyee) explained how she adapted a very strategic approach to posting. After joining TikTok in mid-2020, she spent three months studying the For You algorithm without posting anything, in order to better understand patterns of trending content and tags.

Many creators we interviewed expressed deep personal connections with the content they shared on TikTok. When certain types of content began underperforming by comparison to similar types of content shared in the past, algorithmic gossip served as a defence, to shield creators from self-doubt. As Alex (@alexengelberg) explained,

> You essentially have to put your own self-worth on a pedestal to argue about how the algorithm is screwing you over. It's like by saying, 'Oh, the algorithm isn't doing well. I've made content that deserves to be seen by many people.' And it kind of feels obnoxious to say that. But the reality is that if you're spending time making a lot of stuff, then, um, you definitely deserve to have some amount of transparency into how people are seeing your stuff, which doesn't really exist right now. (Alex (@alexengelberg))

Alex's response speaks to the frustration expressed by several interviewees that, even after taking all the steps to 'satisfy the algorithm', they were still not getting consistent engagement numbers. Black box recommender systems have minimal transparency, leaving TikTok creators to wonder: 'Is it me or is it the algorithm?' Or perhaps there is an elusive third option hinted by Alex: 'Is it the people who see my stuff?'

Socially creative features

As noted in the introduction, an important aim of this book is to explore the various types of creativity that take place on TikTok. In this section we focus on *social* creativity, understood as a set of creative, collaborative, and cumulative actions that are enabled and enacted by social activity (see e.g. Montuori & Purser, 1999; Lebuda & Glăveanu, 2019). Social creativity is a well-established research topic, studied by psychologists interested in the holistic and social aspects of creativity (e.g. Amabile, 1983). The literature finds that social creativity often takes place in group settings (Barron, 1999), requires some form of social validation (Csikszentmihalyi & Sternberg, 1988), and can be understood as a communicative process (Sobrinho & Glăveanu, 2017).

Glăveanu (2020) understands social creativity as a cyclical sociocultural creative process in which new perspectives drive group creativity and foster dialogues that uncover new affordances, which in turn open new perspectives.

When studying these creative processes on TikTok, we focus on the affordances that structure and shape social creativity, and we refer to the features that underpin these affordances as *socially creative features*. Socially creative features are platform features that directly enable users to participate in creating new content together with other individuals or groups. We follow Burgess & Baym (2020), who conceptualize 'platform features' as protocological objects that structure and exercise control over the specific social situation on which they are brought to bear (Galloway, 2004). Users may subvert or work around the intended use of these features and, in doing so, can reveal the politics, relationships, and cultures of use (Bucher, 2013). TikTok's socially creative features facilitate participation through their intended uses as well as in the many ways users have subverted and re-appropriated their affordances. In the next sections we briefly describe four socially creative features on TikTok that play crucial functions in enabling and structuring socially creative practices on the platform: Duet, Stitch, Video Reply to Comments, and Use This Sound.

Duet

Duet works by allowing users to scroll through TikTok videos, find a video for duetting, and tap a dedicated Duet button on the TikTok sharing interface (Figure 2.1). The TikTok platform downloads the video and opens the video recording interface to shoot or import a video, which appears side by side with the original used for duetting (Weir, 2020). Duet was a popular and trademarked feature on Musical.ly (The Nation, 2018; see Figure 1.9). Musical.ly's Duet feature was itself reminiscent of another Duet feature, on the social singing platform Smule, which allowed users to create harmonies with themselves or with other users (Smule, 2015). The key difference was that Musical.ly's Duet did not allow additional audio to be recorded when it was introduced for users to dance or lip-sync alongside others (Musical.ly, 2017). Duet was added to TikTok in 2019, alongside another feature, React, designed to be a 'launchpad of creative activities as people re-interpret other peoples' content and create unique experiences' (TikTok, 2019a). The corporate language used to announce Duet and React reflects the maxims of social creativity already discussed, according to which creativity is enacted in groups and informed by others' perspectives (Barron, 1999; Sobrinho & Glăveanu, 2017). TikTok's version of the Duet feature was initially silent, but the React feature did allow users to add their own audio and thus respond to other videos. Duet's functionality was updated in the second half of 2020 in order to allow users to record audio during duets more easily and reposition the layout of the duet, enabling more creative chains of duets (we will return to the topic in chapter 3).

Figure 2.1a and 2.1b. The basic Duet feature (left) and a Duet chain (right).

Stitch

The Stitch feature improved on the React feature, which it replaced, by allowing users to clip a short segment from a previous video and place it at the start of a new video (TikTok, 2020d). The 'stitched' video clip encapsulates the video, the audio, any visual effects, and the onscreen text (see Figure 0.1 in the introduction). Users who stitch other videos can determine the length of the stitch and add new content as normal. The press release announcing the feature again highlighted the potential for social creativity, 'Like Duet, Stitch is a way to reinterpret and add to another user's content, building on their stories, tutorials, recipes, math lessons, and more' (TikTok, 2020d). Before the introduction of the Stitch feature, short-video users could create the same jump-cut effect by editing together multiple clips, either internally on TikTok or using third-party platforms.

By integrating the Stitch feature, ByteDance developers acknowledged how users were contesting established modes of creative interaction on TikTok, beyond the Duet and React functions. Stitch is an excellent feature for showcasing the input of multiple perspectives that feeds the cycles of social creativity (Glăveanu, 2020). For example, a group of indigenous North American TikTokers explained how they used Stitch to engage, explain, or educate other users who may have questions or are misinformed about indigenous communities (Hickey, 2021). Stitch also opens new avenues for trolling or cyberbullying (Hutchinson, 2020). In recognition of this, the announcement indicated how users can disable the option to stitch before posting a video (TikTok, 2020d).

Video Reply to Comments

Video Reply to Comments is another socially creative feature: it allows TikTokers to spotlight a comment left on a previous video and create a new video in response to the comment or to the commenter (Figure 2.2; Abidin et al., 2020). The new comment appears onscreen in the response video and users can edit its timing and placement for creative effect. Video Reply was teased in March 2020 and officially announced in June 2020, three months before Stitch (Siddiqui, 2020). The press release that accompanied the feature's debut nodded to the role of audiences in the socially creative process (Potts et al., 2008), stating: 'There's nothing quite like the connection between creators and their fans. So often, that connection forms in a video's comments section, where viewers can share jokes, offer commentary, ask questions, and ultimately build community with other users' (TikTok, 2020e).

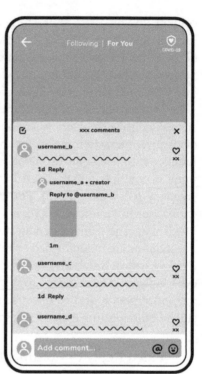

Figure 2.2a and 2.2b. Video Reply to Comments.

The announcement also provided three examples of the feature's use. Users could respond to comments that requested them to make a specific video, for example a song or recipe. Users could use a comment reply as an FAQ, to answer a question asked by multiple other commenters. Users could provide tutorials in which they explained how they created a certain effect or how other users could participate in the trend or in the challenge depicted in the video. In our interview, Kapono (@kaponowmusic) explained that he used Video Reply to Comments mainly to address racist and abusive comments that appeared in his comment section. Kapono noted that, although not as positive as in the examples provided in the TikTok press release (TikTok, 2020e), the feature was still an effective and creative way to 'educate' users who posted toxic or trolling comments by calling them out. As he explained, 'I don't want to call them out for clout. I call them out so they can like understand what they did wrong and maybe they can learn from their mistakes' (Kapono @kaponowmusic, 2021).

Use This Sound

The fourth socially creative feature, Use This Sound, traces back to Musical.ly. Creatively using music in videos was a major appeal for making lip-sync videos on Musical.ly. Like its early competitor Flipagram, Musical.ly had an internal library of sounds that users could select for inclusion in their videos. Musical.ly's audio feature also had a function that allowed users to upload and employ their own sounds by uploading an Mp3 file from internal device storage. Tapping on the sound, located as an icon at the bottom of the video, would show users other videos that employ that sound, and would allow them to create a new video with the same audio. This feature was expanded into 'Use This Sound' on TikTok. Use This Sound is accessed by tapping on the sound badge, a rotating vinyl record icon at the bottom right of the main video viewing window. The platform assigns each video a named audio file, which scrolls across the bottom centre of the screen, to the left of the sound badge. Tapping on the sound badge opens the sound's profile page – a screen that gives the name of the original creator, the total number of videos that use that sound, and a feed with the most popular videos that feature it (see Figure 1.3). At the bottom of the sound profile page is a bright red, pulsating Use This Sound button (see Figure 1.1). As on Musical.ly, here too Use This Sound opens a video creation screen and makes a new video, in which the audio is being used. When a video is posted, the reused or original sound featured in the video can be easily taken and employed by other users through the Use This

Sound function. This is slightly different from the behaviour of other socially creative features. At the end of the native video creation process, users are given the option to disable other users from using Duet or Stitch or from leaving text comments, but in mid-2021 there was still no option to disallow Use This Sound.

Use This Sound is a socially creative feature particularly when the sound being used is an original sound from another user. Like the three features discussed previously, using the sounds of others requires the participation of at least two users. There are also many ways for users to reinterpret meanings or add personal perspectives (Glăveanu, 2020) when creatively using others' sounds. We return to the socially creative aspects of Use This Sound later in this chapter, when discussing the *aural turn* in memes on TikTok (Abidin & Kaye, 2021).

In-app video creation and editing features

A successful design decision made by TikTok was to ensure that video creation and editing are as streamlined and simple as possible. In many other video-sharing apps, the focus is on *sharing* the videos, while the creation and editing of these videos are expected to be done in other apps. But in TikTok these features and functions are part of the app, which facilitates both creative expression and commercial exploitation. In this section we will explore effects and filters on the TikTok platform and will also discuss a relatively recently introduced feature that actually departs from the short-video format – live streaming.

Effects and filters

Effects and filters are creative features that allow users to add a variety of content to their video without manual editing. The effects page, accessed via the video creation screen, has an ever-expanding library of effects content organized by theme. In addition to general filter categories such as 'beauty', 'funny', 'world', 'animal', and 'music' effects, there are categories for green-screen effects, interactive filters, and video-editing tools. Like the Use This Sound function, visual effects and filters in use are automatically displayed as an interactive badge on videos if the video is edited in the native TikTok video editor. Subsequent viewers can tap the filter badge to create a new video that uses the same filter. Filters and effects are not novel to TikTok: platforms such as Snapchat and Instagram previously introduced filters that change users' appearances, add augmented reality effects, and so on. But filters on TikTok have more options and higher complexity than these traditional social media platforms. For instance, since audio is such a central aspect of the TikTok experience, audio filters, sound effects, and songs paired with other visual features are all important creative features on the platform.

In a side-by-side comparison, filters and effects are areas of significant divergence between TikTok and Douyin. Beyond the obvious cultural and language-specific filters, it is also interesting to note that a beautification filter is enabled as default on the Douyin platform. This default filter smoothed one's facial appearance and made skin tones appear slightly lighter, replicating a popular camera effect in China known as *meibai* ('beautify whitening') (Kaye, Chen, & Zeng, 2021). *Meibai* filters can replace costly plastic surgery or time-consuming cosmetic makeup to produce the dominant beauty standard of *wanghong* (Chinese internet celebrities): 'big eyes, double eyelids, white skin, a high-bridged nose, and pointed chin' (Li, 2019, p. 3023).

Live streaming

While TikTok is primarily a platform for sharing pre-recorded short videos, a live-streaming function enables users to broadcast themselves in real time for their followers, and also for others who scroll the For You page. The live-streaming system is another major infrastructural difference between TikTok and Douyin (Kaye, Chen, & Zeng, 2021). Live streaming is a privilege on both platforms, 'gated' and protected through a minimum follower count threshold: only users with 1,000+ and respectively 50,000+ followers are allowed to live-stream on TikTok and on Douyin. If they want to access and watch live streams on TikTok, users must swipe a finger across the screen to get into their Following page, where they see badges of followed users who are currently live; or they must find the live stream randomly, while scrolling through their For You pages. TikTok also notifies users, through messages in their inbox, about certain live streams such as sponsored ones, streamed events, or live streams by popular or followed users. On Douyin, by contrast, next to the For You and Following pages, there is a TV-shaped icon that enables users to scroll only through live streams (see Figure 1.11). As we will see in detail in chapter 5, live streaming is a major component of TikTok's platform economy. TikTok's internal economy relies on a virtual currency that can be purchased through the platform and gifted to other users. In mid-2021, the only way to spend this internal virtual currency on TikTok is via live streaming.

Social media platform features

TikTok certainly is a music-centric mobile short-video platform, but it also belongs to the broad category of social media platforms. Being in that category, TikTok has many of the standard features that one would expect in most other social media platforms, such as @ mentioning, hashtags, commenting, and sharing. In this section we show how these features have been implemented on TikTok's platform and we discuss functions and features that are designed to make the platform accessible to users with a wide range of abilities.

@ Mentioning

The @ symbol followed by a username, as used in video text or comments,[4] creates a hyperlink to the mentioned user's profile, and the mentioned user is notified. The @ can be used to 'summon' other users to a video by commenting @mentions on a video or by chaining together comment threads with multiple users, all tagging the same person. In our interviews with TikTokers, they described instances of @summoning in their comment sections 'offline celebrities' – that is, famous people without a social media presence and often without smartphones – such as the Grammy award-winning artist Lizzo or the chef Gordon Ramsay, as well as some of the biggest TikTok stars, for example @BellaPoarch and @Khaby.Lame. Celebrity TikTok comments create opportunities for more social creativity, such as posting a comment reply video to express shocked excitement, or even posting a Duet or a Stitch of the original video by celebrities themselves. During our interview, Gabbi (@fettuccinefettuqueen) explained her surprise when @summoning brought to her comment section the American celebrity Wayne Brady, who complimented her for writing the songs and composing the music for *Ratatousical*, or *Ratatouille: The TikTok Musical*.[5] Of course, @summoning can also bring friends, mutuals, or random TikTokers to one's page, making them engage in unexpected and distributed creativity.

Hashtags

Hashtags on TikTok can be either included in the video texts as metadata or embedded in the comments. When tapping on a hashtag in either place (video text or comment), users will be shown a hashtag page that displays the videos that use the hashtag in question and presents the option to 'use this hashtag' in a new video, just as one would 'use this sound'. On TikTok as on other digital platforms, hashtags are important mediators for visibility. Branded hashtags may appear on videos that neither are sponsored by the brand nor have anything to do with the promotional campaign. Similarly, nonsensical hashtags such as #xyzbca have no deeper meaning beyond that of .phatic communication designed to boost visibility on the platform. In mid-2021, over 1.2 trillion videos included #fyp – the For You page. As will appear shortly, #fyp is one of many strategies for navigating the For You page black-box recommender systems. Hashtags are useful for creating ad hoc publics, fluid communities anchored in certain topics or tags (Bruns & Burgess, 2015).

Likes, comments, shares

The TikTok main viewing window is designed to be minimalistic, with only five tappable buttons on the right-hand side of the screen and five menu buttons at the bottom (see Figure 2.3). The first is the user profile picture, which functions the same way as an @mention: one has to tap in order to view the creator's profile. The fifth button is the audio badge, which allows users to tap into the Use This Sound feature. In between the profile and the audio are three features very familiar to social media users: the ability to like, comment, and share.

Like. The Like feature functions just like on other social media platforms, for example Twitter and Instagram. This means that TikTokers can 'like' a video or a comment; this is represented by a heart icon, which saves the video to one's favourites list and sends a notification to the original poster. In the platform's privacy settings, users can indicate whether their list of liked videos is visible to other users. In mid-2021, likes on TikTok were not disambiguated into reaction emojis, as on Facebook's and Twitter's direct messaging service. As on other platforms, on TikTok, too, likes are a key measure of engagement. They constitute one of three statistics displayed

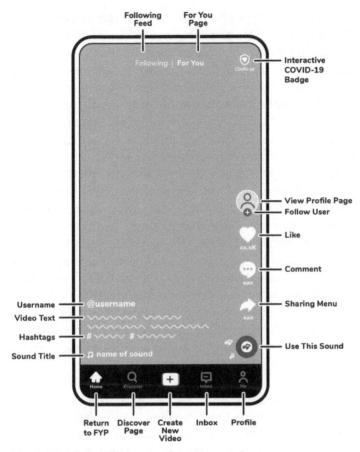

Figure 2.3. Labelled TikTok main video viewing window.

at the top of a user's profile page, the other two being the number of followers and number of other users followed.

Comment. Text comments on TikTok follow the conventions of the short-video format by limiting comments to 150 characters. In 2021, TikTok's comment character limit is the lowest among competing international digital platforms.[6] Users can type comments of their own, can 'like' the comments of others and can reply to comments. The original creator of the video can choose to reply to a comment with text or with a video. Comment sections are automatically sorted by language and by followed users. In other words, commenters would see comments from the users they follow placed above the most popular comments in the thread (Abidin et al., 2020). For example, users who have their internal language profile set to Japanese will see Japanese comments first, before seeing comments in other languages. Comments are also automatically filtered so that abusive ones are removed. Comment filtering is enabled by default, but users can adjust their comment filters in their account privacy settings. The first option is 'all comments', which means that comments will be hidden until approved by the user. The second option is spam and offensive comment filtering; this is the default filter setting. Offensive comments are determined according to an internal algorithmic language-processing system. The third option is keyword filtering, which means that comments will be removed if they contain keywords specified by the user, in addition to the default filtering.

Share. The Share feature allows users to share content (e.g. videos, sounds, user profiles) with other users on TikTok, copy a URL to the content, or share content through other linked social media platforms (e.g. Facebook, Twitter, WhatsApp). The option to share content creates one of the main aesthetic differences between the TikTok and Douyin interfaces. Douyin includes far fewer sharing options than TikTok and, unsurprisingly, all are designed to integrate with Chinese digital platforms (Kaye, Chen, & Zeng, 2021). The Share button is also the omnibus entry point for the additional menu items when viewing a video. The first option is to report the video for any community guideline violations. Tapping the Report button opens a form-entry screen where users can select the type of violation and submit their report. The somewhat unintuitive location of the Report feature has caused controversy in the past, when disturbing or graphic content circulated on underage users' For You pages and parents did not know where to find the Report button (Matamoros-Fernandez & Kaye, 2020). The second option is the Not Interested button, which lets users skip the video while also ostensibly 'instructing' the TikTok recommender system not to recommend similar content. Next to Report and Not Interested are buttons for engaging in the socially creative features Duet and Stitch. Finally, there are three options to archive the video by downloading it (if the option to download has been enabled by the original creator), by sharing the full video as a GIF, or by taking a 'live photo' using clips from the video.

As discussed elsewhere in this book, the Like, Comment, and Share features are prominent fixtures of the TikTok algorithmic imaginary (Bucher, 2017). Several interviewees' tactics of boosting visibility relied on liking, commenting, and using the Share function. In the videos they posted, some would ask viewers to engage in any combination of the three so as to help their video grow. Among the videos they found while scrolling, many would make sure to like, comment, and share the ones posted by both friends and strangers, even without fully watching them.

Accessibility features

A final aspect of TikTok's familiar features relates to features that improve its accessibility to the widest possible range of users. Accessibility features include seizure warnings, which are automatically tagged on videos with flashing lights, and features for hearing-impaired users, for example closed captioning and text to speech (IUKB, 2021). TikTok has faced criticism for its sluggish and reactionary approach to supporting accessibility features. An auto-closed captioning feature was added to TikTok in 2021, several months after the Instagram competitor Reels had added the same feature (Perez, 2021a). In May 2021, a Canadian voice actor sued TikTok for using her voice for the text-to-speech function without her consent and without compensation (Criddle, 2021). As news of the lawsuit spread, debate arose between users who wanted people to stop operating the function because of abusive practices and users who urged people to continue availing themselves of it for practical accessibility reasons (Kastrenakes, 2021). Other accessibility issues, such as the ability to reuse audio and particularly the voices of other users, are more endemic to short-video platforms. In one example, a neurodivergent creator shared a video asking for advice on how to lock the audio on their video so that others could not reuse it to mock, harass, or bully disabled users (Kaye, Rodriguez et al., 2021). In response, commentators highlighted strategies facilitated by TikTok with the help of which the creator would avoid having his or her voice or audio used in unexpected ways.

Emergent platform practices

The features discussed in the sections above underpin the affordances that enable and constrain TikTok users' ability to create and communicate via the platform. As TikTokers engage in socially creative processes enabled by these features, they uncover new affordances, and this eventually leads to the development of platform-specific norms and practices (see Glăveanu, 2020, discussed earlier in this chapter).

In this section we explore a number of such user-driven practices, which have emerged with or without encouragement from the platform. These norms and practices are inherently fluid, but we choose to focus on a set of them that we deem are currently central to the TikTok platform: lip-syncing, challenges, calls for engagement, and attribution practices.

Lip-syncing

Lip-syncing was the main theme for short videos on both Dubsmash and Musical.ly. According to the Musical.ly creation mythology, lip-syncing was made a central component of the platform after the app creators noticed a spike in app downloads on Thursday evenings during the TV game show *Lip Sync Battle*. Users were required to find a song or an audio clip and learn it well enough to perform it as one's own. Similarly, a main selling point of Flipagram was its licensed internal audio library, from which users could select their favourite songs, to go with their short videos. Lip-syncing continues to be a foundational practice on the TikTok platform and has evolved over time into song memes, into well-travelled lip-syncing memes based on stand-up comedy bits (e.g. Anjelah Johnson's 'Nail Salon' bit),[7] or into a form of political commentary, such as Sarah Cooper's (@whatchugot-forme) ironic lip-syncing to Donald Trump's musings about the benefits of injecting your body with disinfectant.[8] We will continue the topic of lip-syncing practices in chapter 4, when we explore lip-syncing as a form of TikTok activism.

Challenges

Challenges, which may feature lip-syncing to audio, dance routines, comedic skits, and many other forms, have become one of the defining features of TikTok. Such memetic challenges are seemingly trivial, but they can 'highlight affect, political views, reactions, key information, and scenes of importance' (Highfield & Leaver, 2016, p. 48). TikTok challenges are multimodal meme templates, shaped by platform norms and algorithmic systems into aesthetically similar content (Leaver et al., 2019). Multimodal communication is layered across different communicative modes such as 'image, writing, layout, music, gesture, speech, moving image, soundtrack and 3D objects' (Kress, 2009, p. 79).

Semiotic modes, similarly, are shaped both by the intrinsic characteristics and potentialities of the medium and by the requirements, histories and values of societies and their cultures (Kress & van Leeuwen, 2021).

Ravelli and van Leeuwen (2018) revisit communicative and semantic modes in the context of digital platforms, calling for a deeper understanding of new variables and of changes to existing variables that configure the meaning and orientation of multimodal content. For example, new methods now exist to analyse the modality of digital music by pairing a textual analysis of lyrics with an analysis of sonic classifiers previously built on the original creators' work digital platforms: '(1) the scale of the audience with which young people can share their performances; (2) the scale at which they can access other versions of performances of the same music; and (3) the fixity of the media they use'. On top of these significant shifts in scale, access, and fixity, the onscreen recorded actions – in this case, sign language and hand gestures – are yet another independent modality on Musical.ly, and now on TikTok, alongside music, lyrics, text, metadata, and video clips. The interactions among these numerous short-video modalities create a communicative environment of TikTok that constitutes a 'dynamic structure... open toward being appropriated and navigated in different ways and in negotiation of potential consequences' (Schellewald, 2021, p. 1451). Situated in that environment are headline-grabbing, viral, fame-inducing, adult-mystifying TikTok challenges, described as 'an easy way for people on TikTok to feel like they're part of the community' – which is achieved through a series of videos 'attempting to do the same thing' (Alexander, 2019a, p. 1).

Zulli and Zulli (2020) offer two explanations for the prevalence and success of TikTok challenges. First is the level of participation among elite users – TikTok internet celebrities with millions of followers and extremely high visibility. The second is the notion of liveliness – the idea that users are immediately engaged with the social realities of other users by participating in challenges. Building on these explanations, Zulli and Zulli coined the term 'imitation publics', which designates 'a collection of people whose digital connectivity is constituted through the shared ritual of content imitation and replication' (2020, p. 11). The activities of catering to and profiting from imitation and replication, they argue, explain why TikTok promotes multimodal mimesis on the platform with users fluidly embedding meaning that is decodable by different configurations of publics.

Visual challenges such as the 2014 Ice Bucket Challenge often display an image or a video of the individual(s) who participate(s) in the challenge. Audio, by contrast, can more easily become disconnected from the original creators. This was especially the case up until late 2020, when TikTok automatically assigned any audio as an original sound. In response, TikTokers developed a variety of strategies designed to overcome infrastructure flaws.

Calls for participation

Earlier in this chapter we discussed how algorithmic folklore shapes user practices. One such myth, expressed in the press (Matsakis, 2020) and by a handful of creators interviewed for this book, is that the For You algorithm initially shows videos to a small number of users and then exponentially to more users, depending on how the video performs in the initial group. Like other types of algorithmic lore, this story, true or false, shapes the actions of creators who seek to appease the algorithm.

This is not novel to TikTok. It is nonetheless useful to show how audience interaction and engagement manifest themselves on short-video platforms. Consider the call to action for audience participation on other social media entertainment platforms; think of YouTubers who urge their audiences to 'smash that like button', 'drop a comment below', and 'hit the bell to get notifications', or podcasters who ask listeners to rate and review their content, or live-streamers who directly speak and respond to viewers' input in the chat (Peterschmidt, 2015; Sehl, 2020). The simple act of consuming also contributes to engagement metrics, represented by the number of views or streams; but calls to action demonstrate that creators place a higher value on active participation than on mere passive consumption.

Abidin (2021) describes how the interactions between TikTokers and audiences are manifested through the platform's frenetic attention economy (see also Goldhaber, 2006). TikTok creators call on their audiences to participate directly with their videos through

- *ownership practices,* or asserting creative claims over content by asking audiences to credit them in subsequent reuse,
- *algorithmic practices,* such as by 'press[ing] random buttons' to improve visibility of their account or content, and
- *interactive practices,* calling on audiences to get involved by creating content of their own, using the socially creative features to Duet or Stitch videos. (Abidin, 2021, pp. 85–92)

Each of these visibility labours (Abidin, 2016) relies on a combination of assumptions that creators make about audiences and vice versa, namely that engaging in these practices will have the desired effect, be it stimulating viewers to engage or helping to boost a creator's visibility.

Visibility labour on TikTok may also involve calls to *inaction* whereby creators, in order to command viewers' attention for the full 15–60-second video, assertively ask audiences to 'stop scrolling' in the first few seconds. These 'pausing practices' are more passive, yet still very much active ways to engage with attention economies on TikTok. They are passive in the sense that creators or TikTokers are literally asking viewers to wait for a few moments and not touch anything. This can constitute a big ask on short-video platforms, where brand new, highly personalized, and bite-sized content is always just a swipe away. Interviews with musical TikTokers revealed pausing practices to be a popular tactic among musical artists who hope to promote new music through cross-platform traffic. The template for this meme begins with immediately asking viewers to stop scrolling right at the start of the video; this is meant to pique interest and is usually followed by a heartfelt story about the song or album that ends with a call to stream the song on a music streaming platform or to use it in TikTok videos, and then perfectly loops back to the beginning.[9] The ask here is at first for viewers to be passive – to pause from an activity – but quickly shifts to a call on them to be extremely active – it goes as far as encouraging them to leave TikTok and open another app.

In addition to having visibility, audience interactions are naturally involved in co-constructing the experiences of others on TikTok. Audiences are deeply entrenched in the power dynamics that shape digital media (Livingstone, 2019). These power dynamics can have serious repercussions in terms of trolling, bullying, and harassment on platforms in general, but on TikTok they can also shift the ballast of one's entire experience. In 2020, clashes between members of queer communities on TikTok – what was described as 'Alt TikTok' – and the more mainstream side of the platform, known as 'Straight TikTok', prompted the publication of guides on how to stay on one's preferred 'side' (Segaetsho, 2020). TikTokers were advised to take a hands-on approach to curating their For You page recommendations by deliberately liking or commenting on certain videos and tapping to select the option Not Interested for others. To go a step further, they could even post videos that asked for audiences to interact with their content not so as to boost the visibility of their content but so as to help them navigate back to their preferred communities (Segaetsho, 2020).

Being on different sides of TikTok can significantly impact one's experiences both as a viewer and as a creator. Violet, a non-binary creator, initially received overwhelmingly negative interactions on their videos. Violet explained that they thought about quitting the platform, but kept going when they would receive supportive comments. It was not until after they posted their first viral hit that their experience began to change.

> I've been on the wrong side of TikTok for most of my career. I was bullied. It wasn't until really recently I started blowing up on the other side of TikTok. Now the energy I'm receiving is all very positive and super supportive. (Violet (@violetbutnotaflower))

When asked what the 'wrong' and 'right' sides of TikTok were, Violet explicitly named Straight and Alt TikTok. Violet went on to recount how their early posts were frequently reported for community guideline violations, which sometimes resulted in videos being removed, although in Violet's view these videos did not depict anything that would warrant a violation. Violet explained that trolls from Straight TikTok who found Violet's account would spam report Violet's videos as a form of harassment. After Violet navigated to Alt TikTok, a few weeks before our interview, the steady stream of reports drew to a halt.

This process of audiences shaping experiences is multi-directional. In the example of Straight versus Alt TikTok, TikTokers deployed strategies of audience participation to get away from the uncomfortable sides of TikTok. Audience participation can also be responsible for putting them there.

Sarah (pseudonym),[10] a TikToker with fewer than 100,000 followers who normally posted meme videos, went viral after sharing a politically charged video that reached wider audiences outside her usual viewership. The video landed on the For You pages of users with opposing political viewpoints, who began interacting with the video by sharing it or by commenting on it, as well as by using socially creative features to troll or harass Sarah. Videos that stitched or duetted Sarah also began going viral among communities that comprised the 'bad side' of TikTok, so far as she was concerned. Because many of the subsequent videos contained embedded links that sent back to her original video or account, Sarah's videos were brigaded by an influx of combative viewers. This is a phenomenon previously observed on digital platforms that host users with a variety of opposing viewpoints and have moderation features or policies that may obscure the extent of the abuse (Matamoros-Fernandez, 2017). On TikTok, however, the high amount of traffic and engagement from hostile audience members signalled to the recommender system that Sarah might also be interested in seeing other content relevant to her new visitors. She explained that her For You page changed after that incident and became filled with content she found confronting, problematic, and deplorable. She felt trapped on the 'bad' side of TikTok and stopped using the app altogether for a few days. When she returned, she posted videos asking members of friendly and familiar communities, the 'good' side of TikTok, to interact with her content in order to help her escape.

Attribution

TikTok is a digital environment that invites users to reuse and remix content. In such environments, automated attribution systems are commonly used to maintain a link between the original content creator and subsequent users of that content (Monroy-Hernández et al., 2011). When these systems fail to identify the correct user or are deliberately circumvented by users, original creators can miss out on the benefits associated with their audio going viral. Drawing on platformization research (Duffy, Poell, & Nieborg, 2019), Kaye, Rodriguez et al. (2021) conceptualize attributional platform practices as the type of actions in which a user tries to ensure that an original creator is properly attributed his or her work, without relying on an automated attribution system.

Attributional platform practices exist on a broader continuum of illicit and permissible sampling (Behr, Negus, & Street, 2017). They may involve using a single onscreen reference to an artist or creator whose work is featured in a subsequent TikTok video. They may also involve a combination of practices such as hashtagging, manually renaming audio clips, and giving verbal mentions during the video. In some cases, creators develop their own practices of manually giving credit to the original without diminishing their own creativity or the creativity of others. For example, they add hashtags and other metadata to identify the original creators, while also promoting the TikTokers who previously built on the original creators' work.

To improve issues and errors with its automatic attribution system, in late 2020 TikTok introduced a sound-matching system designed to identify songs uploaded to the platform by creators incorrectly listed as original audio. But it is questionable whether the current sound-matching tool is an improvement, or whether it only complicates the appropriate crediting and attribution of creative content. TikTok's sound-matching system can seemingly identify individual clips of popular songs. However, in many cases of misattribution on TikTok, sound matching would be just as ineffective or inapplicable as the automatic attribution system. For example, a sound-matching system would have difficulty identifying more complex audio clips such as two mashed-up songs, individual creator voices, or audio clips drawing on other media sources – say, TV shows or films. The issues that can arise from these everyday practices further highlight the importance of complementary attributional platform practices.

In a digital environment that thrives on spreadability (Jenkins et al., 2013) and where attributional issues are platform-facilitated and user-perpetuated cultural norms

(Meese & Hagedorn, 2019), the creators' ability to assert authorship of their original works is limited. As we discuss later on in this book, TikTok's approach to attribution creates economic value for the platform but may do little to motivate creators, if they feel that their creative labour is going unnoticed. Yet the additional effort required from other creators to acknowledge original authorship through (mis)attribution practices can build 'emotional value' (Monroy-Hernández et al., 2011, p. 3428), which contributes to community building and incentivizes creativity. Through these relational aspects, attribution practices on TikTok can be construed as part of a platform-specific, best-practice model of giving credit that is acceptable to the creative community.

Appropriation

While they represent a step in the right direction, attributional platform practices are not enough to redress the harm caused by more serious forms of misattribution such as cultural appropriation. Allowing white creators' cultural appropriation of pieces produced by black, indigenous, and people of colour (BIPOC) creators has been a recurring critique of TikTok, particularly in the United States, where practices on TikTok have deep historical roots connected to race, power, and supremacy. According to Hall (1997), 'the pattern of separating the art from the people leads to an appropriation of aesthetic innovation that not only "exploits" Black cultural forms, commercially and otherwise, but also nullifies the cultural meaning those forms provide for African Americans' (p. 32). Young (2008) characterizes cultural appropriation as profoundly offensive, since it 'strike[s] at a person's core values or sense of self' (p. 130). Analyzing racialized practices on one of TikTok's main competitors, Stevens (2021) argues that Instagram's affordances encourage users to 'engage in more physical, phenotypical, and embodied forms of appropriation' (p . 7) that commodify black identity. As we discuss in chapter 1, elements of templatability that encourage replication and mimesis on Instagram (Leaver et al., 2019) are augmented by socially creative features on TikTok. Duet, Stitch, and Use This Sound can add new dimensions to the ways in which white creators engage with and appropriate content from BIPOC creators.

Dance challenges are a clear example of cultural appropriation on short-video platforms. As we noted in chapter 1, features designed to imitate and replicate dances were key selling points for short-video platforms Musical.ly, Dubsmash, and later TikTok. In *Renegades: Digital Dance Cultures from Dubsmash to TikTok*, Boffone (2021) analyzes how cultural forces such as homophobia, sexism, and racism shape identity construction and participation for young creators on short-video platforms. Boffone begins by describing the eponymous Renegade, a dance challenge originally choreographed by Jalaiah Harmon, a 14-year-old black creator from Georgia, then popularized (among many others) by Charli D'Amelio, a 15-year-old white creator and the first one to surpass 100 million followers. Several months after Harmon posted the original dance, a *New York Times* profile credited her as the original creator of the dance. In response to public outcry, Boffone notes that D'Amelio shifted to crediting choreographers for the dances she performed on TikTok. Even so, the Renegade and subsequent incidents highlight how attributional platform practices of giving credit where due fall flat in instances of cultural appropriation.

As another example, in April 2021 Addison Rae Easterling, a popular TikToker, appeared on the American late night talk show *The Tonight Show Starring Jimmy Fallon*. In her segment, Easterling 'taught' Fallon how to do several dance moves that had garnered her millions of views on TikTok. During the two-minute segment, Fallon held cards with the names of dance challenges that Easterling performed while accompanied by the house band The Roots. After the show aired, the segment drew backlash against the fact that

Easterling, a young white female creator, had been invited to perform these dances without any acknowledgement that they were originally created by BIPOC artists. A video of the segment entitled 'Addison Rae Teaches Jimmy Eight TikTok Dances' was viewed more than 5 million times on YouTube and attracted further criticism for failing to credit the original BIPOC dance creators. One observer remarked:

> The fact they have no idea how offensive this is, is sickening. This is systemic racism at its finest. This white women [*sic*] is benefiting from a broken system & was highlighted on national TV, while the choreographers & actual artists that made the songs weren't even mentioned smh. (@WhosTYE, as quoted in Andrews, 2021)[11]

In response to the backlash, Fallon aired another segment in the following week, inviting the original creators[12] of the dance challenges to share the story of their routine and to perform it. Fallon began the segment by saying:

> On our last show we did a bit with Addison Rae where she taught me eight viral TikTok Dances. We recognize that the creators of those dances deserve to have their own spotlight so right now some of the creators will join me to talk about how their dance went viral. (Fallon, 2021)[13]

There was no admission of guilt, ownership of mistake, or acknowledgement of cultural appropriation. In fact, the segment was framed as though it were *The Tonight Show*'s idea to revisit TikTok dances, as opposed to its being compelled to give credit where credit was due in response to public outcry. Such a reaction exhibited a familiar unwillingness to engage with race, power, and white supremacy in the United States (Di Angelo, 2018; Hughey, 2021) or to apologize for the profound offence of cultural appropriation (Young, 2008). These repeated public failings have normalized new attributional platform practices such as including IB ('inspired by') or DC ('dance credit') and @mentioning the original creators. As we will revisit in later chapters, these practices alone cannot bridge the divide between the marginalized creators who originate popular trends and the mainstream TikTokers who commodify them.

Conclusion

In this chapter we argue that TikTok is an inherently music-centric, mobile, and socially creative platform. We discussed TikTok's For You algorithm and the feed of recommended videos that it generates for the platform's users. We also discussed the folklore and the mythology surrounding this opaque system and how these myths give rise to various opportunistic strategies intended to boost the visibility of the users' posts. We also explored a range of TikTok features – socially creative features, in-app video creation, and editing features – and the mundane but essential features that are found on most social media platforms. Finally, we discussed how these features structure and shape platform practices and norms that have become established components of the TikTok creative ecosystem. In the next chapter we turn our attention to the emergence of different types of TikTok communities.

3

TikTok Communities

Social media platforms have facilitated the emergence of online communities built around professions (Mahrt, Weller, & Peters, 2014), political beliefs (Bruns & Highfield, 2013), ethnicity (Abidin & Zeng, 2020), and other forms of identity. As explained in chapter 2, the connectivity between users on TikTok is predominantly content-centric rather than network-centric. This form of creativity-driven sociality shapes how communities – together with the sense of community – are created on TikTok. Emphasizing such specificities, we discuss in this chapter the coexistence and contestation between different types of communities on the short-video platform. To study the nuances that differentiate between these communities, we rely on Tönnies' classical concepts of *Gesellschaft* and *Gemeinschaft*, which will be introduced in the first section of the chapter. In the subsequent section we discuss the pop-cultural 'mainstream' side of TikTok, home to the platform's most popular creators, major trending, and viral content. We explain how members of these communities are a mixture of new users native to TikTok and nomadic short-video users who migrated to TikTok when other international short-video platforms such as Vine were shuttered.

Next, we explore niche communities that form on TikTok. We use an in-depth case study of one such community to show how community bonds are formed through algorithmic influence, human agency, and creative interaction.

Building community through short video

Inspired by the mobile communications scholar Rich Ling (2012), we draw on the notions of *Gemeinschaft* ('community') and *Gesellschaft* ('society') proposed by Ferdinand Tönnies in 1887: we will think about the community-building capability of short-video platforms with the help of these two concepts (Tönnies, 1965 [1887]). In German, both nouns designate types of communities divided by societal tensions. *Gemeinschaft* is close, intimate, and interpersonal; it brings smaller groups of individuals together through emotional connections or feelings. *Gesellschaft* is formal, calculating, individualistic; it separates individuals according to personal beliefs, values, and imperatives. Tönnies suggests an inevitable shift towards the *Gesellschaft* type of formation as societies become more urban and disconnected, 'when the village and the town develop into a city... the transition takes place from gemein-schaft to gesellschaft' (Tönnies, as quoted in Ling, 2012, p. 187).

In his analysis of mobile communication as a technology for social mediation, Ling (2012, p. 187) explains that, while mobile communication is an important mediator for *Gesellschaft*, such technologies also foster a sense of digital *Gemeinschaft* – a sense of kinship among intimate groups such as friends, family, or members of insular communities embedded in society. In the field of internet studies, scholarly discussion of a digital platform's affordances in fostering this digital kind of *Gemeinschaft* is dominated by studies of social networking platforms such as Facebook and Twitter. In recent years, however, a handful of studies have provided insights into how communities emerge on short-video platforms as well.

Studies of Chinese short-video platforms have indicated that, amid a widening gulf between urban and rural communities in the country, short-video platforms have been able to create new links between the village and the metropolis. For instance, Lin and de Kloet (2019) describe the emergence of an 'unlikely creative class' of marginalized rural short-video creators who build their influence through depictions of everyday life outside the bustling megacities. Wang and Wu's (2021) study of rural communities on Douyin further illustrates how the tension between the ancestral rural and the contemporary metropolis is negotiated through short videos.

A few TikTok studies also show that, although strong-tie interpersonal networks are not central to the platform, connectivity, intimacy, and a sense of belonging can be fostered through discursive participation and cultural practices. For instance, issue publics[1] emerge when TikTokers participate in challenges, fighting for social advocacies such as climate campaigns (Hautea et al., 2021). The wide employment of TikTok by health workers and scientists (Southerton, in press; Zeng et al., 2021) also illustrates the emergence of profession-based communities on the platform.

In the following sections of this chapter we will discuss TikTok communities, focusing on the coexistence and tension between their *Gesellschaft*-related and their *Gemeinschaft*-related characteristics on the platform. Short-video community dynamics can propel TikTokers to widespread fame, making them visible to a more mainstream community, which we characterize as *Gesellschaft*, and they can also help to return TikTokers to a smaller, collective community, which we characterize as *Gemeinschaft*.

TikTok *Gesellschaft*-type communities

As TikTok increased its user base, it also started to get attention from a group of *New York Times* journalists who chronicled their journey of diving into the 'strange and beautiful world of TikTok' (Poniewozik et al., 2019, p. 1). TikTok's account creation process does involve asking new users about their personal interests (Kaye, Chen, & Zeng, 2021). But, even after answering these questions, users spend the first few days on

TikTok training the platform, through conscious or unconscious acts, in what they like and what they dislike, so that they gradually build an accurate profile of content on their For You pages. During this onboarding process, new users are likely to be presented with the most widely popular TikTok celebrities and trends that the TikTok recommender system expects will go down well with newcomers to the platform (Rodriguez & Kaye, 2020).

The celebrities the newcomers are met with on TikTok can be referred to as 'microcelebrities' or 'internet celebrities'. Microcelebrities are known to niche groups, they create public personas, engage affectively with their audiences, and consider their online following to be a fan base (Marwick, 2013).

Abidin (2018) distinguishes internet celebrities from other forms of microcelebrities online (Senft, 2008; Marwick, 2013) through a variety of factors: a larger following, multiplatform presence, considerable audience reach, and impact. Internet celebrities rely on a high degree of sustained visibility in what is a highly competitive online environment (Abidin, 2018; 2021). Among the most commercially successful internet celebrities are social media influencers, who can build lucrative careers in social media entertainment (Abidin, 2018).

TikTok's format and features provide an arable space for individual creators to grow careers in, as influencers sustained through participatory and self-branding practices that are commonplace in the social media entertainment industry (Khamis, Ang, & Welling, 2017; Cunningham & Craig, 2019). TikTok does not publish an official chart of its influencers by follower count. There are, however, unofficial charts that provide some useful data. These charts are not always in agreement, but by combining some of the data sources we have been able to compile Table 3.1. The table gives a snapshot of the 50 TikTokers who had the highest number of followers in mid-2021.

Table 3.1. Top 50 TikTokers by follower count, October 2021. Created by the authors. Based on data from https://www.socialtracker.io/toplists/top-50-tiktok-users-by-followers; https://socialblade.com/tiktok/top/50/most-followers; and https://insiflow.com/tiktok/top.

Rank	Profile	Followers	Likes	Nationality	YOB
1	Charli D'Amelio	125.8M	9.9B	United States	2004
2	Khabane Lame	115.3M	1.8B	Italy	2000
3	Addison Rae	84.1M	5.4B	United States	2000
4	Bella Poarch	83.6M	1.9B	United States	1997
5	Zach King	65.6M	814M	United States	1990
6	Will Smith	62M	340M	United States	1968
7	TikTok	57.6M	260M	United States	–
8	Dixie D'Amelio	55.2M	3.1B	United States	2001
9	Spencer X	55M	1.3B	United States	1992
10	Loren Gray	54.1M	2.9B	United States	2002
11	Kimberly Loaiza	52.5M	3B	Mexico	1997
12	Michael Le	50.5M	1.4B	United States	2000
13	Jason Derulo	50M	1.1B	United States	1989
14	CZN Burak	48.6M	904M	Turkey	1994
15	Riyaz Aly	44.4M	2.1B	Bhutan	2003
16	BTS	42.4M	702M	South Korea	–
17	Domelipa	42.2M	2.4B	Mexico	2001
18	Brent Rivera	40.9M	1.3B	United States	1998
19	The Rock	40.8M	219M	United States	1972
20	YZ	39.1M	794M	Germany	1998
21	Junya/じゅんや	38.6M	654M	Japan	1992
22	Avani Gregg	37.2M	2.6B	United States	2002
23	JoJo Siwa	37M	1.2B	United States	2003
24	Kris HC	36.7M	1.6B	Canada	1996
25	ROD	36.5M	2.1B	Mexico	1999
26	Kylie Jenner	36M	426M	United States	1997
27	Selena Gomez	35.9M	196M	United States	1992
28	James Charles	35.8M	909M	United States	1999
29	Joe Albanese	35.8M	1.3B	United States	2001

Rank	Profile	Followers	Likes	Nationality	YOB
30	Baby Ariel	35.7M	1.9B	United States	2000
31	Billie Eilish	34.7M	187M	United States	2001
32	Kirya Kolesnikov	33.8M	716M	Russia	1997
33	Gil Croes	33.6M	823M	Netherlands	1993
34	Scott	33.1M	669M	Netherlands	1994
35	Carlos Feria	32.8M	1.5B	Colombia	1996
36	Faisal Shaikh	32.2M	2B	India	1995
37	Chase Hudson	32.1M	1.7B	United States	2002
38	Wonjeong	31.7M	803M	South Korea	1997
39	Alina Kim	31.5M	548M	Kazakhstan	2003
40	Stokes Twins	31.4M	810M	United States	1996
41	Lucas and Marcus	31.1M	855M	United States	1999
42	Noah Beck	30.7M	2B	United States	2001
43	Kyle Thomas	30.5M	1.4B	United Kingdom	2004
44	Brianda Deyanara	29.6M	2.1B	Mexico	1995
45	wigofellas	29.5M	750M	United States	1994
46	Savannah LaBrant	29.2M	1.5B	United States	1993
47	Darian Rojas	29.2M	1B	Mexico	1996
48	Liza Koshy	29M	364M	United States	1996
49	Liza Anokhina	28.9M	918M	Russia	2007
50	Montpantoja	28.7M	1.5B	Mexico	2002

Among other things, Table 3.1 shows that the median year of birth is 1998 and that the youngest TikToker on the list is born in 2004. When ByteDance acquired Musical.ly in late 2017, most of the platform users were part of the generational bloc labelled 'Gen Z' (Robehmed, 2017), that is, individuals born between 1997 and 2012 (Parker & Igielnik, 2020). The table shows that four years later, in 2021, the composition of the most popular TikTok creators still reflects the young ages of Musical.ly's and TikTok's early adopters. The general notion that TikTokers were young carried over from public perceptions of the estimated 200 million 'Musers' who migrated to TikTok from Musical.ly. Musers were certainly young. As noted in previous chapters, Musical.ly was founded as a short-video MOOC platform and incorporated strategies and features that were supposed to appeal to a younger demographic (Spangler, 2016). Musical.ly was also home to some of the youngest social media users on any platform (Herrman, 2016).

In addition to noting the young age of the top-ranking TikTok celebrities, we find established offline celebrities, including movie stars (e.g. The Rock, Will Smith) and pop stars (e.g. Billie Eilish, Jason Derulo, Selena Gomez). We also find official or organizational accounts (e.g. TikTok) and internet celebrities who built followings online, but not on short-video platforms (e.g. Zach King, James Charles, Junya). The remaining accounts on the list are those of short-video celebrities, some of whom initially gained traction on international short-video platforms that preceded TikTok but are all now undeniably famous on TikTok.

Fame on TikTok builds fast. On the more traditional social media entertainment platform YouTube, the Swedish gaming YouTuber PewDiePie became the first individual creator to surpass 100 million subscribers in 2019 – a feat that took nearly ten years to accomplish (Alexander, 2019b). The most followed TikToker in the middle of 2021, Charli D'Amelio, passed the same milestone in November 2020, 18 months after posting her first TikTok in May 2019 (Kastrenakes, 2020).

We can further note that the top 50 TikTokers are primarily individuals as opposed to multi-channel networks, legacy media companies, or official platform accounts. Over half of these top 50 are Americans, which reflects Musical.ly's and, later, TikTok's push to establish a presence in the US platform market. The top 50 also reflect the wider geographic diversity of the mainstream TikTok community: accounts are from from Bhutan, Canada, Colombia, Germany, India, Italy, Japan, Kazakhstan, Mexico, the Netherlands, Russia, South

Korea, the United Kingdom, and Turkey. As we noted in chapter 2, issues of attribution and appropriation on TikTok highlight skewed power dynamics between white creators and black, indigenous, and people of colour (BIPOC) creators. This is also evident when looking at the list of the top 50 most followed TikTok accounts: two-thirds are American and the majority of the most popular American creators are white. Earlier in this book, we introduced Khaby Lame, a BIPOC creator, who was celebrated by TikTok for becoming the second creator to surpass 100 million followers in August 2021 (TikTok, 2021f). Khaby is not from or based in the United States, where TikTok has faced intense criticism of racial bias (Ohlheiser, 2021). His viral success, therefore, stands in contrast to the success of other BIPOC creators from the United States such as Will Smith, Dwayne 'The Rock' Johnson, and Selena Gomez, who were established celebrities before joining TikTok, or internet celebrities such as Zack King, Spencer X, and Brent Rivera, who built a following on digital platforms that migrated to TikTok. As Shout explained in a follow-up interview conducted in October 2021,

> When it comes to Black creators, when we see that Khaby Lame has surpassed 100m followers of course the first thought will be 'good for him, a black guy getting a lot of traction on TikTok.' But then you dig deeper you find that his main content is just not talking, and I mean it's funny but it's also not problematic for TikTok. And you dig a little deeper and you think I wish he would talk about some other things, especially things going on in the nation right now, then you realize he's not even from America... When I saw that, of course I was happy for his success. But do I think anything changed? Absolutely not. (Shout (@vocaloutburst))

Far fewer young American BIPOC creators have found the same kind of viral success as their white counterparts. Moreover, several creators in the top 50 who rose to fame on short-video platforms (e.g. TikTok, Musical.ly, and Vine), as did Charli D'Amelio, Addison Rae, and Noah Beck, cemented their TikTok fame by lip-syncing to hip-hop or performing dances choreographed by BIPOC creators (Boffone, 2021).

Nomads and natives

While international short-video platforms struggled to find footing, a platform such as Vine was nevertheless able to expand its user base to 200 million users. Creators who built sizable followings on Vine suddenly found themselves without a short-video home after the platform was shuttered in 2015. YouTube was an obvious choice for some, while others migrated to the recently started Musical.ly, which offered many of the familiar short-video features, albeit with a longer length and a lip-syncing gimmick. Users and creators who had migrated to Musical.ly soon found themselves uprooted again when ByteDance acquired the platform in late 2017, then absorbed it into TikTok in April the following year. By 2020, short-video creators who had persevered since Vine were once again met with the all-too-familiar news that they would have to move on when the governments of Australia, India, and the United States declared that they were preparing a ban on TikTok by reason of security concerns.

As for TikTok users with a background in, and experience of, other short-video platforms, we refer to them as 'nomads'. There are several nomads among the top 50 TikTok users. The American R&B singer Jason Derulo is an example of a traditional celebrity who made an early shift to short video: he began with music marketing campaigns launched on Vine and Musical.ly and later became a viral sensation on TikTok.[2]

It was necessary for internet celebrities who came to TikTok from Snapchat, YouTube, or Instagram to learn the ropes of the short-video format quickly. Like traditional celebrities, YouTubers and influencers who learned to create content that was less produced and more spontaneous were embraced on TikTok faster than others.

Some adjustment was necessary even for nomad creators who came to TikTok from other short-video platforms. Musical.ly was significantly different from Vine, both in length and in platform features, and this meant that Vine stars needed to adjust their expectations by at least nine seconds when shifting to Musical.ly. TikTok, by contrast, was similar enough to Musical.ly for celebrity Musers be able to slip into their new mantle of TikTokers with relative ease. Some of the most popular Musers who migrated to TikTok are Loren Gray and Ariel Martin, who were respectively 14 and 15 when they began posting to Musical.ly, and Jacob Sartorius, who was 13 when he found viral fame on that platform but had been only 11 when he started uploading short-video content to Vine (Elle, 2016).

The natives are not a distinct group of TikTok celebrities; by this description we refer to a number of successful TikTok creators who began their careers on TikTok without any previous experience, acquired from other short-video platforms. In mid-2021, the two most followed TikTokers were (and still are) native to TikTok. Two American teens – Charli D'Amelio and Addison Rae Easterling – rose to fame in July 2019 by participating in popular dance trends and challenges. The pair cultivated their successes separately, and quickly professionalized their presence on TikTok in such a way that, by the end of 2019, they were part of an inaugural LA-based collective known as the TikTok Hype House (discussion to follow). Although both had a background in competitive dance, which is a useful skill to have on a platform that frequently features new viral dance challenges, they started in much the same way as many other native TikTokers, by going randomly viral and capitalizing on their success.

TikTok-famous

The expression 'TikTok-famous' describes individuals featured in viral content on TikTok. Online virality refers to the process by which content circulates rapidly and 'spill[s] over into other social platforms and mainstream media' (van Dijck, 2013, p. 77). On digital platforms, viral content is often associated with memes, cultural information that quickly passes from person to person, scaling into larger social phenomena (Shifman, 2013, p. 365). Marketing and advertising experts are fixated on strategies designed to make content become memes and go viral (Haenlein et al., 2020) but in many cases memes are created organically, unexpectedly, or accidentally (Katz & Shifman, 2017).

Sophie Fraser, known by her stage name Inoxia, or known as @inoxiasounds on TikTok, is an Australian songwriter and vocalist who went viral on TikTok in November 2019.[3] Fraser had been steadily building her music career busking on the streets of Melbourne when, that November, a random passer-by happened to record a video of her cover performance of the popular song 'Dance Monkey' by the breakout Australian recording artist Tones and I (Toni Watson) and posted it on TikTok. The video, which did not credit Fraser as the performing artist or Tones and I as the original recording artist, went viral. Fraser was not a TikTok creator or user at the time, and in 2020 she admitted that she 'had no idea what the app was' (Sophie (@inoxiasounds)). The video had already accumulated over 2 million views by the time Fraser created her own TikTok account, so the first short video she posted from it shows a visceral emotional reaction to the success of the anonymously uploaded video of her performance.

After creating her own TikTok account, Fraser uploaded a longer and higher-quality version[4] of her 'Dance Monkey' cover that also credited the original artist. In the accompanying video text, Fraser implored TikTok to 'make her video go more viral than the video that was uploaded without crediting her'. Her call was heeded by millions and, indeed, this second version went far more viral than the original, uncredited video uploaded by the TikTok user who so unexpectedly catapulted Fraser's professional music career forward. 'It sparked interest among all the major labels. I got flown over to LA and I met all these celebrities, music executives, and was taken to all these fancy dinners' (ibid.). In mid-2021, Fraser's re-uploaded video had over 110 million views.

Creators can find success posting silly videos or dance challenges on TikTok; but, for Fraser, the platform has become a professional calling card: 'Because I have such a big following on my TikTok I feel like I have to be professional... I have to upload strictly singing videos... Like a portfolio for labels' (ibid.). This contrasts with her profile on other platforms that still function as 'normal' social media for the young artist, such as Instagram: 'I let my personality show through a lot more on my Instagram than on my TikTok' (ibid.). Fraser stated that TikTok has now become the primary vehicle for boosting her musical career.

Fraser's rise was cut short by the global COVID-19 pandemic, which required her to shelter at home. To maintain her viral digital profile, her manager encouraged her to become a TikTok 'content creator', which means that she should engage with other logics of TikTok such as dance challenges, memes, and other trending content. But she did not welcome this prospect: 'I didn't know if that would benefit me at all because I'm a musician first. I never thought I would be a content creator or be in this position. My mindset is all about singing, writing, and performing.' Fraser posted several videos while in lockdown, but explained that she was more interested in biding her time before she could get back to the streets and to making music.

Two of the most popular TikTokers in the world owe their TikTok fame, similarly, to accidental virality. One of these, Khabane Lame, has been presented in the introduction. The other is Bella Poarch, a Filipina American creator who went viral in August 2020, after posting a video[5] lip-syncing to a clip from the song 'M to the B', by Millie B; only her face was visible on the screen. Using the Face Zoom visual effect, the camera followed Poarch's expressive lip-syncs to the popular audio through TikTok's Use This Sound feature.

Bella Poarch and Khaby Lame illustrate several aspects of accidental virality on TikTok. First, they had a rapid rise to success. Poarch joined TikTok in April 2020 and Lame joined in March the same year. Slightly more than a year later, in mid-2021, both Poarch and Lame had about 70 million TikTok followers. Second, both went viral for doing simple activities that used creative short-video features. Compared to others (mentioned here) who became TikTok-famous by dancing or singing, Poarch and Lame posted relatively mundane yet replicable templates, and they did it through Use This Sound, in order to take part in audio meme trends, or through Stitch, in order to take viewers by surprise.

Immediately after a first viral success that came by accident, both posted a string of videos that followed the same formula: Poarch did more face-zoomed lip-syncs and Lame posted more life hack-debunking videos. Their ability to capture and sustain fame on TikTok has translated into new opportunities on and off that platform. In May 2021, Bella Poarch debuted a song[6] that credited two TikTok famous musicians, the producer Sub Urban and the songwriter Salem Ilese, and featured a cast of famous TikTokers and influencers in the official music video. Khaby Lame's viral Stitches have inspired the #learnfromkhaby challenge, which in mid-2021 has more than two billion views, and he has signed sponsorship contracts with brands such as the Italian pasta maker Barilla (Adams, 2021).

Accidental virality can open new avenues of professionalization for the handful of TikTokers who can translate their overnight fame into a career as an influencer. (The theme of accidental virality continues in chapter 5.) The three cases discussed so far highlight the individualistic nature of mainstream TikTok: Inoxia, a solo street performer, and Poarch and Lame, who first went viral by posting videos from the solitude of their respective bedrooms. There are, however, attempts at building collectives among mainstream TikTokers, and this is what we will discuss in the next section.

Hype houses

TikTokers who happen to be caught up in the whirlwind of accidental virality and want to maintain their presence must find creative ways to keep the process going. With 700 million TikTok users worldwide (Iqbal, 2021), the accidental viral successes of Inoxia, Bella Poarch, and Khaby Lame is clearly an anomaly that can hardly be translated into a sustainable business strategy. However, in an attempt to overcome the inconsistency and randomness associated with accidental TikTok fame, some mainstream TikTokers have turned to the power of community.

Collaborative houses (collab houses) are a familiar fixture in the social media entertainment industry (see Cunningham & Craig, 2019). The o2LHouse was an early collab house among a group of popular YouTubers who banded together to develop their YouTube Fame in 2012 (Jarvey, 2015). The collab houses were extended to early short-video influencers; so was for instance an apartment building dubbed '1600 Vine' in Hollywood, California, which became a haven for Vine stars and other influencers in 2014 (Wakabayashi, 2017). The trend continued in the TikTok era, the houses being now rebranded hype houses (Lorenz, 2020a).

The original TikTok Hype House was formed in December 2019 through the partnership of two TikTok famous teens: Thomas Petrou, who had previously lived in a collab house for YouTubers, and the popular TikToker Chase Hudson (Ward, 2020). The house, a lavish mansion in Los Angeles, California, served as the base of operations for 19 famous TikTokers, four of whom lived there full time; their job was to create collaborative content. The method proved to be a success, as co-founder Thomas Petrou noted:

When we moved in, Chase [Hudson] had 3,500,000 followers. If he went and got an apartment by himself, he might have 5 or 6 million now but not 9 million. Also, when you have a house, everyone wants to come over... Now, we can invite every big creator to the house. (Quoted in Ward, 2020, p. 1)

It was no secret that the goal of the Hype House (the group) was to create more content and to groom and expand the already sizable followings of the foundational members, the most notable being Charli D'Amelio and Addison Rae. The hype house model inspired several other TikTok hype houses; some copied the recipe exactly, putting up mansions inhabited by young influencers in Los Angeles, while others catered to different audiences. For example, a group of TikTok influencers in London formed ByteSquad (BBC, 2020) and a group of TikTokers in Atlanta, Georgia, formed the Collab Crib (McRady, 2021). Political hype houses appeared during the 2020 US election cycle, when a Republican hype house was followed shortly by a rival Democratic hype house (Galer, 2020).

Hype houses illustrate the precarity of trying to sustain TikTok fame through communities of the *Gesellschaft* type. Accidental virality happens frequently on TikTok, but harnessing overnight fame and turning it into a sustainable career is a different story altogether. For rising and aspiring TikTok celebrities, the hype house model was an appealing proposition. These small communities were strategically assembled to maximize output and leverage members' followings. A 2020 exposé on TikTok houses in Los Angeles documented increased competition as new houses appeared, rivalry that emerged between houses, and internal conflicts that brought many hype houses projects to an end (Ward, 2020). Living in a Los Angeles hype house meant paying exorbitantly for events and for real estate, creating new content non-stop, and making virtually no money. As one member of the short-lived hype house Girls in the Valley noted, 'I was there for a good five months living in the house. We didn't earn a dime' (as quoted in Jennings, 2020, p. 1). As hype house communities were built on a foundation of growing individual fame and profit, it is no surprise that many of them ended in interpersonal fallout or saw roommates going their separate ways.

*

The *Gesellschaft* type of communities described above reflect both the TikTok platform's commercial logic of generating capital through mass appeal and viewing time and the commercially oriented TikTokers' logic of boosting personal visibility and promoting their self-brand. But another type of TikTok community exists that follows a completely different logic. We refer to communities of this type as *Gemeinschaft* communities; and in the next section we will explore three of them.

TikTok *Gemeinschaft*-type communities

Just as there are many diverse subcommunities configured as subreddits on Reddit, or as groups on Facebook, or as fandoms on Tumblr, niche communities on TikTok make up the long tail of its content and creators. They are a form of networked publics, 'space[s] constructed through networked technologies' and an 'imagined collective that emerges as a result of the intersection of people, technology, and practice' (boyd, 2010, p. 39). While not directly influencing participant behaviour, networked publics 'configure the environment in a way that shapes participants' engagement'. Drawing on conceptions of networked publics, Zulli and Zulli (2020) describe TikTok as a site for imitation publics, based on repeated memetic interaction facilitated by TikTok's content creation and engagement features. The For You page matches viewers with content created by other users, who aim for interesting, relevant, or familiar content. Viewers can directly engage in dialogue or play with the content in the endless scroll, through socially creative features such as Duet and Use This Sound, or just by stopping from scrolling for a moment.

The *Gemeinschaft* type is characterized by the warmth and strength of relationships – familial, kindred, and neighbourly (Inglis, 2009). The relationships formed among niche TikTok communities are the threshold of digital *Gemeinschaft*. In our interviews with TikTokers, interviewees frequently commented on how close they were with many of their mutuals (see Gattolari, 2021):

> I met some people through this app that I talk to every week. We [virtually] hang out every Saturday, I text some of these people, FaceTime some of them, I'm planning to see some tomorrow. I feel like I've genuinely made some good friends [on TikTok] that I wouldn't have made otherwise. (Bri (@souparstarbri))

Countless communities extend across linguistic, geographic, cultural, and content boundaries. The edges of these communities are not defined as they would be in a Facebook group or subreddit forum. In some instances, they can be partially constituted by familiar features, such as hashtags or specific challenges. In other instances, they are vague amalgamations of creators, content, and viewers.

In the next sections we present one of these communities, JazzTok, that serves as a useful example of a lively and dynamic *Gemeinschaft* community on TikTok.

JazzTok

On 24 December 2020, the newly created @JazzTokOfficial uploaded its first video.[7] The video begins with a beaming keyboardist ringing out the introduction of Mariah Carey's classic 'All I Want for Christmas Is You'. The camera slowly pans out to reveal a grid with four horn players, a rhythm section, and a singer. As the screens shift, different configurations of band members are shown, playing the hits, grooving through the chord changes, and dancing in their own little boxes. Each is in their own box on the screen, filmed separately from the players' homes, arranged onscreen to resemble the TikTok Duet feature. After 55 seconds the song ends with the iconic chorus, and the video loops to begin again.

The origins of the @JazzTokOfficial TikTok account go back to a live stream in November 2020 hosted by pianist and co-founding member, Lisa (@utzig). A handful of musical TikTokers were viewing the stream who had all developed a friendship after repeated interaction and collaboration on TikTok.

> [Lisa] was streaming and I had never seen her do a live-stream before. I don't think I had ever even heard her voice before. [Lisa], [Gabbi (@fettuccinefettuqueen)], and [Kyle (@felonious_skunk)] and I were in the chat. I remember saying JazzTok is the best ____Tok. And [Lisa] was like 'Jazztok is the best ____Tok... hey I have an idea. Do you want to start a discord server?' and I was like 'YES. That sounds awesome, that's a brilliant idea!' The next morning I wake up to a notification inviting me to the [Discord] server. (Ben (@bensrightbrain))

The short pause before 'Tok' indicates a platform vernacular that refers to the many different sides of TikTok, just as some interviewees referred to the niche subcommunities that exist on other platforms, for example ad hoc publics on Twitter (Bruns & Burgess, 2015) and vernacular creator communities on YouTube. The platform vernacular to signify communities on TikTok is to add 'TikTok', or simply just 'Tok', after the community classifier term, say, 'Alt' in Alt TikTok or 'Straight' in Straight TikTok. 'JazzTok' is an example of one such community name. 'AltTok', 'KinkTok', 'FoodTok', 'ScienceTok', and countless other Toks are examples of other such communities.

A few weeks after Lisa created a server for JazzTok on the social messaging platform Discord, Ben created the TikTok account @JazzTokOfficial, together with an Instagram account of the same name, for cross-promoting posts. The @JazzTokOfficial profile included a link for any viewers to join the open Discord server and become a part of the JazzTok community – an expansive network for musical creators and jazz enthusiasts to connect and collaborate.

Interviews with 19 members of the JazzTok community offered a variety of perspectives about the significance of JazzTok. JazzTok emerged through a combination of opportunity, timing, and circumstances in 2020. The COVID-19 lockdowns forced millions of musicians and performers worldwide to practice social distancing, which meant no rehearsals, jams, or live performances. Many interviewees admitted that they joined TikTok out of boredom, while stuck at home, and were pleasantly surprised to find a musical outlet on the short-video platform. The second main reason why JazzTok was formed on TikTok, and not on any other digital or social media platform, was TikTok's platform-specific infrastructure and features.

Discovery

Before the debut of @JazzTokOfficial on TikTok, JazzTok was a loosely associated constellation of creators, all posting and interacting with similar types of musical content. Some creators used the hashtag #jazztok to indicate the style of their video, just as they used other tags for the musical genres or instruments that they played in the videos. Kyle (@felonious_skunk), a multi-instrumentalist who shared videos in which he played keyboards, melodica, and harmonica, noticed a change in his For You page:

> I started posting a lot of synthesizer content, so then I would start seeing more synthesizer content. And then I realized that [people were using] these hashtags, like #SynthTok, #MusicTok and #JazzTok, which have now kind of become their own little communities. (Kyle (@felonious_skunk))

Despite not using #SynthTok originally, Kyle saw more synthesizer content on his For You page after sharing videos that featured synthesizers and were seen by viewers also interested in synthesizer content. Seeing these other videos encouraged him to use #SynthTok to tag his videos too.

The first major factor that constructs a community on TikTok is how users discover and join that community. Whether intentionally or not, JazzTok members first connected by repeatedly appearing on one another's respective For You pages, since TikTok's machine-learning models and recommender systems labelled the users' content as 'similar'. This content-based connection was mirrored in the personal connections they saw, which encouraged them to interact more than they would on other platforms. Anthony reflects:

> I'll just keep comparing TikTok and Instagram. There's a much different community there. On TikTok, people are more likely to comment, like, share or add something. On Instagram, people 'like' the videos and then keep scrolling. With TikTok, I think it's a much more open community... like 'Hey, I saw your video. I'll like it, I'll give you a comment on something you should do next or share something I liked about it'. (Anthony (@ewokbeats))

Seaver (2017, p. 5) positions algorithms not as 'technical rocks in the cultural stream but... rather just more water', in that they flow along with other human practices that collectively become culture. Viewed as culture, algorithms are part of larger social and political systems in which communities form, converge, and fracture.

Several interviewees specifically named the recommender algorithm, the For You page, as the main feature that enabled them to discover other 'like-minded people' on TikTok. Like other TikTokers, JazzTok members began with more mainstream popular content that had millions of views and shares. Over time, they began narrowing their interests to the constantly fluctuating landscape of TikTok niche communities. After using the platform more, they found themselves in a variety of niches from the mainstream:

> Occasionally I'll get one of those videos with millions of views, like if you were advertising TikTok this is what you would show. I'm definitely not on that Tok and I'm cool with that. I like the community that I'm in, it's good that that community gets to embrace itself... I like the eclecticness of my FYP[8] if I can make up a word. (Kris (@musixicn_kris_))

The everyday interactions with the For You page recommender system show how algorithmic processes continuously shape the user experience on the basis of wilful or incidental human input (Willson, 2016). TikTokers may find themselves gradually or suddenly among new niche communities without fully knowing why. For example, maybe they set their device down to attend to something else and a video looped a few extra times, signalling to show more of a certain type of content. However, in our interviews, many TikTokers stated that they perceived themselves as having a considerable degree of agency and as being able to take control of their feed in order to build and grow the JazzTok community.

Interviewees described how they trained their For You algorithm so as to keep themselves away from mainstream TikTok and comfortably within their preferred communities.

> My FYP is extremely diverse; multiple different cultures, multiple different ethnicities. That all comes down to the fact that I want to see that content on my page so I go out of my way to make sure I'm being shown diverse types of videos. (Tai (@thctai))

None of the creators interviewed professed to have any detailed or technical understanding of how it worked. That said, the For You page was the topic of frequent algorithmic gossip, theories, and folklore shared by users of platforms who attempted to make sense of their experiences with black box algorithms (Bishop, 2019). Bri (@souparstarbri), for example, would share links of videos with friends and family members, and would share them even with those who did not use TikTok. She told them they did not need to click on the link to the video, as she was sharing only to train the TikTok algorithm that this was content that she liked. Kyle also took an active approach to maintaining connections with like-minded users:

> For a while, every time I saw a musician on my FYP, even if I didn't actually like it, I would hit 'like' on the video, leave a comment, and follow them... because I want to try to build as much community as I can. (Kyle (@felonius_skunk))

The same practices have been used to negotiate community on other platforms, such as Twitter, YouTube, or Facebook, which also feature recommender systems that match users with content (van Dijck et al., 2018). Bishop (2019) describes the many ways in which creators on YouTube actively inter-rogate algorithms to make sense of their experiences and to optimize their feed.

As we note in chapter 1, a key to ByteDance's competitive success in China and internationally is its algorithmic recom-mender system. Interviewees echoed the perception that the TikTok's For You page was different from recommen-dation systems on other social media platforms, and even on other short-video platforms. One interviewee who had used Vine before it was shuttered characterized the algorithmic matching on TikTok thus:

> The FYP is unique... how it recommends certain things based on your interests. There are all these branches of TikTok... so many communities that you can find. And it's so easy to connect with mutuals, which I don't remember being as much of a thing on Vine. I've definitely built more of a community on TikTok than on Vine. I've made more friends, 'internet friends', but still friends. (Erynn (@rynnstar))

Erynn's reflections speak to the For You algorithm as an important socio-technical mediator of community building on TikTok. On the one hand, users have a sense of agency about influencing their recommendations and maintaining strong relationships with other users through their own actions and inputs on TikTok. On the other hand, some interviewees felt the algorithm was doing the heavy lifting:

> These people I've met through TikTok... we gel so well and are such great friends. I think it's partially because the [For You] algorithm put us together. We were on each other's For You Pages. It's a little scary. I wouldn't have met these people without the algorithm. (Jake (@jakedoesmusicsometimes))

A final aspect of the For You algorithm discussed by our interviewees was the possibility of encountering new and unexpected content. There are many ways in which new content may end up on a user's For You page that barely connects to their interest, if at all. Perhaps a video goes viral among a group of mutual friends or acquainances, or perhaps a new account accidentally goes viral globally. As one interviewee explained, the For You page is open to discovery – as opposed to the Following page, the other main mode of viewing that consists only of videos from followed users:

> If you only scroll through your following page and don't really go to the FYP, if the people that you follow, who have the same worldview, the same experience and do the same things that you like to do, you can live in a world where that's all you see. I don't find that particularly interesting. (Rachel (@rvmillz))

Viewed in this way, the Following page may invite phenomena of selective exposure and homophily, which are commonly associated with the notion of filter bubbles and echo chambers that other JazzTok members addressed directly. In late 2020, Emerson (@emersonbrophy), an Australian JazzToker who frequently posted political satire, joined Gabbi (@fettuccinefettuqueen), RJ (@rjthecomposer), and many others by participating in the *Ratatouille* phenomenon (see chapter 2). After Emerson posted his original song, his feed was dominated by *Ratatouille* content interspersed with the usual political content. Emerson mentioned the TikTok musical to a friend who was a political TikToker, 'and he said what's that? This was right when [the *Ratatouille* musical] was making the news and everything. That really drove home for me that people have completely different [For You page] feeds.' He went on to raise concerns that the TikTok For You page could and does foster extremism of the kind encountered previously on Facebook and YouTube, adding, 'it's kind of scary. History is in danger of repeating itself.'

Bruns (2019) and others (specifically DuBois & Blank, 2018) contest the existence of hermetically sealed, impermeable filter bubbles or echo chambers, noting: 'we cluster, we do not segregate' (p. 50). On the For You page, such curtailment is effectively impossible, given the black box nature of the recommender system and the randomness of virality. Even if users stick to their Following page, they might still encounter other types of content through TikTok's socially creative features such as Stitch and Duet.

Participation

Moving on from discovery, the second most important factor for community building on TikTok is participation. In interviews with the JazzTok community, the most frequently cited reason why these musicians connected – a phenomenon leading up to the formation of @JazzTokOfficial – was the existence of socially creative features of TikTok, particularly Duet, which enabled them to participate in musical collaboration. Previous research has explored digitally mediated musical participation in the context of education and teaching (e.g. Waldron, 2012) and task-oriented remote collaboration (e.g. Biasutti, 2018). In the following sections we look at Sawyer and DeZutter's (2009) framework of distributed creativity, conceptualized as case studies of live improvisational theatre performances, and apply it to the spontaneously creative practices found on JazzTok.

Distributed creativity is best illustrated by groups of individuals who join together to generate a new and creative output, which ranges from being 'relatively predictable and constrained to [being] relatively unpredictable and unconstrained' (Sawyer & DeZutter, 2009, p. 82). The concept of distributed creativity builds on processes of collaborative emergence (Sawyer, 2003), which are particularly likely to be found in group activities with the following charateristics:

(1) the activity has an unpredictable outcome, rather than a scripted, known endpoint;
(2) there is moment-to-moment contingency: each person's action depends on the one just before;
(3) the interactional effect of any given action can be changed by the subsequent actions of other participants; and
(4) the process is collaborative, with each participant contributing equally. (Sawyer & DeZutter, 2009, p. 82)

Non-musical examples of collaborative emergence can be found in many different sites and communities on TikTok, through duet chains (see Figure 2.1). Duet chains build on the basic two-video duet, as multiple people add new duet content and chain duets together. As mentioned in chapter 2, an update in late 2021 afforded TikTokers the ability to rearrange the placement of videos in longer duets, giving rise to intricate mosaics of duet chains and unexpected social creativity.

In May 2021, @Marcus.DiPaola, a TikToker who became TikTok-famous for his short-video journalistic reporting during and after the 2020 US election, shared a video that introduced his girlfriend. Both Marcus and his girlfriend, Brittany, were visible only from the waist up, parts of their upper torso being cropped on either side of the frame. The original video was duetted by another user, who held a toy gun positioned to look as if it were Marcus' offscreen arm.

Next came other duets, adding missing legs; they were followed by the room and by a hostage negotiator outside the room. The duets continued ad nauseam, adding new characters and context, police response, news coverage, and random people at home who pretended to view the news coverage. Within two weeks, the flurry of duets rendered the original post nearly unrecognizable beneath a self-referential cinematic universe built around the faux hostage situation.[9]

Duet chains like this one illustrate the playfulness and randomness of collaborative emergence on TikTok. The eventual cinematic outcome was certainly not anticipated when the original user posted an unassuming video that introduced his girlfriend. Nobody asked for the video to be duetted by others but, once the duets began, each subsequent video depended on the previous actions of other users. The course of the creative duet chain was altered by individual TikTokers; thus the first video that introduced the imaginary hostage situation opened possibilities for the imaginary police to get involved.

TikTok's other creative features allow for similarly spontaneous forms of collaborative emergence. Audio memes that are circulated through Use This Sound can be recontextualized by creative TikTokers, who build on previous uses; and they can evolve through subsequent contributions. The same is true for longer chains that use the Stitch feature and blossom in unexpected directions, or reply to comments with new videos inspired by or in rebuke to others' content.

Returning to JazzTok, which is our case study, before the formation of @JazzTokOfficial, community members often participated in musical collaborations using the Duet function that we term 'duet jams'. Duet jams can take many forms. For example, a guitarist may share a new guitar solo for a bassist and drummer duet to round out the rhythm section; a beatmaker may share a newly produced instrumental track for a lyricist or vocalist duet to add new meaning; an artist and a songwriter may release a new song and members of the community begin to remix it in real-time. Duet jams are a form of memetic internet creativity, built on a foundation of remixing and bricolage (Literat, 2019). Duet and the For You page are, both, examples of features that enable the co-occurrence of community processes on TikTok. In the early days of JazzTok, the For You page helped prospective members to stumble upon interesting musical content, and Duet let them engage directly with that content and its creator. Interviewees commented that the simultaneous randomness and specificity of the TikTok algorithmic recommender system fuelled their spontaneity.

Duet jams are also a useful way of cultivating a following on TikTok. Anthony explained that it was a duet jam that propelled his TikTok profile to new and unimaginable heights, after he posted a duet drumming behind a creatively remixed version of the jazz standard 'Fly Me to the Moon' shared by another TikToker: 'and overnight it got like 10,000 views when I had just about 50 followers. I was pretty shocked to see that kind of growth happen' ((Anthony (@ewokbeats)). As a rhythm section player, Anthony reflected, 'my page was basically built off of Duets with people because I've noticed that people don't just want to watch the drums or drum covers' (ibid.). Before long, Anthony had built connections with a handful of other musical TikTokers by repeatedly duetting their content to add drums.

JazzTok exemplifies the spontaneous, improvisational ethos of distributed creativity. Alex (@alexengelberg), who worked part-time as a musical accompanist for an improv comedy theatre in his home city, explained that duet jams were the perfect embodiment of the 'yes and...' philosophy of theatrical improvisation, where each new addition contributes to the ongoing performance rather than trying to steal the spotlight. RJ (@rjthecomposer) described the social, technical, and creative interactions facilitated by TikTok and Duet jams as 'the ultimate fusion of social media and [creative] content', a fusion that allowed him to make new friends and join communities while also sharing his creative musical ideas. Ralph (@theboneguy) concurred, remarking that, after spending his entire adolescent and adult life on social media, he 'never had a chance to reach out [to a stranger] and be like "I would love to work with you" then get a response and have a platform to immediately [make music together] all in one contained box'.

Distributed creativity through duet jams creates edgeless virtual musical ensembles with rotating members. Several interviewees mentioned that they would often jump into a Duet jam in progress when they saw that one or more of their friends were already participating. Duet jams also make it easy for communities to grow each time new faces appear in the chain. In many cases these communities remained undefined and amorphous, but in others, like JazzTok, they could crystallize into a *Gemeinschaft* that transcended TikTok.

The in-depth case study of the JazzTok community shows how the affordances of discovery and participation on short-video platforms mutually shape community. There is no denying that TikTok and other short-video platforms are gradually moving in the direction of further commercialization, but our interviewees from the JazzTok study were nevertheless amazed by the spirit of *Gemeinschaft* they found on TikTok:

> TikTok has brought me a network of people that I would never have met. I've never even been overseas... [TikTok] just brought me so many friendships that I never would've seen coming at all. (Gabbi (@fettuccinefettuqueen))

Conclusion

In this chapter we framed TikTok as a mobile social mediation technology in order to illustrate how different kinds of communities constitute themselves on and through the platform. Mainstream communities represent the most visible 'side' of TikTok, demonstrate the rapid and unexpected growth of TikTok fame, and are characterized as individualistic and profit-oriented. Niche communities constitute the many subcultural 'sides' of TikTok. Our case study, JazzTok, showed how platform affordances shape algorithmic discovery and participation and enable distributed creativity and *Gemeinschaft*.

In the next chapter we build on the analysis of TikTok communities and examine how such entities can form themselves through collective activism.

4

TikTok Activism

As a platform championing viral funny videos, TikTok is one of the most light-hearted corners of the internet. However, for many of the platform's 700 million users (Iqbal, 2021), content on TikTok is not merely jokes of little value and trivial entertainment but also communicative devices for coping, learning, and community building. Moreover, seemingly worthless lip-syncing, dance routines, and comedy skits are also used by TikTokers to mobilize people to support various social and political causes. For example, TikTokers have been deploying the platform to advocate for climate change (Hautea et al., 2021), human rights issues (Kuo, 2019), and racial injustice (Janfaza, 2020). In these and other cases, video memes are used as the primary communication device for activism.

In this chapter we will discuss the vernacular styles of TikTok activism: social and political campaigns deploying TikTok in order to mobilize support. We will first examine two cases of TikTok activism – #forClimate and #saveTikTok – then, in the last section, we will use the concept of *circum-scribed creativities* to summarize how platform affordances and logics empower and limit collective actions on TikTok.

#forClimate: Green memes on TikTok

Climate change is one of the most urgent issues of our time, and the past years have seen a new generation joining the global campaign for climate: Gen Z. This young generation of climate protestors is more vocal and more coordinated than its predecessors (Marris, 2019). Following Greta Thunberg and many other teenage activists, more than 1 million school kids from over 100 countries participated in the Fridays for Future school strikes in mid-March 2019 (Taylor, 2019).

From a generation of kids glued to their phones, Gen Z has turned into a vocal social force capable of showing an active social conscience. Motivated by various social ideas and causes, Gen Z activists from across the globe have become vocal campaigners of progressive policy change on various social issues. In parallel with their offline protests, Gen Z activists engage with the social media to support environmental causes; and, as a platform that found its early adopters among kids and teenagers, TikTok has become one of the most important online arenas for Gen Z-led online climate campaigns. Goofy or serious, performing or lecturing, the short-video format has become an essential tool for raising awareness about the climate emergency. For instance, under hashtags such as #forClimate and #climatechange, TikTokers have created hundreds and thousands of videos that by mid-2021 had been viewed more than a billion times. #forClimate was the hashtag officially endorsed by TikTok as one of the first campaigns that were part of the platform's TikTok for Good initiative. In 2019, partnering with the International Federation of Red Cross and Red Crescent Societies (IFRC), the platform officially promoted the #forClimate campaign in more than 100 countries in order to raise awareness on climate-related issues.

In their study of climate activism on TikTok, Hautea et al. (2021, p. 2) argue that 'climate-related expressions on TikTok take place in a complex social media ecosystem in which earnest activists compete with mocking satirists, playful attention-seekers, and bored time-killers for visibility and clout'. Young TikTokers' engagement with climate activism has its unique communicative features, such as the centrality of sound templates and the particular generational zeitgeist of

Gen Z. In what follows we discuss such practices using two specific styles of TikTok climate activism.

Lip-sync activism

'We are killing the Earth and that is really fun. No one believes us cause we are young...', @willow.sky starts her singing of 'Dear 2045' in a TikTok video. The ukulele melody is jolly, but the words are sulky. As the 55-second song continues, @willow.sky sings: 'sea levels are rising and icebergs are melting, the coral reefs are dying, and no one is helping'.

@Willow.sky posted 'Dear 2045' in November 2019, and it quickly became one of the 'anthems' for climate change activists on the TikTok platform. By mid-2021, the video had been viewed 36 million times and had received over 6.7 million likes. It epitomizes the sentimentality shared by many young people on the platform who use short video to communicate their despair and frustration. On the one hand, 'Dear 2045' is a dirge for the gloomy future the younger generation is facing. The closing line goes: 'Dear 2045, I don't think we're gonna survive. If you end up hearing this story, I just want to say, I am sorry.' At the same time, the song is pointing a metaphorical finger at world leaders and at the older generation: both are blamed for damaging the planet and for doing little to save it.

@willow.sky's 'Dear 2045' struck a chord with fellow TikTokers and the song has become heavily memefied. By mid-2021, more than 300,000 users had been inspired by the song to create new climate change videos featuring @willow.sky's music. Meme re-creation based on a sound template is far more than a simple content imitation process. As shown by videos that respond to 'Dear 2045', new videos were enriching the original content primarily by adding visual narration. While @willow.sky's original video features only herself singing in front of the camera, new videos created 'music videos' for her song, adding visual storytelling to accompany the audio narrative. For instance, one commonly used pattern in the videos inspired by 'Dear 2045' is live sketching that narrates how our planet is deteriorating with rising temperatures and is gradually melting down. In another popular TikTok genre, makeup artists lip-sync to 'Dear 2045', while painting their faces and bodies to illustrate how the earth responds to global warming and eventually becomes unliveable (Figure 4.1).

The impersonation of mother nature, as in the example in Figure 4.1a–c, is a common approach used by TikTokers who participate in climate activism on the platform. Mini dramas, made with the TikTok greenscreen effect, about the warm future of the planet tell stories of rising sea levels and hungry polar bears. One feature shared by such meme videos is their reliance on appeals to fear. Like the messages delivered in 'Dear 2045', a large share of the videos depict a dark and scary future for our planet. This reliance on fear in TikTokers' communications is interesting, as it goes against conventional climate change communication practices: those follow

Figure 4.1a–c. Illustrated consecutive snapshots from a video titled 'The Earth Is Crying' by @beiya02, lip-syncing to 'Dear 2045' (https://www.tiktok.com/@beiy02/video/6779776506135694594).

the doctrine that the use of fear-inducing content is risky and ineffective (O'Neill & Nicholson-Cole, 2019; Reser & Bradley, 2017). But in TikTokers' climate messages fear is not only an effective tool for attracting attention; it is also a young generation's cry for help. It is common among Gen Z to identify the climate emergency as the most urgent issue faced by our world (Barbiroglio, 2019), and these videos reflect this fear and the associated frustration.

This example also encapsulates a form of meme creation around climate causes that are centred around music and sound. The TikTok platform's features that enable its users to recycle sounds from other videos facilitate the emergence of what Zeng and Abidin (2021) refer to as 'lip-sync activism': a form of 'synchronised yet personalised meme advocacy, which is not restricted to actual performances of lip-synchronisation but is extended as a metaphor to demonstrate the networked participation of users delivering a united message through individualised narration' (p. 2470). The ability to reuse a sound or a song gives TikTok activists a united voice, to which they add their own personal storyline or their own visual narrative. A shared song, such as 'Dear 2045', brings climate change activists together and builds the momentum that is necessary for the campaign to have impact beyond the platform's realms, in the real world.

Generational mannerism

Scrolling through climate change campaigning TikTok videos, one finds no shortage of awareness-raising content that aims to promote an eco-friendly lifestyle. Educational content on TikTok is generally more focused on showing than on telling, and the hands-on tutorial is a popular genre on the platform (e.g. Zeng et al., 2021). This genre can also be observed in climate activism memes, where Gen Z TikTokers try to teach their generational peers how to reduce their carbon footprint or how to make eco-friendly everyday gadgets.

One characteristic of such call-to-action messages from Gen Z TikTokers is that an eco-conscious lifestyle is presented as a form of generational mannerism. Environmental awareness, including their shared grievances against older generations, is part of Gen Z's self-identity.

An interesting example of this kind of teenage mannerism is the 2019 #VSCO girl trend. The name 'VSCO' came from a photo-editing app that featured a filter that was used to generate a specific social media visual aesthetics. Beyond the filter, what made #VSCO girls distinctive was their eco-conscious posturing and fashion style. A #VSCO girl, commonly from a white middle-class family, had an iconic look marked by an oversized T-shirt, multiple scrunchies, a Fjällräven backpack, a Hydro Flask water bottle, and a puka shell necklace (see Figure 4.2).

Figure 4.2. #VSCO girl aesthetics (https://www.tiktok.com/@luanndiez/video/6728834426651856133).

Besides this stereotypical look, #VSCO girls are also known for loving turtles and hating plastic straws. With 'Save the turtles!' as their mantra, #VSCO girls are described as 'manic pixie ecowarriors' (Aronoff, 2019; Harper 2019) who exhibit their eco-consciousness via conspicuous consumption (Jennings, 2019).

On TikTok, #VSCO girls' mannerism is commonly used for parody or self-deprecation, but the significance of eco-consciousness in this urban teen subculture showcases how environmentalism and consumerism are combined as part of teenagers' 'visibility labour' (Abidin, 2016). As we explain in chapter 3 and as Abidin (ibid., p. 90) puts it, visibility labour is 'the work individuals do when they self-posture and curate their self-presentations so as to be noticeable and positively prominent' to their audiences. #VSCO girl memes fizzled out by the end of 2019, but this form of ecological visibility labour continued on the platform, being carried out especially by eco lifestyle TikTokers who promote and teach how to live an eco-friendly life.

A common trope used by social media influencers in their visibility labour is to show how they are leading extravagant and aspirational lives (Abidin, 2016). Such tropes do exist on TikTok[1] as well: TikTokers engage in what Marwick (2013) refers to as 'aspirational production', that is, seeking attention by posting videos that signal high social status. But the eco lifestyle TikTokers documented in our analysis of #forClimate videos are less interested in presenting a high social status and more interested in demonstrating a high *moral* status. These TikTokers use the platform to teach their peers how to live an environmentally friendly life, have a zero-waste lifestyle, and make their own soap, toothpaste, or deodorant.

This eco mannerism sometimes goes beyond making educational how-to videos; it moves to calling out, even shaming, other TikTokers who do not live up to the required standards. As documented in Zeng and Abidin's (2021) study of #OkBoomer memes on TikTok, Gen Z expresses its grievances against boomers[2] in viral videos that condemn their role in damaging the environment. In the course of our analysis we found that this shaming of other TikTokers is not only intergenerational but extends to other members of Gen Z itself: they, too, who can be targeted. One example is a video from a self-identified #VSCO girl who attempted to 'cancel' Charli D'Amelio – the biggest TikTok star, with over 118 million followers[3] – through a compilation of video clips wherein Charli D'Amelio is seen using plastic straws.

*

The cases of climate campaigns on TikTok discussed here illustrate how young people employ short videos to bring attention to environmental issues. With humour and catchy music, youths creatively use memetic videos to raise awareness of the gravity and urgency of environmental issues. At the same time, these video memes functioned as political weapons insofar as grievances were vented through them. In the next section we discuss how TikTokers united to respond to political controversies rather than environmental issues.

#saveTikTok

During the second half of 2020, the US government led by President Donald Trump made several attempts to shut down TikTok (or to sell TikTok's US operations to an American owner), as it was considered to be 'a threat to America's national security' (M. Singh, 2020). TikTok had 100 million American users at the time (Lorenz, 2020c); and the possibility of having TikTok taken away from them made these users display fear, uncertainty, and even hysteria on the platform. #SaveTikTok,[4] together with many other hashtag challenges, emerged on the platform to label virtual petitions that expressed support for the app.

Videos protesting against the looming TikTok ban were created by TikTokers worldwide, because the shutdown of US TikTok would have a wide impact on the global TikToker community. After all, the United States' share of the market and contribution to TikTok's hall of fame[5] makes this country the creative engine of the platform.

Content under the #SaveTikTok campaign is diverse. While some TikTokers share technological solutions to circumvent the ban, most videos are used for the delivery of political and sentimental messages. On the one hand, TikTokers used this campaign to let out their complaints against Donald Trump and his conservative politics. On the other hand, they expressed a common sense of loss when their favourite app was about to be taken away. In the following sections we will discuss different memes associated with these two types of sentiment.

Ban the Official Trump 2020 App

As the key figure pushing the TikTok ban in the United States, Donald Trump naturally became the target of many TikTokers' anger and frustration. Consequently, the #saveTikTok campaign took a direction summarized in the hashtag #banTrump.[6]

After Trump's announcement of the potential TikTok ban, a large number of TikTokers organized a counterattack that sought to remove the Official Trump 2020 mobile app from Apple's App Store. The plan was based on a widespread misconception that mobile apps with a large number of one-star ratings by users are removed from the App Store. Mocking Trump's rhetoric on TikTok, TikTokers wrote trolling reviews of the Official Trump 2020 app, accusing it of 'stealing' too many personal data or describing it as 'Chinese spyware'. Some examples of such comments are given in Figure 4.3. While the app was never removed from the App Store, TikTokers contributed to bringing the average rating of the Official Trump 2020 app down to 1.2 stars.[7]

★ ★ ★ ★ ★ September 19, 2020   2

WHY U BANNING TIKTOK BRO ITS NOT RIGHT U DOING TOO MUCH NOBODY LIKE U BE-
CAUSE YOUR SO RUDE

★ ★ ★ ★ ★ August 7, 2020   2

I need tictok

★ ★ ★ ★ ★ August 7, 2020

HORRIBLE. racist and homophobic? 🤮, sorry man thats a no go for me, 🙅 ▢ and boring too
🙄 ugh. - a gen z ▢💚

★ ★ ★ ★ ★ August 4, 2020   2

This app is horrendous. It's like a virus on my phone that I can't get off. It's very spazy and
wants me to Tweet racist and homophobia messages. It also asks for a bunch of personal
information. I'm positive it's selling my stuff to other countries, and i don't appreciate the
spam calls.

★ ★ ★ ★ ★ August 2, 2020   3

Steals all your personal information! Might be Chinese Spyware??? Many people are saying
it. Smart people. Don't download!

Figure 4.3. Examples of reviews posted to the Official Trump 2020 mobile
app. Usernames and profile pictures have been removed.

TikTokers in support of Joe Biden's presidential campaign

TikTok is used by supporters of both Trump and Biden, but
during the 2020 presidential election Biden was not expected
to go ahead with the TikTok ban. As part of the #saveTikTok
theme, some TikTokers posted and remixed videos promoting
Biden as the hero who would save the American TikTok
community. Videos[8] pushed the slogan 'if you want to save
TikTok, vote for Joe', which became an integral part of the
#saveTikTok movement (see Figure 4.4).

Figure 4.4. TikTok video depicting Joe Biden as the 'TikTok President' (https://www.tiktok.com/@itsjohnwalsh/video/6847570828255579397).

Some other anti-Trump messages were delivered in a more typical TikTok way – creatively memetic, humorous, and sarcastic. The meme 'Me trying to convince Trump to let us keep TikTok' is one case in point. As a comedy skit, this meme presents a storyline in which a TikToker visits Trump at the White House to try to convince him not to ban TikTok. In the most popular style, the video uses the 'green screen' effect to set the picture of Trump in the background, in front of which the creator him/herself performs a sexually seductive dance, with captions such as 'me going to white house to seduce trump into not banning tiktok'.[9] In similar videos, creators embed captions such as 'Take one for the team', 'Me being human sacrifice in exchange for TikTok'.

Other versions of the meme are made without presenting Trump in the video. For instance, @morganpeoples made a video of herself in the car, speaking; the caption sticker reads 'Me trying to keep TikTok from being banned'. In the video she delivers the following speech:

> President Donald Trump is the best president the USA has ever had. His tan does not remind me of Cheetos. It reminds me of sunset over the ocean. I am going to volunteer tribute to help build the wall. I support the wall. Last but definitely not the least, all life matters.[10]

In this 16-second video, @morganpeoples manages to mock Donald Trump for his narcissism, tan, anti-immigration policies, and white supremacy. Like in other videos that play with this meme, @morganpeoples takes a sarcastic stance in order to respond to the crisis she perceives. Humour was used as a weapon – not pragmatically, to stop the app from being banned, but rather as a communicative device, to express people's resentment towards Trump and his politics in general.

Generational social media

Futuristic scenarios of Gen Z TikTokers in old age is another recurring meme genre that expresses a form of imaginary nostalgia. In such memes, Gen Z people portray themselves as being middle-aged, reminiscing about the app of their generation, or explaining to their imaginary kids about TikTok.[11] In a #POV[12] video by @itsdianalore, the creator tells the story of her meeting TikTok in heaven, telling TikTok how precious it had been to her childhood, and being told by TikTok how the latter was unfairly terminated by Trump as part of his COVID-19 revenge on China.[13]

Other TikTokers took a more personal approach: they shared their own experiences of using TikTok. For instance, under the caption 'Crazy that a Kids' app Can change lives',

@.meech posted a video[14] compilation of his own TikTok highlights, with a touching story at the background of the compilation:

> We all made fun of this app at first, said it was only for kids, and downloaded it as a joke... The silly app helped us to laugh through quarantine. But for most of us, it helped us cope with things in our lives. At least it did for me.

The sentiment in @.meech's video was echoed in many personal stories that were shared as part of the #saveTikTok campaign. TikTok was described as a special place, where people can be themselves. As many pointed out, the seemingly pointless time-waster brought them more than just joy and laughter: it brought them a sense of belonging, too. In the face of the potential ban of TikTok, there is a general feeling of loss. Despite the wide variety of social media available, many young TikTokers showed great frustration at the thought that they may be forced to migrate to uncool social media platforms.[15]

Intergenerational discord

As illustrated by the examples presented here, Gen Zs consider TikTok as a social media platform that is specifically theirs. It is not uncommon to see TikTokers draw generational borders between social media: Gen Zs dance to TikTok, millennials post Instagram stories, Facebook belongs to boomers. Since Gen Zs claimed TikTok to be 'theirs', the TikTok ban was treated as a direct attack on this group.

The Schadenfreude that the TikTok ban stirred in boomers is often featured in #saveTikTok-related memes. For instance, in one video[16] from @nickythomasalt, the creator re-enacted a conversation between himself and a woman labelled 'Facebook Boomer'. The Facebook Boomer begins the mini-drama by saying: 'Thank god we are getting rid of that *Chinese virus app*'. After arguing that TikTok's data collection practice is not that different from the practice of American social media companies, @nickythomasalt replies: 'if they are going to take my data I would rather American government take my data'.

This fictive conversation shows young TikTokers' resentment of baby boomers, whom they perceived to be conservative and xenophobic and whom they generally blamed for the looming threat of a TikTok ban. On the matter of data safety, to many Gen Z, the ban on TikTok was hypocrisy. The rhetoric of 'US companies are no better', 'we should not trust the US government either' were commonly seen, both in the contents of videos and in their comment sections.

*

The #saveTikTok campaign is our second case (the first one was #forClimate) of how Gen Z TikTokers unite and use platform-specific affordances, norms, and practices to drive a cause they believe is important. Since the TikTok ban was interwoven with American politics and with the 2020 US presidential election, this campaign also provided an influential venue for Gen Zs to engage in public political debate.

Circumscribed creativity

Both cases presented in this chapter exhibited how youth activism employs TikTok in order to acquire a collective voice on different social issues. In this section we will discuss the particular character of TikTok activism around the concept of *circumscribed creativity*.

As explained at the beginning of the book, circumscribed creativity refers to the creative potential of individuals when a platform's technological infrastructure and logics give them both affordances and constraints (Kaye, Chen, & Zeng, 2021). In the context of TikTok, the concept of circumscribed creativity underlines how the platform on the one hand introduces various features designed to stimulate creativity and productivity, but on the other hand actively uses regulatory and algorithmic mechanisms so as to draw boundaries. We will discuss both these aspects in the forthcoming sections, using TikTok activism as a source of examples.

Youth vernacular

Simply as a result of the demographic characteristics of the community of TikTok users, TikTok activism is different from activism on platforms such as Instagram, Facebook, or Twitter. The fact that Gen Z constitutes such a significant proportion of this community has led to the emergence of specific vernacular creativities (Burgess, 2006) of visual and audio storytelling. As demonstrated by the #VSCO girl memes discussed earlier, the unique style of consumerism-driven Gen Z green message is influenced by the urban teenage girl culture in the United States.

TikTok activism largely manifests the generational spirit of youth, and especially that of Gen Z members. The rhetoric promoting a collective generational identity is prominent in both cases investigated in this chapter. TikTokers' advocacy for climate-related causes differs from conventional environmental campaigns in the sense that it focuses on framing climate issues as intergenerational injustice, which triggers public discussion around the theme of what the older generation owes to the young (Thew et al., 2020; Zeng & Abidin, 2021). Similarly, as we have seen in the case of #saveTikTok campaigns, many youngsters perceive TikTok as an app that belongs to Gen Z and describe their experience with TikTok as a form of shared generational memory.

The vernacular storytelling by young TikTokers features prominently the usage of memes as the main communicative device. Both the example of #forClimate and that of #saveTikTok campaigns demonstrate how memes serve as 'discursive weapons' (Nissenbaum & Shifman, 2017, p. 495) for expressing collective condemnation and, at the same time, as congregation points around which communities are formed. The role of memes in the advocacy for a wide range of social and political causes such as human rights issues (Vie, 2014), the anti-sexual harassment movement (Zeng, 2020), or anti-racism campaigns (Abidin & Zeng, 2020) has been documented in a rich body of internet studies. In the next section we will discuss how the TikTok platform's specific features and logics shape the discursive power of memes and make TikTok-based activism different from the brands of activism we find on most other image-based social media platforms.

Platform affordance and limitations

The circumscribed creativity of TikTok activism is shaped by youth vernacular and by the platform's idiosyncratic technological features and policies.

In terms of functionality, TikTok provides a streamlined video (re)production process and a meme-friendly ecology. As explained in chapter 2, TikTok introduces a variety of standardized templates and features that stimulate user engagement and remixing. For instance, its Duet feature allows TikTokers to respond directly to one another's videos by grafting a new one to the left of the original. Another example is that reusable special effects and audio clips offer 'templatability' (Abidin, 2021, p. 80) for memefied content production on TikTok.

As we have seen in chapter 2, content discovery on TikTok is largely algorithm- and trend-based. TikTok users discover videos from the For You page, where the platform algorithmically curates and recommends video feeds. For creators to increase the likelihood that their videos end up on other users' For You page, it is vital that they follow the right users, react to the right videos, and tag their videos with the right hashtags. The practice of 'free-riding on a trend' is widely used on TikTok. This has consequences for TikTok activists, as it can jeopardize the impact and efficacy of their causes. For example, campaign-related hashtags can be easily hijacked once they become trending on TikTok.

One distinctive form of campaign hijacking on TikTok is what Zeng and Abidin (2021, p. 2472) describe as meme merchandising and bandwagoning. During social and political campaigns, making and selling campaign-themed merchandise became a popular meme genre, and corporations also capitalize on trending activism to launch advertising campaigns.[17]

Another issue associated with TikTok activism is the platform's capacity for agenda setting in terms of visible social activism. Official endorsements from TikTok or ByteDance can prioritize certain causes while side-lining others; and they can do so by determining which campaigns will receive the enigmatic 'blessing' to be promoted by the For You algorithm. For instance, in late May 2020, TikTok made the headlines for a glitch that made videos tagged with #GeorgeFloyd and #BlackLivesMatter appear as though they had no views (Pappas & Chikumbu, 2020). Rather than giving their blessing, representatives of TikTok were forced to apologize to the black communities as the Black Lives Matter protests were building momentum (we return to this topic in chapter 5).

Despite being the creative impetus behind some of the most iconic challenges and trends on the platform, black creator communities remain subject to racial biases embedded in TikTok's platform logic. For example, in 2020, black creators and their allies used iconic images connected to the Black Lives Matter movement as profile pictures and also as hashtags (e.g.#ImBlackMovement, #ImBlack, and #BlackVoicesHeard), in protest against unfair censorship of black creators on TikTok (Elassar, 2020). Some interviewees we talked to also described instances in which they managed to engage in meaningful dialogue about race and racism on TikTok, but seeing some of the most popular white creators on the platform treating the Black Lives Matter movement as a TikTok trend unquestionably caused more harm than good, particularly without support from the platform. As will be seen in the next chapter, TikTok responded to controversies by pledging to support black creators through initiatives such as a limited-run mentorship program. Creators have also used hashtags to respond to other instances of racism and cultural appropriation on the platform. In May 2021, groups of East Asian creators used the hashtag #AsianFishing to call out white creators who profit from appropriating East Asian culture, through makeup and filters that promote offensive stereotypes.

Conclusion

Using the example of #forClimate and #saveTikTok, this chapter has demonstrated how a platform that is sometimes painted as a trivial playground for tweens can be used by the younger generation for political expression and collective action. Focusing on how the youths' causes are communicated in the form of memetic short videos, we argued that communicative styles of TikTok activism are the manifestation of what we described as circumscribed creativity. On the one hand, TikTok's meme-driven platform logic encourages the collective participation and empowerment of content creators. On the other, the efficacy of TikTok-based activism can be undermined by free-riders and by the platform's agenda-setting practices.

After discussing the social and political relevance of the platform, we will use the next chapter to investigate its economic aspects in the digital media ecosystem.

5

The TikTok Economy

The competition in the digital media platform market is fierce. TikTok and other platforms on this multisided market (Nieborg & Poell, 2018) are vying to attract and generate superior value for advertisers, sponsors, e-commerce partners, intellectual property rights holders, and a spectrum of users and creators – all at the same time. Like most platforms that are on a trajectory of rapid growth, TikTok has been prioritizing its users and creators since its very launch. This strategy is based on the fact that digital media platform markets are heavily governed by network effects (Wilken, 2018). This means that it is essential to get the virtuous circle going: that is, a situation where success leads to more success and to exponential growth. The platform with the market's largest user base is also best positioned to attract advertisers and sponsors and to negotiate effectively with intellectual property rights holders. Hence user growth is priority number one. This priority shows, as TikTok has positioned itself with the mission statement to 'inspire creativity and bring joy' to its young creators and users.

Since its inception, TikTok has become a hub of funny and memetic videos for the internet, as viral videos from TikTokers are routinely propagated on Instagram, Facebook, and YouTube. But while TikTok certainly brings laughter to its users, it is primarily an advertising-funded enterprise. This means that the platform's core capability is to get its users to stay on the platform for as long as possible and to package and target these users for advertiser messages. While TikTok has been successful in growing its advertising revenues since its launch, there are no publicly known financial data that may be available. In 2020, however, when there were plans to sell parts of the company to a US-based entity, some financial data did emerge. At that point, TikTok was forecasted to generate in 2021 US$ 6 billion in revenue, primarily from advertising sales (Wang, Wu & Zhu, 2020). While US$ 6 billion is the figure of a sizable business, it should be noted that TikTok is not a major component of the ByteDance group's total revenue. As a point of reference, in early 2021 ByteDance's China-based business was projected for that year to have an annual turnover of US$ 40 billion; and its Chinese sibling Douyin is forecasted to contribute about 60% of that turnover (Zhu & Yang, 2020; Huang, 2021).

When we explore the economy of the TikTok ecosystem in this chapter, we emphasize the mutual shaping of technology, economic models, and content creators (van Dijck et al., 2018), and our discussion highlights the power dynamics in TikTok's interplay with cultural practices and other social sectors. In particular, we are interested in how the *infrastructurization* and *cross-sectorization* of a short-video platform impact the trajectory of that platform's economy. Infrastructurization can be understood as digital companies' practice of extending their service scale and ubiquity, and of eventually obtaining infrastructural status (Plantin et al., 2018; Plantin & de Seta, 2019). Cross-sectorization refers to the process through which technology companies collect and connect personal information and behavioural data from multiple sectors (van Dijck, 2020). Due to their establishment and global dominance, Silicon Valley platforms are often used in academic discussions of platform infrastructurization and cross-sectorization (Van Dijck, 2020; Plantin et al., 2018). Where Chinese social media are concerned, prior scholarship discussing their development into integrated platforms often focuses on their particular Chinese characteristics.[1] TikTok, on the other hand, offers a unique instance, in which it is possible to look at how non-Silicon-valley platform logics influence and operate in the international platform ecology.

Infrastructurization and cross-sectorization are important manifestations of digital platforms' economic and societal power. Zhang's (2021) recent study of Douyin shows how TikTok's Chinese sibling follows an infrastructurization strategy and is transforming itself from a creative entertainment community into an integrated digital platform (p. 221). Douyin's integration of online education, tourism, and e-commerce, as mentioned in Zhang's study, exemplifies the short-video platform's ambition for cross-sectorial influence. Such ambition to become an infrastructural video platform is also evident on TikTok. Rhetorically, TikTok still places itself as a creative entertainment hub, as mentioned earlier; but it has proactively engaged with educational, cultural, and governmental sectors to diversify its source of influence and profit.

In the following sections we will look at the dynamics and complexity of TikTok's platform economy from four different perspectives: TikTok as an advertising platform, its integration of e-commerce, its creator economy, and its interplay with the music industry.

These perspectives offer the possibility of a multifaceted interrogation of TikTok's platform economy. We analyse TikTok's integration of e-commerce at the platform level to demonstrate how the short-video platform has diversified its business model by emulating Douyin in order to develop an infrastructural ecosystem for commerce. We investigate how the platform's affordances empower and restrict TikTokers' ability to monetize or leverage their influence. We also discuss how the music recording industries have responded to the TikTok phenomenon. But, first of all, we explore TikTok's primary revenue stream: advertising.

TikTokers for sale

Premium media services with strong brand recognition and a high dependence on professionally produced content – sevices such as Netflix, Spotify, *Economist*, or *New York Times*[2]

– generally rely on user subscription fees as their principal source of revenue. On the other hand, media companies that can build their businesses without having to pay high fees for professionally produced content and whose strategy is to maximize their user base need to think differently. For these companies, growth is their top priority, and it is vital that their service can be offered to users for free. Without a steady flow of subscription fees, these companies generally turn to advertising to fund their business. Most social media platforms are in this category; that includes Twitter, Facebook, and YouTube. Some of the incumbent social media platforms (e.g. Twitter and YouTube) have been trying to develop a subscription business, but in 2021 they are still completely reliant on advertising revenues.

The ByteDance platforms, including TikTok and Douyin, are no different, and during TikTok's first years in operation advertising has been its principal source of revenue. The purpose of TikTok's For You algorithm is to keep its users scrolling and engaging with the platform's content for as long as possible. The more the users engage, the more detailed the platform's profile of its users is – a profile that the platform sells for a premium to its advertisers. Since advertisers most often combine ads in multiple platforms in their campaigns, the platforms must develop advertiser tools and mechanisms that can be coordinated by advertising agencies and fit in a large-scale multiplatform campaign. This means that digital advertising formats tend to be quite conventional, which is also the case on the TikTok platform. TikTok offers advertising products such as in-feed ads, Brand Takeover, and TopView, which are similar to formats used by many other mobile social media services.[3]

An in-feed ad is a video posted by an advertiser that is integrated into users' For You page and is intended to have the same aesthetics as a normal user video. Users can interact with the ad by liking and commenting, but normally it is not possible to use on it creative features such as Duet or Use

This Sound. In 2021 TikTok was experimenting with a feature that extends in-feed ads to allow users to promote their posts, a feature that is well established on platforms such as Twitter or Facebook (Weiss, 2021).

The other two advertising formats mentioned earlier are also well established in the world of digital advertising. Brand Takeover is TikTok's version of the splash screen ad format and is displayed for three to five seconds at the app's start-up. TopView is also a full-screen video ad, but can run for up to 60 seconds, showing up in the middle of a user's feed rather than when the app starts up.

In addition to these common formats, TikTok has also commercialized some of its creative features and practices discussed in chapter 2. Advertisers can, for instance, pay TikTok to create branded stickers, effects, and filters and to make them available for users during a limited period. Advertisers can also work with TikTok to promote a branded hashtag challenge that follows the same logic as user-driven challenges (see chapter 2). The branded challenges, however, are ensured high visibility on the app by being placed at the top of the TikTok Discovery page and by being given high prominence in targeted users' For You page.

Since TikTok was established, its advertising revenues have increased along with its user base and its recognition as an effective advertising platform. However, the platform's ability to create value for its other stakeholders and, most importantly, for its high-profile TikTok creators has so far been quite underdeveloped. In the next two sections we will explore first how TikTok is expanding its business into e-commerce and, second, how TikTok supports creators' monetization of their creative labour.

#TikTokMadeMeBuyIt

From 'TikTok leggings' that accentuate the size of one's bottom to pretty green chlorophyll water, TikTokers turn products they love (or hate) into viral memes. In 2020, #TikTokMadeMeBuyIt itself became a memefied trend, with which people share random products they saw on TikTok and were inspired to buy themselves. Such videos often start with an intro narration of the form 'things that I did not know I needed but TikTok made me buy it'. As part of a similar trend, #AmazonFinds, with which TikTokers demonstrate 'random stuff I bought online that just makes (no)sense', has received 9 billion views. Apart from inspiring people to buy random things, TikTok also attracts talented independent artists and crafts makers who use the platform as a marketplace for promoting their work. Knowing its marketing potential and its users' buying power, especially in order to reach a young audience, TikTok has begun to experiment with e-commerce by collaborating with the retailer Walmart and the e-commerce platform Shopify.[4] But can TikTok become the new Etsy, or a QVC-like shopping network for Gen Z? Arguably, when it comes to the integration of e-commerce, TikTok is still behind Facebook and Instagram, both of which have various in-app shopping features that enable users to sell and purchase products. However, TikTok's access to know-how from its Chinese siblings in the ByteDance portfolio may be an advantage that helps the platform establish an effective ecosystem for social commerce. For instance, China's well-established Daihuo culture may have a lot to offer in terms of how to build a video-centred e-commerce system.

Daihuo

Daihuo (带货, 'celebrity endorsement and sale of products through live streaming') can be defined as a selling platform based on digital videos (both short and live-streaming) and facilitated by internet influencers or celebrities. In China, the most popular format of daihuo is zhibo daihuo – that is, live-streaming daihuo. Typical daihuo videos often feature creators trying out products and giving aggressive discounts while having entertaining live conversations with reviewers. Alongside offering bargains, *daihuo* videos attract viewers through their strong hedonic value, as playfulness and gamification are often integrated (Wongkitrungrueng & Assarut, 2018).

Video-mediated *daihuo* emerged on Chinese e-commerce sites (e.g. Taobao) in 2017. The phenomenon quickly became an integrated feature in mainstream social media. In 2018, ByteDance introduced the in-app shopping cart feature to its Chinese video platform Douyin, which allowed content creators to integrate links to shopping opportunities in their short videos or live streams. Until 2021, Douyin has established and integrated a *daihuo* ecosystem that includes its own online marketplace (Xiaodian), online payment (Douyin Pay), and product search function. A detailed timeline of Douyin's platformization of *daihuo* is presented in Table 5.1.

Table 5.1. ByteDance's gradual e-commerce development on Douyin. Created by the authors.

2018 March	Douyin launches the Shopping Cart function in collaboration with Taobao (淘宝网) that allows in-video hyperlinks to products on Taobao. (Taobao is a Chinese consumer-to-consumer shopping platform owned by Alibaba.)
2018 April	Douyin introduces the Shopping Window function, which allows merchants to set up an in-app store with links to Taobao.
2019 April	Douyin launches Douyin Xiaodian (Douyin Shops), which allows merchants to sell without going through third-party online retailers.
2019 April	Douyin adds a 'Products' category to its search engine.
2019 May–Nov	Douyin expands its network of retailer partnerships.
2020 May	Douyin's content trading service Xingtu launches new functions to connect brands and Douyin influencers for *daihuo* purposes.
2020 Jun	Douyin establishes an e-commerce division.
2020 Oct	Douyin bans third-party retailer products hyperlinks from live streaming, to only be allowed in short videos.
2021 Jan	Douyin launches its online payment service Douyin Pay.

In their study of the live-streaming industry, Cunningham, Craig, and Lv (2019) point out that China is leading the world in platform e-commerce integration, especially with video platforms. The authors attributed the rapid development of the country's digital economy to what they called 'tech leapfrogging', coining this term (p. 726). They argued that, to serve a fast-growing middle class with a strong desire to consume, China has created its e-commerce ecosystem from scratch with little dependency on outdated retail or finance technologies. According to the country's 2021 Statistical Report on the Development of the Internet in China, 79% of the Chinese population is made up of e-commerce users, the majority of whom are also consumers of live *daihuo* (CNNIC, 2021). In the first half of 2020, the size of China's live *daihuo* business reached $87 billion (Wen, 2020).

The country's mature live-streaming influencer industry[5] is another factor that contributes to the rapid growth of this *daihuo* trend. Live-streaming anchors can have a great influence over the public's consumption choices. For example, during a single special shopping event on 20 October 2020, the country's two top *daihuo* influencers – Li Jiaqi and Viya – achieved a gross merchandise value (GMV) of US$ 1.5 billion (Xinhua, 2020). In China, the current *daihuo* hype is pushed by traditional urban social media influencers, but also by emerging rural microcelebrities – what Lin and de Kloet (2019) referred to as 'the unlikely creative class' (see also chapter 3). One example of such unlikely *daihuo* influencer on Douyin is @pomegranateBrother (丽江石榴哥), a street fruit vendor from Yunan province with over 7 million followers in May 2021. During a live-streaming session in September 2019, @pomegranateBrother made the headlines by selling 120 tons of pomegranate worth US$1 million within 20 minutes (Zhou, 2020). Farmers also use both short and live-streaming videos to sell fresh products directly to nationwide audiences, without middlemen (Zhang, 2021).

Apart from answering questions about their products, farmer broadcasters talk about their everyday lives and show the beautiful rural scenery around them. Such content is refreshing and exotic to their urban audience and, even more importantly, it creates authenticity and intimacy. This form of affective commerce became even more mainstream during the nationwide lockdown in China that followed the COVID-19 outbreak in 2020. In response to sales disruptions caused by lockdown protocols, Chinese technology companies introduced initiatives designed to help farmers use live streaming, and even to mobilize influencers to promote farmers' products (Hao, 2020). According to a survey conducted by the National Bureau of Statistics of China in September 2020, more than 50% of respondents had purchased agricultural products from farmers' *daihuo* videos (Yang, 2020).

TikTok's *daihuo* future

Notwithstanding ByteDance's preliminary success in integrating e-commerce into Douyin, TikTok's exploration of cross-sectoral expansion has its own specificity and challenges. TikTok's particular platform culture and practice require contextualized strategies if it is to develop *daihuo*. One case in point is the divergent live-streaming usage on Douyin and TikTok. As Craig, Lin, and Cunningham (2021) argued in their book *Wanghong as Social Media Entertainment in China*, the Chinese live-streaming industry is characterized by its diversification. Whereas live gaming is the dominant genre in live streaming in many countries, it represents only a small fraction of China's live-streaming industry. Instead, as mentioned above, e-commerce has become one of the most popular genres of live streaming in China. Although TikTok has launched a range of live-streaming events in collaboration with high-profile organizations such as WHO, celebrities, and the retailer Walmart (Perez, 2021b), its live-streaming features of the past year have yet to take off. Without a well-functioning commercial live-streaming culture, it can be challenging for ByteDance to replicate to its international markets the success of its live commerce and live *daihuo* in China.

The lack of a native e-commerce ecosystem is another weakness for TikTok. As previously mentioned, it took Douyin three years, from 2018 to 2021, to build an in-app *daihuo* ecology that integrates its online shops, payment, and logistics (Table 5.1). TikTok still has a long way to go to catch up with its Chinese sibling, as well as with its Silicon Valley, when it comes to e-commerce. For instance, as the COVID-19 pandemic pushed businesses online, shopping features were launched in 2020 on both Facebook and Instagram that allowed small businesses to sell their products online (Facebook, 2020), and an 'influencer marketplace' has been launched to help Instagram influencers to monetize by matching them with brands (Rodriguez, 2021). Although shopping links are available for sponsored commercial videos on TikTok, private merchants' usage of TikTok remains restricted to raising brand awareness and relies on hyperlinks in these merchants' bios to lead audiences to external sites.

Furthermore, TikTok has its disadvantage in terms of the scale of datafication it can implement to target potential consumers. Facebook, for instance, benefits from its internet-wide ecosystem to track and collect user information. Through Facebook Pixel[6] and Facebook Share and Like buttons, the company gathers data from millions of websites.[7] These data, in turn, serve to optimize their targeted and retargeting ads, and also their own in-app commerce. TikTok, on the other hand, relies exclusively on user profiles and on the users' engagement data. With limited insights into its users' footprints outside the platform, TikTok can rely only on the strength of its algorithmic recommendation systems. As discussed in chapter 2, TikTok's proprietary recommendation algorithm personalizes users' For You page and turns it into a highly addictive experience, which is based on user interests. Counting on the efficacy of this algorithm to push relevant commercial videos to potential buyers, in 2021 ByteDance introduced the concept of 'interest e-commerce' (兴趣电商) as the flagship feature of its video-centred e-commerce model on its short-video platforms (Zhao, 2021). Unlike influencer-led e-commerce or search-based conventional online shopping, interest-based e-commerce focuses on impulsive shopping, which is stimulated through the discovery of users' potential interests. The #TikTokMadeBuyIt challenge mentioned earlier is a case in point, which demonstrates the power of meme videos to make people spend money on random things.

To introduce in-stream shopping functions is important to TikTok's platform economy, as this diversifies its revenue sources; and it is even more important to creators, as it generates ways for them to monetize their TikTok fame.

Since mid-2021, TikTok has been (and still is) testing different e-commerce strategies in its international markets. It already works with local partners to experiment with different in-stream shopping features in the United States and Europe, and is now pursuing similar strategies in Southeast Asia. In this region, TikTok is building its engineering teams, which are focused on e-commerce operations, and has launched the 'TikTok Shop Seller University'[8] to teach private merchants how to use TikTok Shop (Liu, Huang, & Turner, 2021).

Creator business models

During the platform's first years of international growth, many TikTokers struggled to translate TikTok fame into wealth after they had accidentally gone viral. Viral processes on TikTok are perhaps even more unpredictable and volatile than on other digital platforms. TikTokers can gain a massive following overnight, but keeping that following engaged and, above all, generating revenue from it is another matter entirely.

The revenue models that are available to TikTokers reflect the logic seen in many other parts of the growing social media entertainment industry. Cunningham and Craig (2019) argue that the social media entertainment industry generates capital and value through brand integration, influencer marketing, and platform labour. The burgeoning industry, they argue, has given rise to a creator culture driven by the convergence of traditional and digital media industries and social media entrepreneurs (Cunningham & Craig, 2021). Making a living in the social media entertainment industry often requires multi-platform strategies and encompasses a wide variety of labour, which is distinctive to, and divergent between, platforms. Van Doorn (2017, p. 908) refers to this kind of platform labour as 'digitally mediated service work' and argues that it is inherently unequal and 'hinges on the gendered and racialized subordination of low-income workers, the employed, and the unemployable'. Drawing on Angela McRobbie's (2016) work on the new creative economy, Duffy and Wissinger (2017, p. 4653) argue that platform labour embodies a *creativity dispositif* that 'both disciplines and incites contemporary cultural labourers offering models for success – as well as a promise of hope – in an otherwise bleak employment landscape'. They make the case that mediated mythologies of platform labour are draped in narratives according to which labour on platforms is fun, free, and authentic; but this view masks the challenging and demanding nature of the work (Duffy & Wissinger, 2017).

A massive gulf separates the opportunities for and the vulnerabilities of creators on TikTok. In chapter 4 we described two competing worlds on TikTok based respectively on *Gesellschaft* and *Gemeinschaft*. The platform labour of mainstream TikTokers certainly presents an aesthetics of being fun, free, and authentic, of living in glitzy LA mansions, of singing and dancing with one's friends, and of making millions in return for posting short videos. Underneath that veneer, the labour conditions for TikTok creators of all stripes can be demanding, even exhausting, and they differ according to privilege (Lorenz, 2021). Even one of the most globally successful TikTokers, Khaby Lame (@Khaby.Lame; see p. 21 in the introduction), is not immune to the inequality inherent in platform labour on TikTok. Khaby, who was born in Senegal but had lived in Italy since the age of 1, was not an Italian citizen at the time of his viral rise. His Senegalese passport began causing problems for him only after he acquired TikTok fame: he had difficulties in obtaining visas to visit and collaborate with creators or brands, particularly in the United States (Horowitz & Lorenz, 2021).

Smaller creator communities in *Gemeinschaft* pockets reflect van Doorn's (2017) grim picture of platform labour as they fight for visibility in a limited attention economy while competing against millions of others. These precarious conditions are exacerbated on TikTok as a result of the limited avenues for direct monetization that the platform offers (Kaye, Chen, & Zeng, 2021). In this section we discuss TikTok creator strategies for generating revenues from platform labour. We will also examine three initiatives intended to make TikTok more attractive to popular creators when they decide which platform should be the main outlet for their creative endeavours. The three initiatives are focused on payments from users, payments from sponsors, and payments from the platform. We begin with direct payments from users.

Gifts, coins, and diamonds

As discussed earlier in this chapter, live streaming is the principal mode of direct monetization on TikTok. The only way for viewers to make direct monetary contributions to creators during a live-streaming session is to use so-called virtual gifts (e.g. Lu et al., 2018; Tabeta, 2018).

A TikTok gift is a non-physical item (usually some kind of animation with a name such as 'Love Bang', 'Italian Hand', or 'Rainbow Puke') that users can purchase from the platform to give to a creator as a sign of their appreciation (TikTok, 2019b). The currency that is used to buy gifts on TikTok is called 'Coins'. Users buy Coins for cash and keep the Coins in their TikTok Wallet. The gifts that a creator receives from his or her fans are translated into another currency, called 'Diamonds', which can then be cashed out, and the money can be deposited into that person's PayPal account. Throughout this transaction chain between users and creators – cash–coins–gifts–diamonds–cash – TikTok retains 50% of the incoming amount.[9]

Like live streaming, the virtual gifting business on TikTok was carried over from Douyin and the robust culture of virtual gifting in China (Zhang, Wu, & Liu, 2019). As presented in chapter 2, live streaming is available on TikTok only for creators who have passed a certain follower threshold; and access to virtual gifts and virtual currency is even more restricted, both being inaccessible to minors.[10] TikTok has also limited the value of the Diamonds that a creator can cash out per week and implemented controls to ensure that users do not buy an excessive amount of Coins on a weekly basis.

Influencer sponsorships

While the virtual gifting business described above is an increasingly important part of the TikTok platform, it would be challenging for any TikToker to rely solely on an income from other users' TikTok gifts to sustain his or her business. A model that has the potential to be more profitable for creators with a large number of active fans is to work for sponsors and engage in what is known as 'influencer marketing' (Abidin, 2021; Craig et al., 2021). The basic principle behind influencer marketing is that a creator is paid to post a message that endorses some kind of product, company, or cause. Influencer marketing involves a spate of self-branding practices aimed at cultivating a specific personal image for commercial gain or at building other forms of capital (Khamis et al., 2017). A significant part of the sponsoring business takes place outside the TikTok platform, often being managed by advertising agencies and influencer agencies such as the Influencer Marketing Factory[11] or Obviously.[12] The fees paid by brands to influencers for sponsored content vary widely, and there are no official 'price lists' for sponsored content on TikTok. The fees can to some extent be based on the number of views of the sponsored post, user engagement with the post, or the number of fans or followers the influencer has been able to attract. While it is obviously in the interest of influencer agencies to inflate the price of their services, some estimates from these agencies (e.g. Whateley, 2020) claim that the average fee for a sponsored post on TikTok is about $0.001–$0.002 per follower. Reports, true or false, about the fees charged by TikTok 'royalty', represented by names such as Charli D'Amelio, place them between $50,000 (Bernardini, 2021) and $100,000 (Cleary, 2020) per sponsored post. D'Amelio had close to 120 million fans in mid-2021; so, if these rumours are true, they translate into something around $0.0004–$0.0008 per sponsored post, which is lower than the agency estimates. Still, these figures show that TikTok can be a profitable platform for top-tier creators. But, as in most celebrity markets, the distribution of fortune and fame is extremely top-heavy: a very small number of creators attract most of the likes, comments, and sponsor revenues.

The top-heaviness of this business is a problem not only for less popular creators who are trying to make a living from their platform labour. It is also a problem for TikTok, because it is not able to get a share of the transactions between sponsors and creators that take place outside the platform. As a way to address these issues, TikTok has been experimenting with what it calls the TikTok Creator Marketplace.

The TikTok Creator Marketplace is an attempt by TikTok to connect sponsors with creators. The design and function of the Creator Marketplace resemble those of the Facebook Business Manager, established in 2014 to streamline inter-actions between sponsors, users, and the Facebook platform (Constine, 2014). Eligible creators can advertise their profiles, interests, and fees on the Marketplace, and, similarly, sponsors can advertise their prospective campaigns and the price they are willing to pay for sponsored content. The Marketplace was launched as an experiment in the United States market, in early 2020 (TikTok, 2020g), and in the middle of 2021 it remains to be seen whether it will develop into a significant business for the platform, the sponsors, and the creators.

The TikTok Creator Fund

In the previous sections we have discussed how TikTok creators can generate revenues from other users and from sponsors. The third and final revenue stream potentially available to TikTok creators is the TikTok Creator Fund announced in July 2020.[13] The announcement committed US$ 200 million in funds and intended to expand it to US$ 1 billion as the program grew (Pappas, 2019). The Creator Fund followed a model similar to that of the Creative Learning Fund launched by TikTok in May 2020 – a fund that pledged US$ 50 million to educational content creators who met certain eligibility criteria. Just as with the Creative Learning Fund, several conditions must be met to access the Creator Fund (TikTok, 2019e).

The TikTok Creator Fund has inspired similar funds to be set up by short-video competitors. In November 2020, Snapchat announced that it was launching a creator fund called 'Spotlight', which committed to paying creators 1 million US$ per day, a promise from which the company walked back in May 2021 (Whateley, 2021). In May 2021 YouTube similarly announced a US$ 100-million creator fund, as part of its experiments with the short-video initiative YouTube Short (Bergen, 2021).

To join the TikTok Creator Fund in June 2021, creators must be at least 18 years of age, have a minimum of 10,000 followers, and have at least 100,000 views from real accounts in the previous month.[14] Initially, access to the fund was restricted to creators based in the United States. TikTok has provided very vague descriptions of how payments to eligible users are made from the fund. The basic principle of the payment model is that TikTok allocates funds to be shared between eligible creators on a daily basis. This daily amount is shared on the basis of these creators' aggregate metrics for engagement and views. The higher engagement and the more views a creator achieves during a day, the greater share of the daily funds he or she gets.

TikTok explains in its official policy documents that the fund is not based on sharing advertising revenues:

> The Creator Fund is not a grant or ad revenue sharing programme. Creators receive funds based on a variety of factors from their videos, and creators will know that performance on TikTok is dynamic – it changes naturally – so your funds will ebb and flow in the same way.[15]

Royalty sharing mechanisms such as the one TikTok is experimenting with in its Creator Fund are inherently difficult to communicate and understand, and differentiating the Creator Fund from an advertising revenue sharing program may be a way to temper expectations among creators who are familiar with advertising revenue-sharing schemes on platforms such as YouTube.

The revenue-sharing model used for the TikTok Creator Fund presents several parallels with the revenue-sharing model commonly used by streaming platforms such as Spotify and Deezer (Wikström, 2020). The music-streaming platforms have struggled for a decade or more to explain to creators how their model works, and still to this day they are criticized for the lack of fairness and transparency of their systems (ibid.). Just like in these debates, TikTokers in our study explained their disappointment with the payments they received from the Creator Fund. For instance, our interviewee Adam (@adamjdorfmanmusic) mused that he had probably made enough money to buy a single loaf of bread from posting content that had received over two million likes on TikTok. These kinds of sentiments are identical to those of composers and artists on music streaming platforms who lament the petty payouts from Spotify, even when their songs have been played millions of times (ibid.).

The opacity of the TikTok Creator Fund distribution model has also generated a plethora of algorithmic gossip similar to what surrounds the For You algorithm (see chapter 2). Our interviewees pointed to vaguely defined terms, opaque payout conditions, and shifting guidelines that resulted in creators being ejected from the fund on what was described as an unclear basis. The most commonly expressed Creator Fund gossip was that joining the Creator Fund caused the views of and the engagement with the creators' videos to go down immediately:

> I resisted [joining the Creator Fund] for a long time because I didn't want there to be any sort of financial incentive to make me chase views... Although, everyone says that as soon as you join your views tank. I thought, 'no, there's no way that's true.' And Benthamite[16] says there's no statistical evidence of that happening. But it happened to me. I'm really trying to not let that confirmation bias make me buy into that mythology of the algorithm. (Ben (@bensrightbrain))

TikTok included this concern on its Creator Fund FAQ page, a clear sign that this is indeed a widely held suspicion in the creators' community:

> Q   Can joining the Creator Fund negatively impact my videos views [sic] or followers as some creators are reporting?
> A   Absolutely not. Joining the Creator Fund will not have a negative impact on your TikTok videos views [sic] or

followers, any drops in video views are caused by in-app fluctuations that naturally occur and have nothing to do with the Creator Fund. But we will continue to keep a close eye on this and are always listening to the feedback we receive from our creator community.[17]

When we were discussing the Creator Fund with our interviewees, Shout (@vocaloutburst), Ebony (@ebonylorenmusic), and Ben (@bensrightbrain) described how they felt that the engagement-driven Creator Fund negatively impacted their creativity. Creators who participate in the fund are incentivized to make sure that content gets more 'engagement and authentic views'. As we discussed in earlier chapters, TikTok already provides socially creative features that encourage users to participate in trends or to use popular templates. In these interviewees' minds, however, the added pressure of a monetary incentive drives creators to jump on the most popular trends and detracts from the spontaneity and freedom of making truly creative TikTok content.

Other interviewees voiced concerns about the Fund on the grounds that some features that are important to social creativity on TikTok, such as Duet videos, are ineligible for monetization in the Creator Fund. In consequence, our interviewees argued that creators who are serious about making money through the Fund might end up removing Duets from their content repertoire. Viewed in this way, the Fund, which was launched to foster and support creativity, may actually have the opposite effect on creators.

TikTok for Black Creatives

In late May 2020, millions of people around the world united in protest over the death of George Floyd, an African American man brutally murdered by a police officer in Minneapolis. Thousands of creators took to TikTok to share emotional reactions, news coverage, and important safety information. In what was later attributed to a technical glitch, videos tagged with #BlackLivesMatter and #GeorgeFloyd temporarily displayed zero views, despite the high engagement evidenced by likes, comments, and shares. On 1 June 2020, TikTok's general manager, Vanessa Pappas, and the head of the creator community, Kudzi Chikumbu, issued a public apology that stated: 'we understand that many assumed this bug to be an intentional act to suppress the experiences and invalidate the emotions felt by the Black community. And we know we have work to do to regain and repair that trust' (Pappas & Chikumbu, 2020, p. 1). The statement promised to establish programs 'geared towards recognizing and uplifting the voices driving culture, creativity, and important conversations on the platform'.

Seven months later, in January 2021, TikTok announced that it would be piloting a new initiative called 'TikTok for Black Creatives', in partnership with MACRO, a multi-platform media agency founded and run by black creatives. As with the Creator Fund, interested creators needed to have a minimum threshold of 10,000 real followers. In addition, the announcement specified that eligible creators needed to apply, as opposed to joining by invitation; each applicant would be individually vetted by TikTok corporate representatives; and the program had a maximum capacity of 100 US-based creators. One month later, in February 2021, during Black History Month in the United States, TikTok inaugurated the first 100 creators into the program. Crucially, this initiative was not an endowment- or revenue-sharing program, like the Creator Fund. TikTok for Black Creatives provided three months of online mentoring sessions with the successful applicants, and the aim was to produce TikTok videos that incorporated the skills and strategies covered in the sessions (Arit, 2021).

Two months after the launch of the incubator, black creators were reminded of how their creative labor is valued on TikTok, as they watched Addison Rae performing dances on the *Late Night with Jimmy Fallon* show, with no credit to the original black, indigenous, and people of colour (BIPOC) creators and choreographers. As we noted in chapter 2, BIPOC representation on TikTok connects to much larger issues of racism and cultural appropriation, particularly in the United States. Shout (@vocaloutburst), who opted not to apply for the program in January 2021, was conflicted about the program's being launched in apparent response to criticism from BIPOC creators: 'I appreciate that [TikTok] did something, but it is never enough... the [Black Creator Initiative] was a disappointing sham'. We return to TikTok's corporate responses to public controversy in chapter 6.

*

TikTok's development of features, functions, and initiatives such as the Black Creatives Incubator, the Creator Fund, the Creator Marketplace, various promotional tools for creators, virtual gifts, virtual currencies, and e-commerce tools all echo similar developments that are taking place on other social media platforms. The initiatives are a sign that TikTok is learning from its competitors and from its Chinese ByteDance siblings. The platform is gradually diversifying its business and evolving from its heritage as a music-centric short-video platform to what may become a fully fledged social media entertainment platform. While this process is unfolding, TikTok still retains its music-centric nature and has become hugely important for the general recorded music economy. In the next section, we will analyse how TikTok is impacting the music industry and the way music is created, discovered, monetized, and enjoyed.

TikTok and the music industry

The past two decades have been a challenging time for the recorded music economy. When internet technologies started to disrupt the music economy at the end of the 1990s, recorded music was sold, distributed, and collected on shiny

plastic discs. The industry struggled to cope with technological change but, after 15 years' sales of recorded music,
it bottomed out in 2014 and began a period of rapid growth
(Figure 5.1). This growth is largely driven by music services
that offer access to a large music catalogue funded through
advertising revenues or through monthly subscription fees.
These are music-streaming services such as Spotify, QQ
Music, YouTube, Apple Music, Amazon, Deezer, and many
others (e.g. Wikström, 2020).

This industrial transformation impacted all aspects of the
music economy: how music is composed, arranged, recorded,
distributed, discovered, acquired, and (re)used. As a music-
centric short-video platform, TikTok touches all these areas.
TikTok and its earlier incarnation, Musical.ly, are part of a
general transformation of the music economy, which has
shifted from the twentieth-century focus on 'retrospective

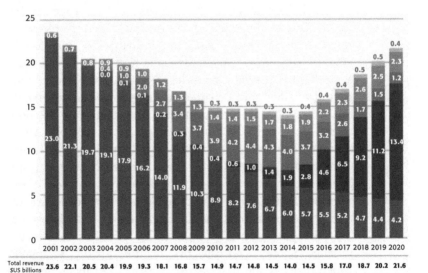

Figure 5.1. Global recorded music industry revenues, 2001–2020 (US$ billions). Created
by the authors. Source: IFPI, 2021.

music collections' to a focus on 'ephemeral listening experiences' (Wikström, 2012; 2013). The detailed dynamics of this transformation lies beyond the scope of the present volume. It is, however, essential for its problematics and interrogation to note that, when the recorded music economy experienced some of its darkest moments at the beginning of the 2010s, there was an expectation that it would never again be possible to convince listeners to pay for music. Out of this desperation emerged a range of music-centric mobile apps that certainly offered some kind of musical experience; yet their main value was to provide not the music itself, but the ability to engage in social and creative music games. Two of the best-known mobile apps of this kind were the London-based RjDj and the San Francisco-based Smule (Wikström, 2013). Smule in particular (mentioned in chapter 2) introduced a number of socially creative features that were picked up by Musical.ly and are to this day integral parts of TikTok's user experience.

This discussion shows that TikTok's DNA lineage can be traced back to the ruins of the twentieth-century recorded music economy. Even though the industry has since found effective ways to get music listeners to pay for music once again, TikTok has not become less relevant. The platform may have diversified and departed from its music-centric roots, but it launches initiatives intended to solidify its position in the music industry. For instance, in 2019, TikTok hosted a talent competition – the All-Star Southeast Asia Talent Competition – judged by a panel of TikTok celebrities from across the region.[18] In 2020 TikTok debuted a new feature, Year on TikTok, which produced a video retrospective of the most popular music and sounds a user had discovered over the past year (TikTok, 2020h). The feature directly imitated Spotify's retrospective feature, Spotify Wrapped, which displays the past year of personalized listening data analytics (Amos, 2021). The success of this TikTok initiative is perhaps questionable, as it prompted some users to duet their own retrospective, wondering aloud how their categories were determined. Regardless of this, in announcing the retrospective feature, TikTok's global head of music, Ole Olbermann, stated the platform's intention 'to work hard to make TikTok a platform that supports artists and encourages musical engagement and discovery' (TikTok, 2020h).

While TikTok is a platform for creative play with music, from a music industry perspective, music discovery is its most important function, mainly thanks to the platform's extraordinary capacity to drive musical memes into a viral spin.

Monetizing musical memes

There are many similarities between the processes that drive a meme to go viral and the processes that propel a pop song into the charts. Musical memes tap into traditions of remix culture and meme culture in which many overlapping voices are simultaneously present, diversely engaged, and endlessly reconfigurable (Lessig, 2008; Milner, 2016; Sinnreich, 2010). Abidin and Kaye (2021) argue that short-video platforms make audio an increasingly central component in memes. They think of the shift as an 'aural turn' in memes and note that it is the presence of audio – interlaced with video, text, effects, and filters – that makes short-video memes so spreadable.

Practices that privilege memetic audio alongside text, images, or video content certainly predate short-video platforms. Since the early days of YouTube, users have engaged in creating and sharing memetic videos that prominently featured music (Burgess & Green, 2018). These creative uses of music in YouTube videos developed their own norms, practices, and cultures (Cayari, 2011; Edmond, 2014), 'augmenting and replicating original audio content, neither merely creating user-copied content nor only redacting or quoting professional content' (Liikkanen and Salovaara, 2015, p. 121).

But combining music with memetic processes of this kind can also cause complications and conflict among the stakeholders involved, who are seeking to profit from a musical meme that, for one reason or another, has gone viral. Memes are generally fluid and iterative (Shifman, 2013) but turning a song into a meme also brings expectations of protection and control inherited from the music industry into the mix (Soha & McDowell, 2016). The Harlem Shake, an early musical meme that spread across YouTube and Reddit and went viral in February 2013, is a useful illustration of these tensions. The Harlem Shake, created by Baauer, an American record producer, was released in 2012 and subsequently remixed, reconfigured, and recontextualized by YouTubers and Redditors into a meme, with new additions and accompanying dance challenges. Critiquing Baauer's attempts to profit from the meme, Soha and McDowell note: 'a meme due in part to its seemingly accidental, collective creation, should not be owned or "authored" in the same way as a song' (ibid., p. 9). Even so, Baauer and his label Mad Descent generated substantial revenue from the Harlem Shake through streams and downloads of the song on digital music platforms as well as from advertising revenue videos that featured the song on the YouTube copyright detection system, ContentID.

The opportunities and challenges of the Harlem Shake are reprised or exacerbated on TikTok. The culture of imitation (Zulli & Zulli, 2020) and features such as Use This Sound streamline and simplify the process by which songs become audio memes. However, as noted in chapter 2, the platform's internal attribution system is prone to errors that can result in audio's being disconnected from its original creators and performers. Further, TikTok's monetization models make it difficult for creators to profit directly from the viral success of video content, let alone from their original audio.

These challenges are inconsequential to TikTokers who have no intent or expectation of making money on TikTok.

But, for those musical artists and companies vying to incorporate TikTok into their business practices, it is essential to understand and control all aspects of audio memetic dynamics. However, memetic processes are inherently unpredictable, random, and difficult to control. Indeed, artists and managers can have some influence on the process, but the history of internet memes (as well as the history of pop songs) is littered with songs and memes that have gone viral without any intention or plan. For instance, Nathan Apodaca (@doggface208) posted a video[19] in September 2020, where he is riding his skateboard and drinking Ocean Spray cranberry juice to the 1977 Fleetwood Mac hit 'Dreams'. The video ignited a meme that brought 'Dreams' back to #21 on the Billboard Hot 100 (Zellner, 2020). In April 2021, @swagsurff posted a video[20] of dancing and joking about the wonderful music of the Nickelodeon show *Backyardigans*, and particularly the bossa nova-inspired episode and song 'Castaways', which was aired in September 2005. 'Castaways' is the perfect fodder for memefication. One month later, on 12 May 2021, 'Castaways' debuted at number one on the US Spotify Viral 50 Chart, where it remained for almost a month before it started to fade.[21]

Intentionally or not, in 2020 TikTok reported that 176 songs had received, each, over 1 billion views on the platform (TikTok, 2020h) and 70 artists had landed record deals thanks to TikTok (Cross, 2021). However, considering the fact that there are hundreds of millions of TikTokers around the world, 176 and 70 are indeed quite underwhelming figures.

These figures and challenges aside, TikTok has a reputation of being a 'meme machine' (Grey Ellis, 2018). There are enough stories about how TikTok memes brought fame and fortune to their creators to persuade millions of aspiring artists to try to get the For You algorithm to work to their advantage. In the next section we will present some high-profile cases where artists have intentionally or unintentionally succeeded through those efforts.

Success stories

Successful outliers provide the stories that build the myths of TikTok's commanding presence in the international music market. In what follows we tell some of these success stories and briefly discuss examples of musical artists whose careers, at different stages, have been elevated by intentional or unintentional memetic processes on TikTok.

1. *Famous by accident.* Sometimes random memetic processes impact a person who is poised and ready to ride the surge of a viral audio meme on TikTok. One such example is 26-year-old Nathan Evans, a Scottish TikToker who went accidentally viral in late 2020 for his rendition of nineteenth-century sea shanties, and specifically of 'Soon May the Wellerman Come' (Rogers, 2019). In this instance, the sea shanty template became the audio meme, more so than Evans' original sound. Evans had recorded and posted other shanties, but 'Wellerman' became the audio meme that established him as the originator of the sea shanty trend. Evans' contested criticism that he was just a 'mailman singing sea shanties' and that it was all no more than a passing craze: 'I'm an actual musician. I've written some songs and hopefully, you'll get to hear some of them this year. Fingers crossed. I'll prove that I've got other things in my locker' (Browne, 2021, p. 1).

Shortly after the 'Wellerman' audio meme, Evans quit his job and accepted his first record contract. His response above alludes to the delicate next steps for accidentally viral artists who wish to avoid being pigeonholed into doing only the thing that made them TikTok-famous.

2. *Professional artists at an early stage in their career.* These artists may be established, yet relatively unknown musical artists who post music on TikTok and other digital platforms in the hope that their song will take off, and with it their career. The patron saint of this method is Lil Nas X, who skyrocketed to

global prominence after his 2018 song 'Old Town Road' went viral on TikTok in early 2019. 'Old Town Road' was recorded in a single day and released on SoundCloud (Molanphy, 2021). Lil Nas X had spent the past years before the release of 'Old Town Road' building his social media skills; and he immediately took to the internet to create memes, share the song, and call for remixes. The song gained traction on several digital platforms, including TikTok, as an audio meme, and soon caught the eye of notable artists such as Diplo, BTS, and Billy Ray Cyrus. Lil Nas X's achievement with 'Old Town Road' is one of the most clearly recognized examples of launching a career successfully with social media savvy. The successful memefication of the song translated into traditional music industry sales, including 19 weeks at the top of the Billboard Hot 100 (Trust, 2019).

Another example of an artist with a slightly higher profile than Lil Nas X whose musical career was also propelled into TikTok fame is Olivia Rodrigo. Indeed, in 2019, Rodrigo was already an actor with a role in the Disney+ series *High School Musical: The Musical: The Series*; but, when she debuted her first single 'drivers license' in early 2021, that took her career to the next level. The song became an audio meme template on TikTok, depicting endless alternative interpretations of the song's melancholic lyrics. The popularity of the meme helped to drive the song to the top of the new Billboard Global 200 chart, where it remained for eight weeks (Trust, 2021). Five months later, Rodrigo's full album *SOUR* debuted at number one on global Billboard charts, and each of the eleven tracks charted in the top 30 (Zellner, 2021). While clearly not responsible in entirety for *SOUR*'s performance, the viral spread of 'drivers license' probably introduced Rodrigo's music to millions of TikTokers.

3. *The well-established pop star.* Further up the music industry food chain, we find established artists who view TikTok as another social media platform on which their presence is

expected. The push to join the platform can come from their label; or it can be their own initiative. In either case, their purpose is to build and maintain their brand and to find a space where they can engage in relational labour with their fans (Baym, 2015). One of the most commercially savvy pop stars in the late 2010s was the Canadian artist Drake. In 2018, Drake's single 'In My Feelings' went viral on Musical.ly and, later, on TikTok as the Kiki Dance challenge, in which users were recorded dancing and lip-syncing to the song alongside a moving car. The viral whirlwind of 'In My Feelings' must have been a good experience for Drake. Two years later he used this experience and tried to replicate the feat when he released the single 'Toosie Slide' in the lead-up to the debut of his new album. Toosie Slide has been described as a 'shameless commercial ploy' (Rolli, 2020) and not 'really a song, just a bald attempt to incite a dance craze on TikTok: a load of noncommittal meandering attached to instructions on how to do the titular move' (Petridis, 2020, p. 1). While the song did not receive much critical acclaim, the 'commercial ploy' worked, and the song and the dance did go viral. Toosie Slide surpassed 1 billion views in three days, earned 55.5 million US streams in its first week, was listed as the top viral hit of 2020, and reached the number one spot on the Billboard Hot 100 (Rolli, 2020; TikTok, 2020h).

The success stories recounted here show how memetic processes on TikTok can indeed elevate a song or a musical career into the stratosphere. These stories inspire millions of hopeful artists to experiment with TikTok's features and to replicate these achievements. The artists and their managers are simultaneously at the mercy of inscrutable algorithms such as the For You algorithm and in a position where they hold the levers that can influence their visibility. Damoyee (@damoyee), an independent artist based in Dallas, Texas, who has 170,000 TikTok followers is just such an example: she described how she used TikTok's features and practices to promote her music. Previously, Damoyee asked her viewers 'please don't let this flop', or started her videos with an alluring hook such as 'I really messed up, and I need your help', followed by a video that promoted the song and let viewers know what they could do to support it. In our interview, Damoyee explained how she took an experimental approach to her TikTok promotional practices and learned from other musical artists on the platform. If her current practices did not work or the trend had moved on, she would continue to explore and test other ways of feeding the meme machine.[22] The music industry is brutal and unpredictable, and it remains to be seen whether Damoyee's TikTok strategies will eventually get the attention that her talent deserves.

As noted in chapter 4, most of the musical TikTokers we interviewed stated that they had aspirations of becoming professional short-video content creators, but many hoped even more to use their TikTok fame to launch a professional musical career beyond the platform's realm. Damoyee featured her original music in the majority of the videos she posted and personally created promotional campaigns in preparation for the release of any new music on other streaming platforms. Sophie (@Inoxiasounds; see chapter 3) turned down offers from TikTok and record labels after she became TikTok-famous in 2019 and was anxious to get back to busking the very moment when the 2020 pandemic lockdowns were lifted. Some interviewees were eager to professionalize their short-video content but were conscious of stigma and the limited opportunities for monetization on TikTok. When asked whether she wanted to use TikTok as a way of achieving her professional goals as a musician, Lisa (@utzig) reflected:

> Yeah. It's one of those things I'm almost scared to even admit. When I first started, I wanted to be a content creator. But it's hard to talk about that because there's such a shallow connotation to that. So I keep it kind of hush-hush. But I do want to grow this platform. I try to make conscious steps

towards doing that. Now that I have more of a following on TikTok, maybe I can branch out and do a little more YouTube stuff or grow my Instagram and make some sort of money doing this. It's one of those things that feels not real. I can see it but I can't grab it. I want it to be a thing but I know that I can't put all my eggs in that basket yet. (Lisa (@utzig))

Antagonizing the memetic processes

Betting on the star-building power of audio memes is an extremely risky move, and attempting to market a 'viral aesthetics' can backfire spectacularly. In April 2021, the American musical trio Tramp Stamps became TikTok-infamous after a video that debuted their new song became a viral audio meme. Members of the PunkTok community were immediately suspicious of the all-girl pop-punk outfit, which was perceived as a thinly veiled attempt by music industry executives to market a pastiche punk aesthetics. In the span of a few hours the band faced a barrage of criticism that made full use of TikTok's socially creative features in comments, duets, and stitches of the original video, as well as in new videos that used the audio of the 'Tramp Stamps' song 'I'd Rather Die'. The band responded to its detractors on Instagram by denying claims that its members were 'industry plants' and calling out the harassment and abuse they had faced since uploading the song (Jennings, 2021).

Equally noteworthy are hits that explicitly do not rely on TikTok for promotion. In May 2021, Nicki Minaj's third mixtape *Beam Me Up Scotty* (which includes the tracks 'Seeing Green' and 'Fractions') was re-released after 12 years. *Beam Me Up Scotty* became the highest-charting re-released mixtape by a rapper and the highest-debuting female rap mixtape in history. In an Instagram post thanking her fans, Minaj announced:

> Singles now r 2–3 mins, catchy hook, #Fractions is just rapping for over 3 mins, no hook). ★ no videos [...] ★ no

RADIO, ★ very little playlisting due to a surprise release [...]
★ no TikTok challenges (which has become EXTREMELY
helpful to all artists, love the app, btw)[23]

The specification that the mixtape was successful despite the
fact that there were no hooks or TikTok challenges, followed
immediately by a caveat that the app is extremely helpful to
artists and that she loves the app, speaks volumes to TikTok's
influence in the music industries. As Minaj points out, her
single 'Fractions' became a hit without the help of a catchy
TikTok hook; this contrasts Minaj with her former Young
Money label mate, Drake, whose 2020 hit single 'Tootsie
Slide' was described as a 'bald attempt to incite a dance craze
on TikTok' (Petridis, 2020, p. 1).[24]

Conclusion

In this chapter we argued that e-commerce features, new and
existing creator revenue models, and audio are core components of the TikTok economy. We examined how the platform
generates economic value for its owners, creators, advertisers,
and other stakeholders. We reviewed monetization features
incorporated from Douyin, such as *daihuo*, and novel initiatives trialled on TikTok, such as the TikTok Creator Fund
and the TikTok for Black Creatives incubator program. We
discussed how TikTok is situated within broader transforma-
tions of the global music economy and how musical artists
seek to capture value from memes. In the next chapter we
move on to analyse the governance of TikTok, as well as
governance by TikTok.

6

TikTok Governance

Like other major social media platforms, TikTok employs automated tools, human moderators, and user reports to identify and remove content that is deemed to be harmful for one reason or another. As a platform with worldwide reach, TikTok is required to negotiate constantly with the local rules, norms, and regulatory frameworks in the regions where it operates. Failing to do so can have vital consequences. For example, for content-related reasons, the platform has been (temporarily and permanently) banned in several countries, including India,[1] Indonesia, and Pakistan. This chapter discusses regulatory concerns, shifts, and controversies that have influenced TikTok's practice of content governance. In the first section we give an overview of platform governance on TikTok, emphasizing some of the particular challenges that this platform faces. The following sections shed light on three aspects of TikTok's content regulation: copyright governance, visibility governance, and the platform-sponsored ambition to promote what TikTok calls 'positive content'.

Platform governance struggle

Although many other social media platforms are faced with ever-growing pressure to regulate user-generated content, three factors have made platform governance *of* and *by* TikTok particularly controversial.

The young demographic of the TikTok community

First, the fact that the demographic of TikTok users is predominantly young raises wide concerns about children's safety. As pointed out by the internet researcher Milovan Savic (2021), during its early development TikTok focused on presenting itself as a parent-free and playful space for underage users. To this end, the platform implemented features that were appealing to the social and cultural practices of a pre-teen demographic. Although the short-video platform is gradually evolving from being a youth subculture into becoming mainstream, its user base remains younger than that of other dominant social media. According to a 2020 report, 40% of TikTok's monthly active users are between 18 and 24 years (Stokel-Walker, 2020b). In the United States, TikTok registered more than 30% of its 49 million daily users as being 14 years old or younger (Zhong & Frenkel, 2020). According to the platform's official data (TikTok, 2021e), more than a third of the removed videos are related to concerns about the safety of minors (see Table 6.1). One source of these concerns is content that depicts child exploitation and abuse; another is TikTok's handling of data from its underage users. In 2019, to settle the US Federal Trade Commission's allegation of Musical.ly's violation of the Children's Online Privacy Protection Act (COPPA), TikTok paid US$ 5.7 million – the highest record of civil penalty ever obtained by the Commission in a children's privacy case (Federal Trade Commission, 2019). Only two years later, TikTok itself was charged with lawsuits that claimed that the app harvested personal data from users. These lawsuits were filed mostly on behalf of minors and made the platform pay US$ 92 million for the settlement (Allyn, 2021). Although TikTok has tightened up its policies and introduced features that grant parents direct control over their kids' activities on the platform, similar legal challenges continue to be made by regulators from the European Union and the United Kingdom (Ridley, 2021).

The short-video format as a conduit for illicit content

Illicit content, especially pornography, is another known problem for TikTok's platform governance. A major contributing factor to this problem is the short-video format itself. TikTok has defined nine types of illicit content that are not allowed on its platform (see Table 6.1).

The multimodality of short videos makes them an ideal conduit for some of the most common types of illicit content listed in Table 6.1, particularly violence and pornography. Live streaming – a feature commonly supported by short-video platforms – is particularly easy to use for disseminating sexually explicit content. China, home to the world's most developed live-streaming industry, has a long history of battling with livestreamers who promote sexual content. After a nationwide crackdown on live-streaming services related to pornography, Chinese live-streaming platforms introduced drastic counter-porno measures, which include even a ban on wearing camisoles and on eating bananas (Wang, 2016). Moderating and filtering video content in real time are resource-intensive and technologically challenging – much more so than applying the same operations to text-based and still image-based communication. This is how TikTok, as well as its Chinese sibling, Douyin,[2] explain why they keep failing to prevent illicit content from entering the platform. As mentioned already, in some of TikTok's biggest markets such as India, Pakistan, and Indonesia the platform has been banned (either temporarily or permanently) for failing to avert content that local governments have deemed to be illicit.

Table 6.1. Nine types of content that are not allowed on TikTok. 'Share' is the percentage of all removed videos and is based on TikTok's biannual (H2) *Transparency Report* of 2020 (TikTok, 2021b); 'Category' is based on TikTok's 2020 Community Guidelines; and the data presented are based, again, on TikTok's 2020 H2 *Transparency Report*. Created by the authors.

Category	Explanation	Share
Minor safety	Content, including animation or digitally created or manipulated media, that depicts abuse, exploitation, or nudity of minors.	36%
Adult nudity and sexual activities	Nudity, pornography, or sexually explicit content.	21%
Illegal activities and regulated goods	Content features trade, sale, promotion, and use of certain regulated goods, as well as the depiction, promotion, or facilitation of criminal activities, including human exploitation.	18%
Violent and graphic content	Content that is gratuitously shocking, graphic, sadistic, or gruesome or that promotes, normalizes, or glorifies extreme violence or suffering.	8%
Harassment and bullying	Expressions of abuse, including threats or degrading statements intended to mock, humiliate, embarrass, intimidate, or hurt an individual.	7%
Suicide, self-harm, and dangerous acts	Content depicting, promoting, normalizing, or glorifying activities that could lead to suicide, self-harm, or eating disorders.	6%
Integrity and authenticity	Content or accounts that involve spam or fake engagement, impersonation, misleading information that causes harm, or that violate any intellectual property rights.	2%
Hateful behaviour	Content that contains hate speech or involves hateful behaviour that attacks, threatens, incites violence against, or otherwise dehumanizes an individual or a group based on their race, ethnicity, religion, etc.	2%
Violent extremism	Content advocating for, directing, or encouraging other people to commit violence.	<1%

The China connection

The third reason why TikTok governance is particularly challenging and controversial is its connection to China. ByteDance, which owns TikTok, is a Beijing-based company that operates within the Chinese legal and political system. Internet companies operating in China serve as part of the country's surveillance apparatus. When 'illegal' activities are suspected, online platforms must comply with authorities' requests to share user information. As a well-known example, Yahoo! provided the Chinese government with information about two users, the dissident journalist Shi Tao and the writer Wang Xiaoning, who shared anti-Chinese Communist Party messages through the Yahoo! email service.[3] The information supplied by Yahoo! was instrumental in causing 10-year prison sentences for Wang and Shi, on the charge of 'incitement to subvert state power', in 2003 and 2005 respectively. The Yahoo! incident received global attention, given the company's international profile and the high profile of the legal charges that the company faced in the United States because of this incident. For domestic Chinese internet companies, censoring and surveilling political criticism and dissident activities is simply part of their survival skills and daily routine. TikTok, on the other hand, has officially declared that its operation is independent of the Chinese government and of any intervention from it and that TikTok does not conduct censorship for the government.[4] Despite such attempts on the company's part to distance itself from the political suppression exercised by China, general scepticism and suspicion over its handling of user data remain. This lack of trust can be further exacerbated in times when tensions with China are on the rise, as demonstrated by TikTok's misadventures in 2020, when it was banned in'India and threatened to be banned in the United States for reasons of national security.

A fragmented TikTok

As the three factors just discussed demonstrate, the high level of scrutiny of, and the controversies around, TikTok's platform governance are the result of particular features of the platform, its user base, and geopolitical power confrontations. While expanding its global markets, the platform is faced by constant clashes and negotiations with local rules, norms, and regulatory frameworks. As pointed out by Flew, Martin, and Suzor (2019), global internet companies have to meet the requirements of different content regulations in their international operations, but without generating a 'splinternet, where their platforms are fundamentally different across territorial jurisdictions in terms of the content available' (p. 39). According to Flew and colleagues' remark on content regulation, TikTok's short-video service is already a 'splinternet' in terms of both localized content governance focus and international geolocation-based content personalization.

The regional idiosyncrasies of content regulation can be illustrated through the uneven distribution of content removal. Table 6.2 shows the top five countries that have removed the largest number of videos uploaded by TikTok, according to TikTok's 2020 *Transparency Report* (TikTok, 2021b).

When interpreting this table, it is vital to note that the number of monthly active users varies between countries and that TikTok also recorded a rapid growth in most markets during 2020. Estimates indicate, however, that India was TikTok's largest market before the ban in mid-2020 (R. Singh, 2020). TikTok's user base in India was approximately twice as big as in the United States, but the table shows that, before the platform was banned from the Indian market, approximately four times as many videos were removed in India as in the United States. It is unclear why so many more videos were taken down in India, but this is a sign of how TikTok

Table 6.2. The top five countries where the largest number of TikTok videos have been taken down. Created by the authors. Source: TikTok 2020 H2 *Transparency Report* (TikTok, 2021b).

2019 H2		2020 H1		2020 H2	
India	16,453,360	India	37,682,924	US	11,775,777
US	4,576,888	US	9,822,996	Pakistan	8,215,633
Pakistan	3,728,162	Pakistan	6,454,384	Brazil	7,506,599
UK	2,022,728	Brazil	5,525,783	Russia	4,574,690
Russia	1,258,853	UK	2,949,620	Indonesia	3,860,156
Global total	49,247,689	Global total	104,543,719	Global total	89,132,938

struggles to navigate different norms and regulatory systems in the countries where it wishes to operate.

Another governance area where it has been apparent that TikTok has limited experience of how to operate a sound-based (or audio-based) social media entertainment platform is copyright, which we tackle next.

Copyright governance

Copyright is a key driving force for platform governance (Gorwa, Binns, & Katzenbach, 2020). For the past two decades, international copyright policy has lagged behind technological advancements in copyright and sharing, from bootlegs to Napster and Instagram (Marshall, 2004; Meese & Hagedorn, 2019). Years of reactive legislation have caused digital platforms to adapt poorly to novel copyright issues or have exacerbated existing power imbalances in this area (Appleyard, 2015). Copyright policy is deeply entrenched in the governance of platforms, in the international laws and regimes that address digital copyright issues (e.g. Yu, 2006). Copyright is also governed by platforms (Gillespie, 2018), when it comes to the internal terms of use and enforcement systems that dictate how copyright matters are understood and addressed on digital platforms (e.g. Gray, 2020).

Copyright governance on TikTok has been shaped by two decades of struggle, colloquially dubbed 'the Copyright Wars', between platforms, large rightsholders, and users. YouTube was a central staging ground for the Copyright Wars, as large media conglomerates, prominently Viacom and Universal Music Group, fought to protect and maintain control of their intellectual property (IP) online (Burgess & Green, 2018). Eventually YouTube emerged from the wars as an industry leader in automated copyright enforcement. YouTube employs a Copyright Match Tool that scans uploaded videos and detects whether the video is already uploaded on the platform. YouTube has also launched the Content Verification Program (CVP), which allows rightsholders to serve notices and takedowns (YouTube, 2021). A third component of YouTube's automated copyright enforcement system is the Content ID system, which scans digital fingerprints embedded in licensed content and enforces rightsholder's predetermined settings to any videos containing matched content (Google, 2018). Content ID is effective at identifying licensed content, but can misidentify content or be overexerted by rightsholders (Gray & Suzor, 2020). Content ID is an example of an automated black box system (Pasquale, 2015), which is inscrutable but still exerts power over stakeholders (Kaye & Gray, 2020). YouTube's copyright enforcement systems have influenced Google services more broadly, and other international digital platforms have followed suit (Gray, 2020), including TikTok.

YouTube has extensive experience in managing copyrighted material on its platform, as it launched its Content ID system as early as 2007. At its own launch in 2018, TikTok had little experience of such techniques and, consequently, a considerably less imposing copyright enforcement system. Copyright policy was included in the platform's terms of service, but TikTok did not indicate that it used a ContentID-equivalent system for the automatic enforcement of copyright

(Kaye, Chen, & Zeng, 2021). Partnerships with major rightsholders are necessary for building up the databases of protected materials that are needed to scan for digital fingerprints, and TikTok did not secure licensing agreements with major music publishers until early 2020 (Ingham, 2020). That same year, TikTok exponentially strengthened its copyright enforcement, as Table 6.3 displays, issuing nearly 45,000 copyright takedown notices more than in 2019.

Copyright governance on TikTok is influenced by different factors, depending on the nature of the dispute. 'Copyright' broadly refers to two distinct types of rights: economic rights, which give artists the power to control the monetary exploitation of creative works; and moral rights, which allow artists to manage personality and reputational interests in creative works (Bargfrede, 2017).

Economic rights are most commonly associated with copyright protections and have played a substantial role in the development of international copyright policies (Drahos, 1996; Landes & Posner, 1989). Issues related to economic copyright often concern right holders' exclusive right to license and profit from their intellectual property.

Issues related to moral copyright, however, are generally concerned with creators' right to have their names properly attributed to creative works (Hansmann & Santilli, 1997). Moral rights are increasingly important on platforms that encourage remix and reuse and that are governed by norms of giving credit (Pappalardo & Meese, 2019), such as TikTok.

Table 6.3. Takedown notices issued by TikTok. Created by the authors. Source: TikTok 2020 H2 *Transparency Report* (TikTok 2021b).

Period	Copyrighted Content Takedown Notices
2019 H1	3,345
2019 H2	1,338
2020 H1	10,625
2020 H2	34,684

The spreadable nature of TikTok's content creates complex entanglements of economic and moral rights on the platform. As an example, in March 2020, a new dance challenge, Deep End Freestyle, began going viral as an audio meme template. The eponymous song lent itself well to the audio meme format, as it begins with melancholy singing followed by a beat drop:

> Singer: I don't think you wanna go off the deep end (x2)
> [Instrumental beat drop]
> Rapper: My body different...

TikTokers participating in the challenge would visually shift along with the tonal shift of the song when the beat drops, through creative transitions and subversions of expectations. Videos that featured #deependchallenge used an audio clip available in the internal TikTok's audio library and videos with the hashtag garnered over 12 million views on the platform. TikTok's automated attribution system correctly connects the song to its original creator, Sleepy Hallow, a Jamaican rapper based in Brooklyn, New York. Sleepy Hallow was also credited as the original artist on digital platforms and music streaming services, with no mention that the song featured or was written by another artist.

In May 2020, a TikToker and musical artist Fousheé (@foushee), shared a video[5] playing the intro bars of Deep End Freestyle on guitar and singing the lyrics. The onscreen text read:

> The irony of this is
> I'm actually the original singer in this sound
> But nobody knows or believes me
> And it's legit making me go off the deep end
> (Fousheé, 23 May 2020)

Fousheé's song was sampled by Sleepy Hallow. The practice of sampling is not itself noteworthy in the music recording industry. The practices and policies of sampling have been developed through decades of innovation and controversy and are well established in 2020. Fousheé's original song, Deep End, had been listed on Splice,[6] a digital audio marketplace where artists and producers can buy and sell samples and sample packs used in digital audio workstations. Splice's terms of use govern licensing arrangements between users; they assign creative commons licences for public tracks and a waiver of rights for public tracks.[7] It wasn't a fluke or an accident that Fousheé's music had ended up on Splice, as she explained in an interview with the music magazine *NME*:

> It started out as one of a collection of royalty-free samples that I had made in 2018, and then Sleepy Hallow picked it up. When I wasn't credited and people didn't know that I was responsible for that sample, I decided to put it out as a full song. (Fousheé, as quoted in O'Reilly, 2020)

Selling songs as free samples is a viable means of creative labour for musical artists and hobbyists who wish to meet the increasing demand for royalty-free catalogues online. In many cases doing so waives artists' economic rights, and in some cases – as with Splice – their moral rights as well. Fousheé did not take legal action against Sleepy Hallow but instead released her own version of the sampled song. By that point the Sleepy Hallow version had millions of views, but slowly word spread that another artist deserved credit for the song's catchy hook.

Foushee's video went viral the day it was published. Viewers began @mentioning Fousheé in the comment sections of the video that featured the Deep End Challenge. Other TikTokers created videos discussing the situation, offering their take, and praising Fousheé for the song. The following day, Fousheé posted a comment that received over 80,000 likes on the original video:

> Y'ALL JUST CHANGED MY WORLD IN A MATTER OF HOURS. I'M TEARING UP. I CAN'T THANK YOU ENOUGH!!!!!!!!! MADE MY MOMMA SO HAPPY (Fousheé, 24 May 2020)

Shortly after the video went viral, Fousheé was retroactively added as a featured artist on Sleepy Hallow's version, and she was able to produce and release a music video for her original full version.

On the one hand, receiving due credit for viral content on TikTok can be life-changing. By asserting her moral right to attribution, Fousheé turned a sample originally sold with no expectation of future profit into a launchpad for her musical career. In August 2020, Deep End Freestyle featuring Fousheé was certified gold by the Recording Industry Association of America (RIAA),[8] and in March 2021 Fousheé was named Billboard's R&B Rookie of the Month (Mitchell, 2021). As a contributing artist, Fousheé now also enjoys the economic benefits of the song's success. On the other hand, not receiving credit can be deeply demoralizing and profoundly offensive to creators who feel their content to have been culturally appropriated.

In June 2021, the entire failure to credit and misattribution phenomenon spurred a call to action among black creators in the United States to go on strike. Several among them called on other members of TikTok's black communities not to create any content – dances or anything – using audio from the artist Megan Thee Stallion's newest single, 'Thot Shit'. The strike reignited debates over the murkiness of copyrighting dance moves in the United States.[9] The American law and culture scholar Madhavi Sunder argues that the strike illustrates the tensions between cultural appropriation and copyright governance in the United States. As Sunder (2021) argues, 'copyright should not be used to prevent individuals from copying dance moves for social purposes... at the same time copyright can prevent choreographers from being exploited by corporations' (p. 1). In earlier work, Sunder (2012) advances a cultural framework of intellectual property built on social values such as participation, livelihood, and shared meaning – a framework that the law must recognize and protect. The absence of such protections can impact participation, damage livelihood, and corrupt the meaning of cultural expressions. Nearly a decade later, Sunder (2021, p. 1) concludes her analysis of the black creator strike on TikTok thus: 'Today, we must do better than this. Social media platforms need to recognize their role in perpetuating norms about what and whose culture is valued.'

Visibility governance

As discussed in chapter 2, the For You algorithm plays a crucial role in content discovery and trend making on the platform. From a content governance perspective, the algorithm creates both opportunities and challenges. On the one hand, the structure of the For You page and logic behind it set a high bar for potentially harmful videos if they intend to make an impact on the platform. Videos need not only to pass the platform's automated system for removing problematic content,[10] but also to be recommendable by the For You algorithm. On the other hand, the opacity of this algorithm makes it difficult to scrutinize potential algorithmic biases and explain why some videos, but not others, become visible and are promoted by the platform.

This black box governance of visibility on social media platforms causes frustration and confusion among users, especially users from marginalized groups who have made allegations against platforms about what is known as 'shadow-banning' – a practice whereby 'their content is made invisible to other users without actually being removed entirely' (Myers West, 2018: 4374). In 2019, a group of YouTubers from the lesbian, gay, bisexual, transgender, and queer (LGBTQ) community sued the video-streaming platform for allegedly discriminating against its members' content by suppressing recommendations (Kleeman, 2019).

Similar allegations of shadowbanning have been made by TikTokers. Frustrated TikTokers share their experiences and folk theories on other platforms and show 'evidence' of how they have been shadowbanned on TikTok. For example, some link their sudden drop in views to a specific video they posted (e.g. where they used too many swear words); others speculate that their 'bot like' behaviour (e.g. login to the same accounts from two different locations) prevented them from getting the visibility they deserve. However, not all allegations on TikTok's visibility governance are speculative. In December 2019, netzpolitik.org, an activist-founded online blog that advocates digital rights, revealed some controversial measures through which TikTok intends to prevent cyberbullying (Köver & Reuter, 2019). On the basis of the information provided by leaked documents and by an informant from TikTok, netzpolitik.org claimed that the platform restricts the viewing of individuals who are perceived as being 'highly vulnerable to cyberbullying' (e.g. people with 'facial disfigurement', 'autism', or 'Down syndrome'): such individuals can feature on a For You page only in their home country and can be viewed only up to 10,000 times. In an interview with netzpolitik.org, one spokesperson from TikTok admitted that the company is aware of this flaw in its system and intends to resort to the restriction only as a temporary solution (Köver & Reuter, 2019). A similar allegation was later made by the Intercept, an online publication according to which TikTok's content moderation suppresses users perceived to be unattractive on criteria such as 'abnormal body shape', 'ugly facial look', 'dwarfism', and 'obvious beer belly' (Biddle, Ribeiro, & Dias, 2020).

The controversies discussed above reveal a disconcerting morality embedded in TikTok's visibility governance practices. According to TikTok's statement, the restriction it placed on certain users' visibility was intended to 'protect' those very persons from potential bullies. However, such visibility manipulation takes a regulatory shortcut, which can be seen as driven by the platform's attempt to manage its risk exposure (i.e. its attempt to avoid condemnation for allowing online bullying) and to save its resources (i.e. its attempt to economize computational and human resource), rather than by a genuine consideration for its users' well-being.

TikTok's practice of labelling and grouping individuals perceived as vulnerable is akin to *social sorting*. According to the definition of David Lyon, a surveillance expert, social sorting refers to the data-driven approach to classify individuals 'according to varying criteria, to determine who should be targeted for special treatment, suspicion, eligibility, inclusion, access' (Lyon, 2003, p. 20). Empowered by the development of big data analytics, social sorting is increasingly used by banks, insurance companies, and the police as an anticipatory surveilling measure to manage risk (Lyon, 2014). TikTok's visibility governance uses video metadata as well as human manual labelling to conduct social sorting in the name of preventing online bullying. However, the conventional logic of anticipatory surveillance requires the identification of potential convicts. Against this logic, TikTok's anti-bully measures focus, on the contrary, on profiling and punishing potential victims. They are punished by being forced into 'enclaved publics' (Squires, 2002) – forced to hide from the view of the dominant public on the platform.

Even if the moderation guidelines uncovered in the two separate cases presented here may no longer be in use, they reveal persistent and recurring issues associated with the kind of algorithmic governance that is implemented by TikTok, as well as by other social media platforms. The algorithmic governance practices of social media platforms are imbued with questions related to their fairness and efficacy (Zarsky, 2016). As Morris (2015: 452) notes, 'today's algorithms and recommendation systems are not entirely autonomous systems. They depend highly on the people who design them and use them.'

The example discussed here shows clearly how the For You page incorporates the TikTok computer scientists' and coders' one-sided imaginations about the users' perceived vulnerabilities and needs. Machine-learning tools allow social platforms to automate and simplify many of their content moderation tasks by turning them into statistical problems for pattern identification; but, as Gillespie (2020: 3) noted, 'the margin of error typically lands on the marginal'. 'Good enough' and 'works for now' algorithms are used as 'temporary solutions', but at the cost of those who are already underserved and marginalized.

In relation to the algorithmic visibility governance practices discussed here, TikTok has implemented a controversial strategy, in an effort to distance itself from the image of a meritless and even harmful platform. This strategy will be discussed in the next section and involves the platform's attempt to promote what it refers to as 'positive content'.

Cultivating 'positive content'

As previously discussed, TikTok has been widely condemned for disseminating potentially harmful content. Its failure to manage these governance challenges has exposed it to massive financial penalties, the permanent banning of its service in some of its biggest markets, and a reputation as a vulgar and dangerous hub for teens and tweens. Improving its image and performance in this general area has become TikTok's top priority; and, when shaping its strategy, TikTok has learned a lot from its Chinese mother company, ByteDance. Since its launch in 2012, ByteDance has been surrounded by criticism over vulgar content hosted across the company's products. For example, in 2018, ByteDance's popular meme app Neihan Duanzi ('Implicit Jokes') was permanently shut down by the Chinese authorities for spreading vulgarity online. In the same year, the Cyberspace Administration of China (CAC) demanded that 'the promotion of core socialist values should always be integrated into short-video platforms' planning of content management' (Cyberspace Administration of China, 2018). In an attempt to win the favour of the regulator, ByteDance vowed to promote core socialist values in its products and launched a Positive Energy campaign on its short-video app Douyin (Chen, Kaye, & Zeng, 2021). To show its determination to combat vulgarity and its alignment with the party line, Douyin collaborated with 2,800 governmental accounts (governmental agencies and state media) to bring official voices from the government and the party to the platform (Xinhua, 2018). Furthermore, the platform also altered its interface to include a Positive Energy section on the app's front page, which was dedicated to videos that promoted 'positive values' such as patriotism and nationalism. Given Douyin's strong endorsement and promotion of such content, its users realized that making videos that explicitly promoted 'positive values' was a shortcut to attaining wide visibility.

Douyin's successful Positive Energy campaign was mirrored by TikTok, which introduced a series of campaigns designed to improve its image as a responsible and positive platform in international markets.[11] Two of the earliest initiatives in this range are TikTok's 2019 #cleanindia and #eduTok campaigns, both of which were launched in its India markets in response to local regulators' warnings about pornographic and other harmful content shared on the platform. The #cleanindia campaign had an environmental focus and invited creators to film themselves contributing to a cleaner India; picking up rubbish from the ground was the most popular theme. With a mission statement of 'democratizing learning for the Indian digital community on the platform', TikTok recruited and mentored local creators to bring educational content (TikTok, 2019d). According to TikTok's own figures, the #eduTok campaign has stimulated the creation of more than 8.8 million videos, which makes it the most popular 'for good' challenge to date.[12]

Notwithstanding that the popular #eduTok campaign did not save TikTok in India, TikTok continues to launch similar campaigns, as it is trying to convince the world of its potential to serve educational purposes. Since the beginning of the COVID-19 outbreak in 2020, TikTok has partnered with the

WHO and many other regional health authorities to inform and educate the youth about the virus. TikTok responded to the large scale of lockdown and school closures caused by the pandemic by introducing a variety of programmes that connected educational institutions and experts to young audiences. In Australia, TikTok collaborated with the Peter Doherty Institute for Infection and Immunity, whose researchers took part in the #scienceathome challenge; there TikTokers shared video clips of themselves doing science experiments at home. In the United Kingdom and the United States, TikTok devoted the #LearnOnTiktok campaign to promoting a wider range of informative, educational, and inspirational videos (TikTok, 2020c). Apart from partnering with organizations and experts, the platform also trains and funds TikTokers, in an attempt to stimulate more grass-roots creation of educational content. For instance, as part of its 2019 #eduTok campaign in India, TikTok delivered workshops to mentor 5,000 creators. In 2020, TikTok US provided a creator fund to support creators in the making of educational content (TikTok, 2020c).

Zeng and colleagues' (2021) study of science communication on TikTok shows that, by comparison with conventional models in science communication, educational videos on TikTok have their own vernacular styles. For example, these videos focus on affective values, visual appeal, and a personalized science communication. The two authors argue that educational content has the potential to be highly efficient on TikTok, thanks to its multimodality and popularity among younger audiences.

However, Zeng and colleagues also show that it is difficult to control campaigns such as #eduTok and other forms of educational content on TikTok. Their study documents a number of incidents wherein science was used to legitimize potentially very dangerous content. In 2019, an unknown TikToker revealed in a video clip that there was a 'mysterious' tablet (it was the moisture-absorbing tablet) inside pregnancy tests. This video triggered numerous viral responses, some claiming that the tablet was a 'plan-B' birth control pill, and some even swallowing the moisture-absorbing tablet in their videos. In another example, one TikToker claimed that one can get high by eating large quantities of nutmeg, and this resulted in a TikTok challenge in which participants recorded themselves consuming large doses of nutmeg.

The memefication of science blurs the border between jokes and knowledge; but this can easily backfire, as these examples demonstrate. While TikTok is determined to push for more educational and scientific content, the platform still struggles to regulate pseudoscience, or harmful science jokes that can easily hijack the platform's promotion of science-related videos.

TikTok's ambition to cultivate positive content is not restricted to promoting itself as a learning platform or as a platform for knowledge exchange. In the past years, TikTok has taken a proactive role in supporting progressive causes, for instance environmental campaigns (e.g. #forClimate challenge; see chapter 4) and campaigns advocating for inclusiveness.

As we note in chapter 5, TikTok partnered with the multi-platform media company MACRO to launch the TikTok for Black Creators initiative during Black History Month in the United States. According to one of the 100 selected partici-pants in the program, black creators were advised to 'follow up on [content] goals with *positive energy* and believe that [their] ideas would win people over' (Arit, 2021, emphasis added). Emulating ByteDance's strategy of creating a *positive energy* trending category on Douyin in respose to criticism from the Chinese government (Chen et al., 2021), TikTok explicitly emphasized that American black creators should incorporate *positive energy* into their content strategies. This was its response to potential criticism.

Regardless of the mixed reception that the Black Creator Initiative received, in August 2021 TikTok announced the launch of another incubator program for black, indigenous, and people of colour (BIPOC) creators. The second incubator program targeted Latino/a creators in the United States and was expanded to accommodate 150 creators. Once again, in partnership with MACRO, the program offered successful applicants similar mentorship opportunities as the Black Creators Initiative and was scheduled to begin at the start of National Hispanic Heritage Month in the United States (Gonzales, 2021).

In addition, TikTok has long been actively presenting itself as an LGBTQ+-friendly platform. Since 2019, TikTok has been engaging with LGBTQ+ influencers and rights groups to celebrate Pride Month and LGBTQ+ History Month in the United States and in Europe. Besides hashtag campaigns and donations to LGBTQ+ causes, TikTok also created special video effects such as Rainbow Sparkles, Pride Flag Cape, Rainbow Eyeshadow, and Rainbow Ribbons.

TikTok's celebration of inclusiveness is significant and Zeng and Abidin's (2021) study of Gen Z memes on TikTok reveals that homosexuality and transgender are key issues around which youths construct their generational identities. Young TikTokers who self-identify as members of the LGBTQ+ community use the platform for community building, as well as to fight older generations' conservative attitudes towards sexuality and gender norms. By sharing and watching personal stories of being an LGBTQ+ youth, queer TikTokers commiserate with and console one another (Ask & Abidin, 2018).

Despite being celebrated as the 'vital community hub' and 'soul of the LGBTQ+ internet' by LGBTQ+ rights groups and media commentators (Fox, 2020; Ohlheiser, 2020), TikTok's promotion of LGBTQ+ inclusiveness has clashed with the platform's ambition to abide by local regulations, as discussed earlier in this chapter. For instance, a number of reports from 2019 and 2020 showed that the platform blocked and restricted the visibility of homosexual content in parts of Eastern Europe and in the Middle East.[13]

As previously discussed, the platform's handling of perceived sensitive content is vitally important to its survival, so TikTok's double standard in treating LGBTQ+ markets comes as no surprise. Especially when it comes to countries such as Russia, where the dissemination of pro-LGBTQ+ content is illegal, the platform may easily get away with its exclusion of these regions in its 'international' celebration of LGBTQ+ inclusiveness.

Conclusion

Platform governance presents an especially thorny challenge in ByteDance's parallel platformization of Douyin and TikTok. As noted in chapter 2, the infrastructures of TikTok and Douyin are very similar. As noted in chapter 5, ByteDance deployed a similar, live-streaming-centric platform business model developed in the Chinese short-video market, and adopted new strategies to capture value in the international short-video market. In this chapter we have explored the governance of and by TikTok, highlighting ongoing tensions and platform responses. TikTok has faced legal action for failing to comply with child privacy laws in the United States and in the European Union, has been banned in India, Pakistan, and Indonesia for hosting illicit content, and has been the subject of intense scrutiny on account of its Chinese origins. Copyright and visibility, as governed by TikTok's internal systems and terms, create issues of misattribution and moderation for creators on the platform. ByteDance has attempted to ameliorate governance challenges by strategically cultivating positive content on both Douyin and TikTok. These responses have generated mixed results; ByteDance managed to appease the Chinese government in 2018, after facing scrutiny for Neihan Duanzi, but has been unable to reverse the ban from the Indian government in 2020. The likelihood of future governance challenges portends an enduringly uncertain future for TikTok.

7

The Future of TikTok

In April 2020, a new short-video platform called Quibi launched in the United States, after nearly two years of development and more than US\$ 1.75 billion of investment. The platform was created by Jeffrey Katzenberg, the DreamWorks Studios co-founder, and backed by the full force of Hollywood's most influential film and TV studios (Anderson, 2020). Quibi was meant to mark a new phase in the evolution of short-form video, combining as it did the storytelling and production value of Netflix and Amazon Prime with the bite-sized accessibility of TikTok. Before Quibi's launch, Katzenberg boldly claimed: 'What Google is to search, Quibi will be to short-form video' (Sweney, 2020). If the era of social media entertainment is heralded by the intersections of Hollywood and Silicon Valley (Cunningham & Craig, 2019), Quibi was a fatal collision. The platform lost billions of dollars, was unable to attract more than 500,000 subscribers at a time when TikTok was on its way to 700 million (Iqbal, 2021), and was ultimately shuttered by its founders six months after launch (Anderson, 2020; Alexander, 2020).

Multiple factors contributed to Quibi's failure to enter the international short-video market. As Sweney (2020) points out, Quibi 'simply failed to deliver content in a way that people want to consume it. Bite-size content tends to be the domain of free, mostly user-generated, models, such as... TikTok.' As this remark indicates, the fact that Quibi was so clearly 'not' TikTok was partly to blame for its failure. Quibi relied on a more traditional media industries approach to content creation practice and platform culture. It relied heavily on its Hollywood backers and on the A-list roster of celebrities under contract to provide exclusive content, which included Jennifer Lopez, Liam Hemsworth, and Reese Witherspoon. This content was professional, it was studio-produced and not user-generated, and it was forcibly broken into short videos.

The saga of Quibi is a cautionary reminder that short video is much more than *bite-size* content; it is also cultural practice, creative expression, and social interaction. For instance, as illustrated in our case studies of different viral content on TikTok, short videos are spreadable, templatable, and imitable. They are spreadable in their penchant for virality, templatable through their socially creative features, and imitable through their sound usage and editing features. Those affordances contributed significantly to TikTok's early growth. Focusing on these specifics of short videos, we will reflect in this last chapter on the future of TikTok, structuring our discussion into a number of topics and areas that have been covered in previous chapters: parallel platformization, short-video creativity, TikTok communities, professional content creators, and, lastly, TikTok and music.

The future of parallel platformization

One perspective we frequently returned to in this book is 'parallel platformization'. We argued that TikTok is one of the first digital media platforms from the Chinese media ecosystem to challenge the Silicon Valley digital media hegemony. We argued that the experience acquired in the short-video market in China, which is more advanced than its counterpart almost anywhere else in the world, is one factor that explains the platform's success. We have also shown how the otherness that is brought on by its Chinese heritage has caused TikTok a range of challenges and existential threats.

From the beginning of TikTok's international launch, the ideological systems, mainly those of the United States and China, were at odds, an opposition that manifested itself in trade wars, aggressive foreign policy, and culpability rhetoric developed during the COVID-19 pandemic. Shortly after its launch, TikTok became a political fulcrum between the two nations, setting the stage for more politically charged clashes that would have dire consequences for its own future. Reflecting on the 2020 geopolitical contestation between the United States and ByteDance, Gray (2021, p. 11) notes:

> On the basis of its data policies and practices, TikTok poses no greater security threat to its users than do its counterparts... In many ways, though, this is a familiar economic story: market incumbents striving to sustain their privileged positions, policymakers seeking to protect strategically important industries.

Silicon Valley's digital media incumbents wasted no time when TikTok's future was uncertain. When TikTok was on the verge of being divested or banned in the US market, Instagram launched its short-video feature Reels; this was followed by Snapchat's launch of its own version of a Creator Fund and by YouTube's beta testing of its short-video feature Shorts. Despite these challenges, TikTok was still in operation in the US market in mid-2021 and after.

Since their inception, most of the major Chinese technology companies have had limited incentive to operate business ventures outside the country's self-sustained domestic market, and the handful of successful attempts in international expansion focused on the Asia Pacific region (Keane & Wu, 2018; McLelland et al., 2017, p. 59). However, ByteDance's successful parallel platformization strategy has shown a path for future interaction and competition between Silicon Valley and China and has inspired more digital companies back home to launch parallel international products (for discussion and examples, see chapter 1).

Notwithstanding this book's focus on the example of the Chinese company ByteDance, the phenomenon of parallel platformization should not be seen as unique to Chinese technology companies that compete in Silicon Valley. As more technology hubs emerge to rival firms from the United States and from around the globe, the future may bring a rise in multidirectional parallel platform competition.

The future of short-video creativity

Creativity has been a central theme throughout this book, as we have identified a number of characteristics and features that promote, facilitate, and reward being creative. TikTok's powerful algorithmic recommender system and socially creative platform features have sparked new opportunities for instant creative practices such as dance challenges, audio memes, or distributed musical jams. Most of these features have been invented by short-video platform ancestors in China and Silicon Valley. By combining them with a highly effective recommender system, TikTok has been able to establish the platform as the leader of the global short-video industry.

However, if TikTok wants to keep its market leadership position, it will have to continue developing new functionalities that maintain user engagement, stimulate social engagement, and expand monetization. There are no indications that TikTok is slowing down on developing new features. In April 2021 alone, the platform introduced six music creative effects, together with automatic caption and playlist functions (Hind, 2021; TikTok, 2021a, 2021c). Many socially creative features, like Video Reply to Comments or Stitch, represent the platform's attempt to appropriate and integrate existing user practices and cultures (Burgess & Baym, 2020). Some instances of feature development, such as auto-captioning, have been necessary steps to keep pace with competitors. It will be interesting to see which current platform practices on TikTok will inform the next popular socially creative features. Further, it will be interesting to observe whether new features on TikTok will continue to set the norm among short-video competitors and how norms on these other short-video platforms will influence TikTok in their turn.

Not only TikTok's short-video features are rapidly changing; so too is its platform culture. We pointed out that, as the early adopters, youthful content creators, and especially members of Gen Z, have shaped the vernacular culture of TikTok. As we argue in chapter 4, TikTok is a *generational social media platform*, a site on which millions of younger TikTokers have creatively used short videos for self-expression, connection, and protest. The cultural demographics of TikTok have shifted after a year of global lockdowns drove international user bases to an unprecedented high. This user base expansion will bring new cultural dynamics and uncertainties to the platform. We cannot know to what extent TikTok still captivates the attention of Gen Z creators, or whether the incursion of their parents, who joined the platform, was enough of a sign to pack up and move on. Perhaps the For You algorithm will learn how to keep these generational cohorts enclaved within separate For You bubbles, with only minimal or incidental interaction.

Additionally, TikTok is steadily rebranding itself: from an entertainment hub, it turns now into a platform for learning and social good. This strategic shift, partially in response to controversies facing TikTok and ByteDance, presumably means more engagement with institutional collaborators, the aim being to promote educational content and advocacy. This shift can be viewed as the manifestation of a survival instinct. To maintain the interest and engagement of older generations of users, TikTok must defend itself against accusations that it houses nothing more than vapid, trivial, or even illicit content. Through the acquisition of Musical.ly, TikTok had the opportunity to learn, from Musical.ly's early blunders, how to build a short-video massive open online course (MOOC) platform. These lessons are evident in TikTok's trialling of an educational For You feed in 2020 (Stokel-Walker, 2020a). Perhaps such initiatives will return; but, like the Positive

Energy trending section on Douyin, the educational feed experiment has not become a permanent fixture at this stage.

The changes we noted in functionalities, shifting user base, and strategic repositioning will all impact what creative expression will look like on short-video platforms in the future. Probably the platform will eventually lose its cool, as it shifts towards being a place for learning rather than a place for making weird memes, and teens' videos are now more likely to be seen by parents and teachers. There is also a new cohort of youths, Gen Alpha,[1] and they are fast on the way to being the new kids on the platformized block. We can imagine the nostalgia of Gen Z reminiscing, in the future, about the 'good old days' of TikTok, just as millennials did with YouTube, as Gen Xers did with MTV, and as boomers did with disco.

Creativity lies at the heart of TikTok's platform culture, where it is nestled alongside its algorithmic recommender system. The company will continue to negotiate and develop creative, social, and cultural dynamics on its platform.

The future of TikTok communities

We have examined the communities that emerged on the TikTok platform and found communities that can be characterized as belonging to the *Gesellschaft* type, individualistic and profit-oriented, and communities rather of the *Gemeinschaft* type, communal and intimate (Tönnies, 1965 [1887]). In a capitalistic platform society, the *Gesellschaft* sides of TikTok are only going to become more *Gesellschaft*. Infomediaries (Morris, 2015) will develop new extractive practices in order to capture value from TikTokers, to the sole benefit of larger creators. Ownership and authorship are likely to be asserted more forcefully by major record labels and other corporate interests through vehicles such as automated copyright enforcement systems (Soha & McDowell, 2016) – systems that TikTok has already strengthened considerably in a relatively short time. Mid-sized creators may attempt to consolidate their power by joining or forming multi-channel networks or independent consortiums. A major shift towards *Gesellschaft* will also probably come from the casual, independent, or hobby TikTokers who, from making short videos for fun, pivoted into an influencer marketing role after one of their videos went accidentally viral. These 'TikTok for TikTok's sake' creators may then suddenly find themselves selling products for a company that has no ongoing contracts available and offers to pay only a pittance. These e-commerce practices on TikTok are inevitable; more *daihou* is coming to TikTok. Whether and how TikTokers embrace the growth of merchandising remains to be seen.

On the other side, revisiting our case study of JazzTok, it may be that the pull of *Gesellschaft* or the push of *daihou* are not the factors that cause the band to break up; it is the realization that they do not need TikTok to preserve their budding *Gemeinschaft* that has that effect. One critique noted by many interviews was that TikTok had severely limited messaging functions; in this respect it was described as being worse than any of its main competitors. To overcome this limitation, members of JazzTok simply decided to go to another platform, Discord, to chat with one another, to host game nights, and to coordinate new arrangements. Similarly, long before the official founding of Duet, some members of JazzTok felt that this function was too restrictive for high-quality musical collaborations. From the beginning in December 2020, JazzTokOfficial used a different platform, BandLab, for remote music-making. Limitations aside, these creators all found one another on their For You page on TikTok, through a combination of their own practices and the For You algorithm. If jazz musicians continue to post and view videos on TikTok, there will continue to be a JazzTok community in some shape or form.

Regarding the actual @JazzTokOfficial account, several founding members of @JazzTokOfficial acknowledged that COVID-19 played an important role in galvanizing the community in late 2020 and wondered what would happen after the pandemic was 'over'. In early 2021, a few months before COVID vaccination figures began to climb rapidly and musicians were cautiously returning to rehearsal spaces and performance venues, the 'head intern' at JazzTok admitted:

> I do have this little fear that when the vaccine is fully public and everyone's gotten it and we can all start going out and seeing each other again, we're not all going to be inside turning to TikTok, so will that community just fall apart? Are people just going to be like, 'yeah, I don't need this anymore'? And then go back to their regular hangouts. I don't know... but I would hate for this community to fizzle out. (Ben (@bensrightbrain))

In our interview, Ben explained the incredible amount of effort that went into coordinating, recording, and producing JazzTok videos. Everything was of course entirely voluntarily sourced from within the community. Perhaps the format of JazzTok would benefit from incorporating a bit of *Gesellschaft*, operating as a kind of TikTok multichannel network or shifting to become an independent label or production studio. Even if the @JazzTokOfficial account fizzles out, the community will persist. The videos on the account can become a memento to what this group of musicians accomplished, during an unprecedented historical time, which opened the doors to countless future professional ends. And it happened on TikTok.

The future of the professional TikTok creator

Short-video creators are a key stakeholder group for the continued viability and growth of the TikTok platform. Earlier in this book we discussed the precarious and challenging life of professional and aspiring creators on the platform.

The pressure to maintain visibility and constantly create new short-video content adds to the challenges of making a sustainable living on TikTok. Rapid production cycles and unpredictable successes cause some young creators to burn out (Lorenz, 2021). Even TikTok's most subscribed creator, Charli D'Amelio, expressed fatigue in 2021 from having amassed such a gigantic audience in such a short time and from the pressure of dealing with expectations and negativity. For D'Amelio and other creators in the top echelons, TikTok ennui can be easily remedied by shifting into other creative industries, such as film and television or music, or onto other platforms where the climate of creative labour is, or is at least perceived to be, less demanding. Smaller creators, however, lack such control over their professional opportunities on TikTok. Live streaming is still the main direct source of revenue on the platform, but it does not offer the same lucrative returns there as it does on Douyin. It is therefore more likely that TikTokers must adopt influencer marketing strategies to build their self-brand, connect with intermediaries, and forge partnerships with brands. Short-video commerce, or *daihuo*, could be a new source of monetization for TikTokers but, as we discussed earlier in the book, the platform infrastructure remains under development.

TikTok has indicated a willingness to support creators by establishing the 200 million USD Creator Fund and by rolling out new tools for self-promotion. The Creator Fund is fraught with criticisms – for instance about its restrictive terms of entry, or about the fact that its black box nature makes creators wary about how it might affect their views, or about the sobering economic reality that millions of views are sometimes not enough for a creator to afford a loaf of bread. TikTok has also announced that the Creator Fund initiative will continue and that the Fund will be expanded to US\$ 1 billion. While more funding for content creation is fundamentally positive, the issues experienced by our informants and other TikTokers will continue to create obstacles for creators, established and aspiring ones alike.

Some TikTokers are also beginning to compare YouTube's revenue-sharing model with TikTok's Creator Fund. YouTube generated close to US$ 20 billion in advertising revenues in 2020 and is expected to pay approximately 55% of that turnover to its creators (Ingham, 2021). TikTok does not regularly publish its revenues, but did make an exception in late 2020, forecasting that its revenues would be at US$ 6 billion in 2021 (Wang, Wu, & Zhu, 2020). If TikTok's Creator Fund were anywhere close to YouTube's revenue-sharing model, the size of the Fund would have to be slightly above US$ 3 billion, which means that the current Fund has a long way to go. Hank Green, a co-founder of the popular Crash Course YouTube series and of the YouTube creator conference, VidCon, expressed his frustrations:

> I've actually been pretty lenient about TikTok. I have been thinking in my head 'Hey this is a different format. They aren't making as much money because the advertising value is probably different.' But I think it's safe to say we should be done with that by now... Where's the value coming from? It's from the people that are making content. (Hank Green (@hankgreen1))[2]

Creators such as Hank Green and other professional social media entertainers do not often rely on a single platform for their work, but rather combine YouTube, TikTok, Instagram, and other platforms, depending on format and the audience they are addressing. However, the competition for talent is still fierce and, if the brightest shining stars perceive that the compensation from TikTok is not worth the effort of operating a presence on the platform, they will certainly abandon it for greener pastures.

The future of TikTok and music

TikTok is changing how audio, and particularly music, is enmeshed in participatory culture and vernacular creativity online. The TikTok platform facilitates creative use and reuse of audio through audio memes, voiceover effects, and dance challenges. As showcased by the JazzTok case, TikTok also fosters the emergence of tightly knit communities of musicians. Through Duet jams and chains, musical artists immediately participate in a form of distributed creativity that produces new and unpredictable music and also develops meaningful collaborations with a global network of other musicians.

TikTok has a music-centric nature that it carefully culti-vates through its messaging and various music industry initiatives (TikTok, 2020h; 2021d). Through these initiatives, TikTok has established a role for itself in the music industry as the latest platform for music promotion and discovery. The music industry, however, is always looking for new ways to cut through the noise and it will be interesting to see how long the platform will sustain its aura of novelty. In earlier chapters we pointed out examples of pop artists who are already distancing themselves from the platform. This may be an early sign of its fading powers.

In addition to TikTok's influence on the music economy, there are indications that TikTok may be changing the way music *sounds*. The history of popular music is intertwined with the development of media technologies. Broadcast radio, television, full-length albums, music streaming, and other media technologies have shaped the sound of popular music. For instance, when streaming music platforms took over as the dominating sites for music distribution, the structure of pop songs changed. On streaming music platforms, a song is counted as a 'listen' only if it is played for more than 30 seconds. Therefore pop songs in the streaming era tend to place the song's 'hook' within the first seconds, so as to make sure that the user doesn't skip to the next song before the creator is getting paid.

In parallel with this development, the purpose of music on TikTok is for it to be played *with*, in other words to be incor-porated in the users' multimodal short-video productions.

This means that, for songs to be successful on TikTok, they must be structured in a way that makes it easy for users to cut the songs into short (say, 15-second) chunks that can be seamlessly looped and creatively combined. There are several examples of successful releases in the first half of 2021 that have followed this recipe, including Lil Nas X's 'hooky, short and wildly loopable' hit 'Old Town Road', Olivia Rodrigo's album *SOUR*, or Bella Poarch's song 'Build a B*tch' (Leight, 2019; Schroeder, 2021). It is still early days for this trend, and it remains to be seen whether it will leave an enduring imprint on the sound and structure of popular music.

Final words

TikTok has made an indelible mark on the platform society. The largest and most influential platform companies have been steadily pivoting into the short-video market to compete with TikTok or to push the format ahead. This competition will continue to intensify, and TikTok's unique features may eventually lose their shiny newness. If YouTube or Instagram manage to reverse-engineer the algorithmic recommender system, or if a new platform enters the fray with a more powerful system, TikTok, the platform, may fall out of fashion and fade into obscurity. Regardless of this, TikTok has helped to usher in a golden age of short video; but the future of TikTok and of the short-video format remains hidden in obscurity. We do know, however, that, whether TikTok remains the world's leading short-video platform or not, the strange and beautiful world of short-video creativity and culture will endure and evolve.

Notes

1 Visit https://www.tiktok.com/@khaby.lame/
  video/6950627842518568197.
2 'Chug Jug with You' (https://www.youtube.com/
  watch?v=Z0Uh3OJCx30) was recorded in late 2018 by YouTuber
  Leviathan, who was 13 at the time. It is a parody of the 2008
  commercial hit 'American Boy' (https://www.youtube.com/
  watch?v=Ic5vxw3eijY) by British musical artist Estelle (featuring
  Kanye West) and is based on an 18-second chorus recorded by
  YouTuber CM Skits titled 'Let's Play Fortnite!!!' (https://www.
  youtube.com/watch?v=7yK5qHDMSXA). In 'Chug Jug with
  You', Leviathan sings, in what was described as 'a squeaky,
  prepubescent voice', 'about a Fortnite item that's no longer in the
  game' (Diaz, 2021). Two years after the recording, in early 2021,
  this piece went viral on TikTok for unclear reasons and has since
  been used in at least 600,000 TikTok videos, which collectively
  attracted billions of views.
3 The short film https://www.tiktok.com/@aatoji/
  video/6936529855475404038 is the original video posted by
  @aatoji.
4 The global platform ecosystem has been divided between Silicon
  Valley and China. Major Chinese technology companies have
  struggled for years to internationalize their core products outside
  China, while many major Silicon Valley platform firms, most
  notably Amazon, Facebook, and Google, have been prevented
  from establishing market bases in China as a result of internet
  governance regulations.
5 Gen Z is generally defined as the generation of those born
  between 1997 and 2012. See Parker and Igielnik, 2020.
6 Scopus is the world's largest database of peer-reviewed scholarly
  literature.

NOTES TO CHAPTER 1

1   For instance, with the Chinese government's shutdown of Twitter in 2019, Sina launched a Chinese equivalent to Twitter: Sina Weibo. Likewise, China's Renren is often considered a Chinese copycat of Facebook, which has also been banned in mainland China.
2   Both platforms would later increase the maximum allowable duration of videos to three minutes (Kuaishou) and five minutes (Meipai).
3   Flash was an early format of online animation; it was created in, and viewed through, Adobe Flash Player. The format supported audiovisual animations that ran on limited bandwidth and were used in web cartoons and online series throughout the early noughties.
4   In 2017, Reddit user Cinango created https://youtubehaiku. net, an open-source web platform for viewing YouTube Haikus online.

NOTES TO CHAPTER 2

1   In May 2021, TikTok's mission statement was to inspire creativity and bring joy.
2   The hashtag #fyp identifies TikTok's For You page. The origin of the hashtag #xyzcba is unclear. But the urban legend that this hashtag can boost the visibility of videos on TikTok has made it commonly adopted and used by creators.
3   For a full list of interviews, see the Appendix.
4   @ mentions placed in onscreen text stickers are not hyperlinked or clickable.
5   *Ratatouille the Musical* or *Ratatousical* emerged through the distributed creativity of musicians, choreographers, thespians, and many others who transformed a memetic premise (What if Disney's *Ratatouille* were a Broadway musical?) into reality (Alter, 2020). Several videos posted in mid and late 2020 imagined what a *Ratatouille* musical might look like, who might be involved, and how it might sound. The viral videos caught the attention of Broadway elites such as Lin-Manuel Miranda, the creator of *Hamilton*, and members of the animated film's original cast such as Patton Oswalt, the voice of the protagonist Remy the rat. The musical was approved for production in

late 2020 and performed in January 2021, being streamed on
the digital ticketing platform TodayTix to over 350k viewers.
It generated in total more than $2M, which was donated to
the New York Actors Fund to support the struggling theatre
community heavily impacted by the COVID-19 pandemic (King,
2021). The viral videos that inspired the musical are available
at https://www.vulture.com/2020/11/ratatouille-musical-tiktok.
html.

6 Comment character limits: Facebook 63,205; YouTube 5,000;
Instagram 2,200; LinkedIn 1,300; Twitter 280; TikTok 150
(Romero, 2020).

7 Visit https://www.youtube.com/watch?v=SsWrY770770.

8 Visit https://www.tiktok.com/@whatchugotforme/
video/6819061413877763334.

9 For an example of a twist of the 'stop scrolling' call for
participation meme by interviewee @damoyee, visit https://www.
tiktok.com/@damoyee/video/6971073779153816838.

10 All interviewees provided informed consent to be named in this
book; however, we chose to anonymize this particular vignette
given the sensitive nature of the events described.

11 Visit https://twitter.com/WhosTYE/
status/1376305508798377984.

12 Some of the dance creators profiled are Mya Nicole Johnson
(@theemyanicole), Chris Cotter (@cchrvs), Dorien Scott
(@yvnggprince), Fur-Quan Powell (@flyboyfu), Camyra
Franklin (@17slumz), Adam Snyder, Nate Nale, and Greg Dahl
(@macdaddyz), and Keara Wilson (@kekejanajah).

13 Visit https://youtu.be/Bdal1YTQjIY.

Notes to Chapter 3

1 According to Burgess and Matamoros-Fernández's (2016, p. 81)
definition, 'issue publics are animated by acute controversies
which are of a different ontological order to issues: they are
discrete and identifiable sites of uncertainty and creativity
around a given issue'.

2 In May 2020, Derulo's use of a viral TikTok audio 'Laxed (Siren
Beat)' in his new song 'Savage Love' led to a brief controversy
about its attribution. The original audio was created by Josh
Nanai (@Jawsh385), a teenage TikToker and producer who lives
in New Zealand. In response to criticism, Derulo added Nanai as

a featured artist on the song and in the official music video. The song was remixed by K-pop megastars BTS and peaked at #1 on the US Billboard charts (Aualiitia, 2020).

3 For an extended discussion of this case study, see Kaye (2020).

4 Visit https://www.tiktok.com/@inoxiasounds/ video/6760948081396681989.

5 Visit https://www.tiktok.com/@bellaporch/ video/6862153058223197445.

6 Visit https://www.tiktok.com/@bellaporch/ video/6962204861312027910.

7 Visit https://www.tiktok.com/@jazztokofficial/ video/6909535106017316102.

8 'FYP' is an acronym for 'For You page'.

9 Visit https://www.tiktok.com/@katelxyn/ video/6959809607661276421.

Notes to Chapter 4

1 E.g. the 'rich friend check' meme.

2 'Boomers' is the general name for people born between 1946 and 1964, during the so-called baby boom period after the Second World War.

3 The account had 118 million followers in June 2021.

4 By December 2020, the #saveTikTok challenge had reached more than 1.6 billion views.

5 In June 2021, 30 of the top 50 TikTokers were based in the United States (see Table 3.1).

6 Visit https://www.tiktok.com/@mehnaz___s/ video/6847574416038104326.

7 Visit https://www.tiktok.com/@nathantriska/ video/6847967798774254853.

8 https://www.tiktok.com/@itsjohnwalsh/ video/6847570828255579397.

9 Examples can be found at https://www.tiktok.com/@ brodywellmaker/video/6847466840088743174, https://www. tiktok.com/@lipstickfables/video/6873984836101491974, and https://www.tiktok.com/@brendanisugly/ video/6846789247563812101.

10 Visit https://www.tiktok.com/@morganpeoples/ video/6856026460721876229.

11 Two examples are https://www.tiktok.com/@simonjosephjavier/

video/6847817135943585025 and https://www.tiktok.com/
@resanu/video/6847847199372578053.

12 POV stands for Point of View. It requires the creator to shoot
videos using the viewer's point of view, and it has become
a common style and a challenge used by TikTokers for
storytelling.

13 Visit https://www.tiktok.com/@itsdianalore/video/
6848416824015588614.

14 Visit https://www.tiktok.com/@.meech/video/
6847509000699890949.

15 Visit https://www.tiktok.com/@anwar/video/
6847674937180769542, https://www.tiktok.com/@leazylilix/
video/6847245062124915974.

16 Visit https://www.tiktok.com/@nickythomasalt/video/
6847236280250584326.

17 As documented by Zeng and Abidin (2021), during campaigns,
craft makers or artists make artefacts related to the cause, for
instance paintings, and often provide links to external websites
where such artefcts can be purchased. On TikTok, commercial
advertisements also engage with popular campaigns, in order to
connect with the Gen Z market.

NOTES TO CHAPTER 5

1 WeChat is referred to as a 'super app' in Chen et al. 2018 and
the term 'hyper-platformization' is used by D. Craig in Craig,
Lin, & Cunningham, 2021, p. 59.

2 Share of total revenues generated via subscription fees in 2020:
Netflix: 100%, Spotify: 91%, *Economist*: 68%, *New York Times*:
67%.

3 https://www.tiktok.com/business/en-AU/apps/tiktok#1.

4 Walmart launched live-streaming shopping on TikTok in 2021
(Walmart, 2021), and E-commerce platform Shopify works
with TikTok to develop in-app shopping features that facilitate
merchants' usage of TikTok (Liu, Huang, & Turner, 2021).

5 For an overview of the influencer industry in China, see Craig
et al. 2021.

6 Facebook Pixel is a tracking tool that enables websites and online
retailers to collect data about their visitors' activities.

7 According to Paris Martineau's (2018) report, Facebook's Like
button appeared on 8.4M websites, the Share button appeared

on 931K websites, and there were 2.2M Facebook Pixels installed on websites.

8   Visit https://seller-id.tiktok.com/university.

9   Visit https://www.tiktok.com/legal/virtual-items.

10   Visit https://www.tiktok.com/legal/virtual-items.

11   Visit https://theinfluencermarketingfactory.com.

12   Visit https://www.obvious.ly.

13   Visit https://www.tiktok.com/creators/creator-portal/en-us/getting-paid-to-create/creator-fund.

14   Visit https://www.tiktok.com/legal/tiktok-creator-fund-terms.

15   Visit https://newsroom.tiktok.com/en-gb/tiktok-creator-fund-your-questions-answered.

16   Visit https://www.tiktok.com/@benthamite. @benthamite is a TikTok account that posts computational experiments using TikTok analytic data. In 2021 the creators behind @benthamite commercialized their TikTok analytics tools creating Statistok.com, a subscription service that offers more in-depth analysis than the native TikTok analytics for business accounts.

17   Visit https://newsroom.tiktok.com/en-gb/tiktok-creator-fund-your-questions-answered.

18   Visit https://activity.tiktok.com/magic/page/ejs/5dc2a8a09a2c594bf2daf3c2.

19   Visit https://www.tiktok.com/@420doggface208/video/6876424179084709126.

20   The video is 'currently unavailable'; visit https://www.tiktok.com/@swagsurfff/video/6948522339294301445.

21   Visit https://spotifycharts.com/viral/us/daily.

22   Visit https://www.tiktok.com/@damoyee/video/6971073779153816838.

23   Visit https://www.instagram.com/p/CPWegwlLZxv.

24   Drake and Minaj, two North American rappers, both got their start in music after being signed to the American rapper Lil Wayne's record label Young Money around the same time, in the late noughties. In the subsequent decade they have both been very successful, but appear to be divided on how to use TikTok to promote music. The quotation given here from Minaj's Instagram post highlights that she was *intent* on not creating songs with hooks that would go viral. According to the music critic Alexis Petridis (2020), Drake did exactly the opposite in his 2020 album *Dark Lane Demo Tapes*. Petridis argues that many of the songs in that album are just extended 'hooks' composed so as to make the songs go viral on short-video platforms. This

was particularly true of the album's hit single 'Tootsie Slide', which in his view 'wasn't really a song... a load of noncommittal meandering attached to instructions on how to do the titular move'.

Notes to Chapter 6

1 India's permanent ban of TikTok in 2020 was introduced in the name of national security concerns, but in 2019 the government banned TikTok temporarily for content-related reasons.

2 In 2020 alone, the Chinese national anti-pornography work group received more than 900 reports on Douyin, which is TikTok's Chinese sibling platform (Wang, 2021).

3 Wang emailed electronic journals advocating reform of China's political system. Shi emailed a governmental document to an overseas Chinese pro-democracy website (Helft, 2007).

4 TikTok US' head of safety, Eric Han, posted a blog on the platform's Newsroom, apologizing for the suspension and 'clarifying' the timeline of events (Han, 2019).

5 Visit https://www.tiktok.com/@kungfou/ video/6829935439818919173.

6 Visit https://splice.com.

7 Visit https://splice.com/terms, Section 5.h.

8 The RIAA Awards Gold certifications to albums or singles that have accumulated 500,000 certification units, calculated by downloads and streams, in the United States.

9 One year before, the actor Alfonso Ribeiro and the artist 2 Milly withdrew copyright lawsuits over dance moves used in the video game Fortnite (developed by Epic Games) after a 2019 US Supreme Court decision on copyright. According to the ruling, 'if the US Copyright Office has not granted or refused a person's application for registration, that person is not legally able to sue for copyright infringement' (Crucchiola, 2019, p. 1).

10 As discussed earlier in this chapter, TikTok relies on tools (e.g. PhotoDNA) for the automated flagging and removal of potentially harmful content. According to TikTok's 2020 *Transparency Report*, over 80% of removed videos were identified before they received any views (TikTok, 2021b).

11 TikTok has launched several campaigns since 2018. A partial, curated list of past TikTok For Good campaigns is archived at https://www.tiktok.com/forgood.

12 The data are retrieved from https://www.tiktok.com/forgood.
13 According to reports from Reuter and the *Guardian*, TikTok's
   Turkish, Russian, Estonian, Bosnian, and Arabic versions
   moderate pro-LGBTQ+ contents (Bacchi, 2020; Criddle, 2020;
   Fox, 2020).

Notes to Chapter 7

1 Gen Alpha is the generation of children born between 2011 and
  2025.
2 Visit https://www.tiktok.com/@hankgreen1/
  vitodeo/6976405761987448069.

Appendix
Interviews

Qualitative semi-structured interviews for this book were primarily conducted in January and February 2021. One additional interview was conducted in May 2020, as part of a separate project (Kaye, 2020), and one follow-up interview was conducted in October 2021. All interviews were conducted remotely, recorded via the Zoom conferencing platform, and automatically transcribed using the Rev transcription service. Twenty-five ($n = 25$) interviews were conducted, nineteen ($n = 19$) with members of the JazzTok community described in chapter 4. Initial interviewees were purposively identified as being musical TikTokers who used socially creative features (i.e. Duet) to make music. The later emphasis on JazzTok emerged from snowball sampling. All interviewees provided informed consent to be identified by name and TikTok account.

The interviewees

Name	Date	Account	Country
Sophie	6May20	@inoxiasounds	Australia
Ebony	12Jan21	@ebonylorenmusic	United States
Emerson	14Jan21	@emersonbrophy	Australia
Kapono	14Jan21	@kaponowmusic	United States
Ben	15Jan21	@bensrightbrain	United States
Kyle	15Jan21	@felonious_skunk	United States
Shout	16Jan21	@vocaloutburst	United States
Anthony	18Jan21	@ewokbeats	United States
Damoyee	19Jan21	@damoyee	United States

Kris	20Jan21	@musixicn_kris_	United States
Bri	20Jan21	@souparstarbri	United States
Lisa	20Jan21	@utzig	United States
Rachel	21Jan21	@rvmillz	United States
Adam	21Jan21	@adamdorfmannmusic	United States
Violet	21Jan21	@violetbutnotaflower	United States
Jake	21Jan21	@jakedoesmusicsometimes	United States
Jay	22Jan21	@jaywebbtrumpt	United States
Alex	26Jan21	@alexengelberg	United States
Ralph	27Jan21	@theboneguy	United States
Stacey	28Jan21	@staceyryanmusic	Canada
RJ	30Jan21	@rjthecomposer	United States
Tai	30Jan21	@thctai	Canada
Erynn	4Feb21	@rynnstar	United States
Gabbi	4Feb21	@fettuccinefettuqueen	Australia
Shout	3Oct21	@vocaloutburst (follow up)	United States

References

Abidin, C. (2016). Visibility labour: Engaging with influencers' fashion brands and #OOTD advertorial campaigns on Instagram. *Media International Australia*, *161*(1), 86–100. https://doi.org/10.1177/1329878X16665177.

Abidin, C. (2018). *Internet Celebrity: Understanding Fame Online*. Emerald Publishing.

Abidin, C. (2021). Mapping internet celebrity on TikTok: Exploring attention economies and visibility labours. *Cultural Science Journal*, *12*(1), 77–103. https://doi.org/10.5334/csci.140.

Abidin, C., & Kaye, D. B. V. (2021). Audio memes. In C. Arkenbout, J. Wilson, & D. de Zeeuw (eds.), *Critical Meme Reader* (pp. 58–68). Institute of Network Cultures.

Abidin, C., Nagel, E. van der, Johns, A., Bailo, F., Rodriguez, A., Valdovinos-Kaye, B., Wikström, P., Gerrard, Y., & Leaver, T. (2020). 'Please read the comments': Commenting cultures across platforms. *AoIR Selected Papers of Internet Research*. https://doi.org/10.5210/spir.v2020i0.11109.

Abidin, C., & Zeng, J. (2020). Feeling Asian together: Coping with# COVID racism on subtle Asian traits. *Social Media + Society*, *6*(3). https://doi.org/10.1177/2056305120948223.

Access to China. (2020). Baidu Alibaba and Tencent. Access to China, 4 May. https://accesstochina.com/chinese-internet/being-found-on-the-chinese-internet/baidu-alibaba-and-tencent-bat.

Adams, P. (2021). Barilla pens rigatoni-themed 'funkytown' parody for TikTok. Marketing Dive, 25 May. https://www.marketingdive.com/news/barilla-pens-rigatoni-themed-funkytown-parody-for-tiktok/600747.

Ahuja, A., & Dalal, M. (2018). Chinese start-up says Helo to India, set to take on ShareChat, Clip. LiveMint, 27 July. https://www.livemint.com/Technology/oanSCMhXkOTx6xINpvGPTL/Chinese-startup-says-Helo-to-India-set-to-take-on-ShareCha.html.

AI Lab. (2021). ByteDance (home page). https://ailab.bytedance.com.

Alexander, J. (2019a). Your guide to using TikTok. The Verge, 2

April. https://www.theverge.com/2019/4/2/18201898/tiktok-guide-for-you-challenge-creator-trend-algorithm-privacy.

Alexander, J. (2019b). PewDiePie becomes the first individual YouTube creator to hit 100 million subscribers. The Verge, 26 August. https://www.theverge.com/2019/8/26/20831853/pewdiepie-100-million-subscribers-youtube-tseries-competition.

Alexander, J. (2020). Quibi will add sharing features as the app struggles to find subscribers. The Verge. https://www.theverge.com/2020/5/11/21255084/quibi-jeffrey-katzenberg-streaming-tv-screenshot-sharing-social-media-subscribers-coronavirus.

Allyn, B. (2021). TikTok to pay $92 million to settle class-action suit over 'theft' of personal data. NPR, 25 February. https://www.npr.org/2021/02/25/971460327/tiktok-to-pay-92-million-to-settle-class-action-suit-over-theft-of-personal-data.

Alter, R. (2020). Broadway is closed, but *Ratatouille the Musical* is cooking on TikTok. *Vulture*, 19 November. https://www.vulture.com/2020/11/ratatouille-musical-tiktok.html.

Amabile, T. (1983). *The Social Psychology of Creativity*. Springer. https://doi.org/10.1007/978-1-4612-5533-8.

Amos, M. (2021). Is TikTok the future of the music industry? RouteNote Blog, 17 May. https://routenote.com/blog/is-tiktok-the-future-of-the-music-industry.

Anderson, J. (2020). Quibi is an innovative, mobile-only streaming video entertainment service with a little something for everyone. TechHive, 5 April. https://www.techhive.com/article/3535820/quibi-has-a-little-something-for-everyone.html.

Andrews, T. M. (2021). Jimmy Fallon addresses controversial Addison Rae segment that didn't credit dance creators. *Washington Post*, 6 April. https://www.washingtonpost.com/technology/2021/04/06/addison-rae-jimmy-fallon-dance-credit.

Appleyard, M. (2015). Corporate responses to online music piracy: Strategic lessons for the challenge of additive manufacturing. *Business Horizons*, 58(1), 69–76. https://doi.org/10.1016/j.bushor.2014.09.007.

Arit, J. (2021). Inside the TikTok incubator program for black creators. *Los Angeles Times*, 29 May. https://www.latimes.com/lifestyle/story/2021-05-27/inside-tiktok-incubator-program-black-creators.

Aronoff, K. (2019). Why VSCO girls are going on strike for the climate. The Intercept, 29 September. https://theintercept.com/2019/09/20/why-vsco-girls-are-going-on-strike-for-the-climate.

Ask, K., & Abidin, C. (2018). My life is a mess: Self-deprecating relatability and collective identities in the memification of student issues.

Information, Communication & Society, 21(6), 834–850. https://doi.org/10.1080/1369118X.2018.1437204.

Aualiitia, T. (2020). Meet Jawsh 685, the New Zealand teen behind the hit song 'Savage Love'. ABC News, 19 September. https://www.abc.net.au/news/2020-09-20/jawsh685-jason-derulo-join-up-for-savage-love-tiktok-viral-song/12677552.

Bacchi, U. (2020). TikTok apologises for censoring LGBT+ content. Reuters, 22 September. https://www.reuters.com/article/britain-tech-lgbt-idUSL5N2GJ459.

Barbiroglio, E. (2019). Generation Z fears climate change more than anything else. *Forbes*, 9 December. https://www.forbes.com/sites/emanuelabarbiroglio/2019/12/09/generation-z-fears-climate-change-more-than-anything-else/?sh=eb993d0501ba.

Bargfrede, A. (2017). *Music Law in the Digital Age: Copyright Essentials for Today's Music Business*. Berklee Press.

Barron, F. (1999). All creation is a collaboration. In A. Montuori & R. E. Purser (eds.), *Social Creativity* (pp. 49–60). Hampton Press.

Baym, N. (2015). *Personal Connections in the Digital Age* (2nd edn). Polity.

BBC. (2020). TikTok UK house: Who's in it and what do you need to know? CBBC Newsround. BBC News, 21 April. https://www.bbc.co.uk/newsround/52354393.

Behr, A., Negus, K., & Street, J. (2017). The sampling continuum: Musical aesthetics and ethics in the age of digital production. *Journal for Cultural Research*, 21(3), 223–240. https://doi.org/10.1080/14797585.2017.1338277.

Bergen, M. (2021). YouTube puts $100 million into creator fund to rival TikTok. Bloomberg, 11 May. https://www.bloomberg.com/news/articles/2021-05-11/youtube-puts-100-million-into-creator-fund-to-rival-tiktok.

Bernardini, G. (2021). Charli D'Amelio makes an insane amount per TikTok video. Distractify. https://www.distractify.com/p/how-much-does-charli-make-per-tiktok-video.

Biasutti, M. (2018). Strategies adopted during collaborative online music composition. *International Journal of Music Education*, 36(3), 473–490. https://doi.org/10.1177/0255761417741520.

Biddle, S., Ribeiro, P. V., & Dias, T. (2020). TikTok told moderators: Suppress posts by the 'ugly' and poor. The Intercept, 16 March. https://theintercept.com/2020/03/16/tiktok-app-moderators-users-discrimination.

Bishop, S. (2019). Managing visibility on YouTube through algorithmic gossip. *New Media & Society*, 21(11–12), 2589–2606. https://doi. org/10.1177/1461444819854731.

Boffone, T. (2021). *Renegades: Digital Dance Cultures from Dubsmash to TikTok*. Oxford University Press.

Bolin, G. (2017). *Media Generations: Experience, Identity and Mediatised Social Change*. Routledge.

Borreau, M., Moreau, F., & Wikstrom, P. (in press). Does digitization lead to the homogenization of cultural content? *Economic Inquiry*.

Boukes, M. (2019). Social network sites and acquiring current affairs knowledge: The impact of Twitter and Facebook usage on learning about the news. *Journal of Information Technology & Politics*, 16(1), 36–51. https://doi.org/10.1080/19331681.2019.1572568.

boyd, d. (2010). Social network sites as networked publics: Affordances, dynamics, and implications. In Z. Papacharissi (ed.), *A Networked Self: Identity, Community, and Culture on Social Network Sites* (pp. 39–58). Routledge.

Browne, D. (2021). Sea shanty sensation Nathan Evans: 'I'm an actual musician'. *Rolling Stone*, 26 January. https://www.rollingstone.com/music/music-features/sea-shanty-nathan-evans-tiktok-record-deal-1118686.

Bruns, A. (2019). *Are Filter Bubbles Real?* Polity.

Bruns, A., & Burgess, J. (2015). Twitter hashtags from ad hoc to calculated publics. In N. Rambukkana (ed.), *Hashtag Publics: The Power and Politics of Discursive Networks* (pp. 13–27). Peter Lang Publishing. http://www.peterlang.com/index.cfm?event=cmp.ccc. seitenstruktur.detailseiten&seitentyp=produkt&pk=84451&conco rdeid=312898.

Bruns, A., & Highfield, T. (2013). Political networks on Twitter. *Information, Communication & Society*, 16(5), 667–691. https://doi. org/10.1080/1369118X.2013.782328.

Bucher, T. (2013). Objects of intense feeling: The case of the Twitter API. *Computational Culture*, 3. http://computationalculture.net/ objects-of-intense-feeling-the-case-of-the-twitter-api.

Bucher, T. (2017). The algorithmic imaginary: Exploring the ordinary affects of Facebook algorithms. *Information, Communication & Society*, 20(1), 30–44. https://doi.org/10.1080/1369118X.2016.1154086.

Burgess, J. (2006). Hearing ordinary voices: Cultural studies, vernacular creativity and digital storytelling. *Continuum*, 20(2), 201–214.

Burgess, J. (2021). Platform studies. In S. Cunningham & D. Craig (eds.), *Creator Culture: An Introduction to Global Social Media Entertainment* (pp. 21–38). NYU Press.

Burgess, J., & Baym, N. (2020). *Twitter: A Biography*. NYU Press.

Burgess, J., & Green, J. (2018). *YouTube: Online Video and Participatory Culture* (2nd edn). Polity.

Burgess, J., & Matamoros-Fernández, A. (2016). Mapping sociocultural controversies across digital media platforms: One week of #gamergate on Twitter, YouTube, and Tumblr. *Communication Research and Practice*, 2(1), 79–96. https://doi.org/10.1080/220414 51.2016.1155338.

ByteDance. (2021). A letter from Yiming. *ByteDance*. https://bytedance. com/en/news/60a526af053cc102d640c061.

Cai, Y. C. (2016). The most successful video messaging app in China. Medium, 26 February. https://medium.com/new-media-photography/new-media-studies-proposal-study-of-the-most-successful-video-messaging-app-in-china-dc81ed7a3f53.

Carson, B. (2016). How a failed education startup turned into Musical. ly, the most popular app you've probably never heard of. Business Insider Australia, 28 May. https://www.businessinsider.com.au/what-is-musically-2016-5.

Cayari, C. (2011). The YouTube effect: How YouTube has provided new ways to consume, create, and share music. *International Journal of Education & the Arts*, 12(6), 1–29.

Chaykowski, K. (2015). Flipagram could be bigger than Instagram. *Forbes*, 23 November. https://www.forbes.com/sites/kathleenchaykowski/2015/11/23/flipagram-pop-stars-music-video-stories-instagram-mini-movie.

Chen, L. Y., & Bergen, M. (2018). 35-year-old unknown creates the world's most valuable startup. Bloomberg, 28 September. https://www.bloomberg.com/news/articles/2018-09-28/35-year-old-unknown-creates-the-world-s-most-valuable-startup.

Chen, X. (2019). TikTok is popular, but Chinese apps still have a lot to learn about global markets. The Conversation, 2 April. http://theconversation.com/tiktok-is-popular-but-chinese-apps-still-have-a-lot-to-learn-about-global-markets-113039.

Chen, X., Kaye, D. B. V., & Zeng, J. (2021). PositiveEnergy Douyin: Constructing 'playful patriotism' in a Chinese short-video application. *Chinese Journal of Communication*, 14(1), 97–117. https://doi. org/10.1080/17544750.2020.1761848.

Chen, Y., Mao, Z., & Qiu, J. L. (2018). *Super-Sticky Wechat and Chinese Society*. Emerald Publishing. https://doi.org/10.1108/9781787430914.

Cheung, M. (2020). Why short-form video apps are so popular in China. EMarketer, 2 January. https://www.emarketer.com/content/why-short-form-video-apps-are-so-popular-in-china.

China Internet Network Information Center. (2021). 第 47 次中国互联网络发展状况统计报告 [The 47th statistical report on the development of the internet in China]. CNNIC. http://www.cac.gov.cn/2021-02/03/c_1613923423079314.htm.

Cleary, D. (2020). Charli D'Amelio reportedly makes over $100K per sponsored TikTok. Dexerto. https://www.dexerto.com/entertainment/charli-damelio-reportedly-makes-over-100k-per-sponsored-tiktok-1391267.

Constine, J. (2014). Facebook's secret new 'business manager' could compete with developer partners for marketing dollars. *TechCrunch*, 15 March. https://social.techcrunch.com/2014/03/14/facebook-business-manager.

Constine, J. (2020). Vine reboot Byte officially launches. *TechCrunch*, 25 January. https://social.techcrunch.com/2020/01/24/vine-byte.

Craig, D., Lin, J., & Cunningham, S. (2021). *Wanghong as Social Media Entertainment in China*. Palgrave.

Criddle, C. (2020). Transgender users accuse TikTok of censorship. BBC News, 12 February. https://www.bbc.com/news/technology-51474114.

Criddle, C. (2021). Actor sues TikTok for using her voice in viral tool. BBC News, 10 May. https://www.bbc.com/news/technology-57063087.

Cross, A. (2021). The future of the music industry is TikTok, and here's why. Global News, 9 May. https://globalnews.ca/news/7836653/tiktok-music-industry.

Crucchiola, J. (2019). Alfonso Ribeiro shimmies away from Fortnite lawsuit over Carlton Dance. *Vulture*, 8 March. https://www.vulture.com/2019/03/alfonso-ribeiro-fortnite-lawsuit-carlton-dance.html.

Csikszentmihalyi, M., & Sternberg, R. (1988). Society, culture, and person: A systems view of creativity. In R. Sternberg (ed.), *The Nature of Creativity: Contemporary Psychological Perspectives* (pp. 325–339). Cambridge University Press.

Cunningham, S., & Craig, D. (2019). *Social Media Entertainment: The New Intersection of Hollywood and Silicon Valley*. NYU Press.

Cunningham, S., & Craig, D. (eds.). (2021). *Creator Culture: An Introduction to Global Social Media Entertainment*. NYU Press.

Cunningham, S., Craig, D., & Lv, J. (2019). China's livestreaming industry: Platforms, politics, and precarity. *International Journal of Cultural Studies*, 22(6), 719–736. https://doi.org/10.1177/1367877919834942.

Cyberspace Administration of China. (2018). 国家网信办：要让网络短视频充满正能量 [State Internet Information Office: To make the short-video network full of positive energy].

Cyberspace Administration of China. www.cac.gov.cn/2018-08/23/c_1123318088.htm.

Dalton, A. (2017). The Vine Archive will keep the videos looping forever. Engadget, 21 January. https://www.engadget.com/2017-01-20-vine-archive.html.

Dave, P. (2017). Flipagram acquired by China's Toutiao. *Los Angeles Times*, 1 February. https://www.latimes.com/business/technology/la-fi-tn-flipagram-toutiao-20170201-story.html

Dave, P. (2018). China's ByteDance scrubs Musical.ly brand in favor of TikTok. Reuters, 2 August. https://www.reuters.com/article/us-bytedance-musically-idUKKBN1KN0BW.

de Kloet, J., Poell, T., Guohua, Z., & Yiu Fai, C. (2019). The platformization of Chinese Society: Infrastructure, governance, and practice. *Chinese Journal of Communication, 12*(3), 249–256. https://doi.org/10.1080/17544750.2019.1644008.

Deahl, D. (2018). Facebook unveils Musical.ly competitor called Lip Sync Live. The Verge, 5 June. https://www.theverge.com/2018/6/5/17429884/facebook-musical-ly-competitor-lip-sync-live.

Deng, I., & Hu, M. (2019). Tencent to invest US$ 2bn in video app Kuaishou in battle with ByteDance. *South China Morning Post*, 12 December. https://www.scmp.com/tech/apps-social/article/3041747/tencent-said-invest-us2-billion-short-video-app-kuaishou.

Di Angelo, R. (2018). *White Fragility: Why It's so Hard for White People to Talk about Racism*. Beacon Press.

Diaz, A. (2021). Fortnite parody 'Chug Jug with You' is taking over TikTok. *Polygon*, 22 February https://www.polygon.com/2021/2/22/22295287/fortnite-parody-american-boy-internet-tiktok.

Drahos, P. (1996). *A Philosophy of Intellectual Property*. Routledge. https://search.ebscohost.com/login.aspx?direct=true&scope=site&db=nlebk&db=nlabk&AN=1432301.

Dubois, E., & Blank, G. (2018). The echo chamber is overstated: The moderating effect of political interest and diverse media. *Information, Communication & Society, 21*(5), 729–745. https://doi.org/10.1080/1369118X.2018.1428656.

Duffy, B. E., Poell, T., & Nieborg, D. B. (2019). Platform practices in the cultural industries: Creativity, labor, and citizenship. *Social Media + Society, 5*(4), 2056305119879672. https://doi.org/10.1177/2056305119879672.

Duffy, B. E., & Wissinger, E. (2017). Mythologies of creative work in the social media age: Fun, free, and 'just being me'. *International Journal of Communication, 11*(0), 4652–71.

Durkee, A. (2020). Snapchat goes after TikTok by letting users add music to Snaps. *Forbes*, 3 August. https://www.forbes.com/sites/alisondurkee/2020/08/03/snapchat-goes-after-tiktok-by-letting-users-add-music-to-snaps.

Dwyer, K. (2016). Why everyone is downloading this new social media app: Have you joined Musical.ly yet? *Teen Vogue*, 17 March. https://www.teenvogue.com/story/musically-becomes-top-app-popular-teens.

Edmond, M. (2014). Here we go again: Music videos after YouTube. *Television & New Media*, 15(4), 305–320. https://doi.org/10.1177/1527476412465901.

Elassar, A. (2020). TikTokers stand in solidarity with black creators to protest censorship. CNN. https://edition.cnn.com/2020/05/19/us/tiktok-black-lives-matter-trnd/index.html.

ELLE. (2016). 90 million tweens, a free app, one goal: Fame. *ELLE*, 20 July. https://www.elle.com/culture/music/a37581/musically-app-jacob-sartorius.

Emekalam, K. (2019). Vskit app's growing popularity in Africa. CGTN, 11 October. https://news.cgtn.com/news/2019-10-11/Vskit-app-s-growing-popularity-in-Africa--KHTQhuKu4o/index.html.

Facebook. (2020). Introducing Facebook Shops, a new online shopping experience. Facebook for Business, 19 May. https://en-gb.facebook.com/business/news/announcing-facebook-shops.

Fallon, J. (2021). TikTok Creators break down and perform their viral dances. *The Tonight Show Starring Jimmy Fallon*, 6 April. https://www.youtube.com/watch?v=Bdal1YTQjIY.

Fannin, R. (2019). The strategy behind TikTok's global rise. *Harvard Business Review*, 13 September. https://hbr.org/2019/09/the-strategy-behind-tiktoks-global-rise.

Federal Trade Commission. (2019). Video social networking App Musical.ly agrees to settle FTC allegations that it violated children's privacy law. Federal Trade Commission, 26 February. https://www.ftc.gov/news-events/press-releases/2019/02/video-social-networking-app-musically-agrees-settle-ftc.

Feng, C., Qu, T., & Lee, A. (2020). Why China's new tech export rules add to US TikTok sale uncertainty. *South China Morning Post*, 31 August. https://www.scmp.com/tech/big-tech/article/3099571/chinas-new-tech-export-restrictions-further-cloud-us-tiktok-sale-and.

Flew, T., Martin, F., & Suzor, N. (2019). Internet regulation as media policy: Rethinking the question of digital communication platform governance. *Journal of Digital Media & Policy*, 10(1), 33–50.

Fox, C. (2020). TikTok admits restricting some LGBT hashtags.

BBC News, 10 September. https://www.bbc.com/news/technology-54102575.

Fung, K. C., Aminian, N., Fu, X. (Maggie), & Tung, C. Y. (2018). Digital silk road, Silicon Valley and connectivity. *Journal of Chinese Economic and Business Studies, 16*(3), 313–336. https://doi.org/10.108 0/14765284.2018.1491679.

Galer, S. S. (2020). US election 2020: TikTok gets pulled into the campaigns. BBC News, 6 October. https://www.bbc.com/news/technology-54374710.

Galloway, A. (2004). *Protocol: How Control Exists after Decentralization.* MIT Press.

Gartenberg, C. (2021). YouTube Shorts arrives in the US to take on TikTok, but the beta is still half-baked. The Verge. https://www.theverge.com/2021/3/18/22334540/youtube-shorts-us-beta-tiktok-competition-launch.

Gatollari, M. (2021). 'Mutuals' basically means online 'friends' – mainly on social media platforms. Distractify, 24 February. https://www.distractify.com/p/what-does-mutuals-mean-on-tiktok.

Gibbs, M., Meese, J., Arnold, M., Nansen, B., & Carter, M. (2015). # Funeral and Instagram: Death, social media, and platform vernacular. *Information, Communication & Society, 18*(3), 255–268. https://doi.org/10.1080/1369118X.2014.987152.

Gillespie, T. (2010). The politics of 'platforms'. *New Media & Society, 12*(3), 347–364. https://doi.org/10.1177/1461444809342738.

Gillespie, T. (2014). The relevance of algorithms. In T. Gillespie, P. Boczkowski, & K. Foot (eds.), *Media Technologies: Essays on Communication, Materiality, and Society* (pp. 167–194). MIT Press.

Gillespie, T. (2018). Governance of and by platforms. In J. Burgess, T. Poell, & A. Marwick (eds.), *SAGE Handbook of Social Media* (pp. 254–278). SAGE Publications. http://culturedigitally.org/wp-content/uploads/2016/06/Gillespie-Governance-ofby-Platforms-PREPRINT.pdf.

Gillespie, T. (2020). Content moderation, AI, and the question of scale. *Big Data & Society.* https://doi.org/10.1177/2053951720943234.

Glăveanu, V. P. (2020). A sociocultural theory of creativity: Bridging the social, the material, and the psychological. *Review of General Psychology, 24*(4), 335–354. https://doi.org/10.1177/1089268020961763.

Goldhaber, M. (2006). The value of openness in an attention economy. *First Monday, 11*(6). https://doi.org/10.5210/fm.v11i6.1334.

Gonzales, T. (2021). Calling all Latine creators, TikTok is looking for you. *Remezcla,* 31 August. https://remezcla.com/culture/tiktok-latine-initiative-creatives.

Google. (2018). *How Google Fights Piracy*. https://blog.google/documents/25/GO806_Google_FightsPiracy_eReader_final.pdf.

Gorwa, R., Binns, R., & Katzenbach, C. (2020). Algorithmic content moderation: Technical and political challenges in the automation of platform governance. *Big Data & Society*, 7(1), 2053951719897945. https://doi.org/10.1177/2053951719897945.

Gray, J. E. (2020). *Google Rules: The History and Future of Copyright under the Influence of Google*. Oxford University Press.

Gray, J. E. (2021). The geopolitics of 'platforms': The TikTok challenge. *Internet Policy Review*, 10(2). https://policyreview.info/articles/analysis/geopolitics-platforms-tiktok-challenge.

Gray, J. E., & Suzor, N. P. (2020). Playing with machines: Using machine learning to understand automated copyright enforcement at scale. *Big Data & Society*, 7(1). https://doi.org/10.1177/2053951720919963.

Graziani, T. (2018). How Douyin became China's top short-video app in 500 days. Walk the Chat, 30 July. https://walkthechat.com/douyin-became-chinas-top-short-video-app-500-days.

Grey Ellis, E. (2018). TikTok is a short-form monetized musical meme machine. *Wired*. https://www.wired.com/story/tiktok-musical-meme-machine-vine.

Haberman, S. (2012). YouTube Haiku: Bursts of comedy gold. Mashable, 15 June. https://mashable.com/archive/youtube-haiku.

Haenlein, M., Anadol, E., Farnsworth, T., Hugo, H., Hunichen, J., & Welte, D. (2020). Navigating the new era of influencer marketing: How to be successful on Instagram, TikTok, & Co. *California Management Review*, 63(1), 5–25. https://doi.org/10.1177/0008125620958166

Hall, P. (1997). African American music: Dynamics of appropriation and innovation. In B. Ziff & P. Rao (eds.), *Borrowed Power: Essays on Cultural Appropriation* (pp. 31–51). Rutgers University Press.

Han, E. (2019). An update on recent content and account questions. TikTok Newsroom. https://newsroom.tiktok.com/en-us/an-update-on-recent-content-and-account-questions.

Hansmann, H., & Santilli, M. (1997). Authors' and artists' moral rights: A comparative legal and economic analysis. *Journal of Legal Studies*, 26(1), 95–143. https://doi.org/10.1086/467990.

Hao, K. (2020). Live-streaming helped China's farmers survive the pandemic: It's here to stay. *MIT Technology Review*. https://www.technologyreview.com/2020/05/06/1001186/china-rural-live-streaming-during-cornavirus-pandemic.

Hariharan, A. (2017). Hidden forces behind Toutiao: China's content king: China, growth, consumer. YC Startup Library. https://

www.ycombinator.com/library/3x-hidden-forces-behind-toutiao-china-s-content-king.

Harper, L. (2019). The rise of the VSCO girl, and how to spot one. *Guardian*, 14 November. https://www.theguardian.com/fashion/shortcuts/2019/nov/14/the-rise-of-the-vsco-girl-and-how-to-spot-one.

Hautea, S., Parks, P., Takahashi, B., & Zeng, J. (2021). Showing they care (or don't): Affective publics and ambivalent climate activism on TikTok. *Social Media + Society*. https://doi.org/10.1177/20563051211012344.

Havens, T. (2014). Towards a structuration theory of media intermediaries. In A. Santo, D. Johnson, & D. Kompare (eds.), *Making Media Work: Cultures of Management in the Entertainment Industries* (pp. 25–38). NYU Press. https://eprints.qut.edu.au/128881.

Helft, M. (2007). Chinese political prisoner sues in US court, saying Yahoo helped identify dissidents. *New York Times*, 19 April. https://www.nytimes.com/2007/04/19/technology/19yahoo.html?ex=1334635200&en=ab9e05d7726fe430&ei=5124&partner=permalink&exprod=permalink.

Helmond, A. (2015). The platformization of the web: Making web data platform ready. *Social Media + Society*, 1(2), 2056305115603080. https://doi.org/10.1177/2056305115603080

Hern, A. (2015). Periscope launches Android app. *Guardian*, 26 May. http://www.theguardian.com/technology/2015/may/26/periscope-launches-android-app.

Herold, D. K., & Seta, G. de. (2015). Through the looking glass: Twenty years of Chinese internet research. *Information Society*, 31(1), 68–82. https://www.tandfonline.com/doi/abs/10.1080/01972243.2014.976688.

Herrman, J. (2016). Who's too young for an app? Musical.ly tests the limits. *New York Times*, 16 September. https://www.nytimes.com/2016/09/17/business/media/a-social-network-frequented-by-children-tests-the-limits-of-online-regulation.html.

Hickey, S. (2021). TikTok: Powerful messaging in 60 seconds or less. Indian Country Today, 1 June. https://indiancountrytoday.com/culture/tiktok-powerful-messaging-in-60-seconds-or-less.

Highfield, T., & Leaver, T. (2016). Instagrammatics and digital methods: Studying visual social media, from selfies and GIFs to memes and emoji. *Communication Research and Practice*, 2(1), 47–62. https://doi.org/10.1080/22041451.2016.1155332.

Hind, S. (2021). Introducing auto captions. TikTok Newsroom, 6 April. https://newsroom.tiktok.com/en-us/introducing-auto-captions.

Horowitz, J., & Lorenz, T. (2021). Khaby Lame, the everyman of the internet. *New York Times*, 2 June. https://www.nytimes.com/2021/06/02/style/khaby-lame-tiktok.html.

Huang, Z. (2021). Leaked ByteDance memo shows blockbuster revenue projections. Bloomberg. https://au.finance.yahoo.com/news/bytedance-grow-ad-revenue-40-035801638.html.

Hughey, M. W. (2021). How blackness matters in white lives. *Symbolic Interaction*, 44(2), 412–448. https://doi.org/10.1002/symb.552.

Hutchinson, A. (2020). TikTok adds new 'Stitch' feature to facilitate video responses. Social Media Today, 4 September. https://www.socialmediatoday.com/news/tiktok-adds-new-stitch-feature-to-facilitate-video-responses/584774.

IFPI. (2021). *Global Music Report*. International Federation of the Phonographic Industry.

IndiaSA Comms Team. (2019). Uber puts safety at the heart of driver experience. Uber Newsroom, 29 January. https://www.uber.com/en-IN/newsroom/uber-puts-safety-at-the-heart-of-driver-experience.

Ingham, T. (2015). Universal, Warner, Sony and Indies license video music app Flipagram. Music Business Worldwide, 17 July. https://www.musicbusinessworldwide.com/universal-warner-sony-and-indies-license-video-music-app-flipagram.

Ingham, T. (2016). This tech startup boss's attitude to music licensing says it all. Music Business Worldwide, 14 March. https://www.musicbusinessworldwide.com/this-tech-startup-bosss-attitude-to-music-licensing-says-it-all.

Ingham, T. (2020). TikTok and Sony Music ink licensing deal for major's 'roster of global superstars and exciting emerging artists'. Music Business Worldwide, 2 November . https://www.musicbusinessworldwide.com/tiktok-and-sony-music-ink-licensing-deal-for-majors-roster-of-global-superstars-and-exciting-emerging-artists.

Ingham, T. (2021). YouTube is generating $32k every minute, but how much of that money is being driven by music? Music Business Worldwide, 29 April. https://www.musicbusinessworldwide.com/youtube-is-generating-32k-every-minute-but-how-much-of-that-money-is-being-driven-by-music.

Inglis, D. (2009). Cosmopolitan sociology and the classical canon: Ferdinand Tönnies and the emergence of global *Gesellschaft*. *British Journal of Sociology*, 60(4), 813–832. https://doi.org/10.1111/j.1468-4446.2009.01276.x.

Instagram. (2020). Introducing Instagram Reels. Instagram Blog,

5   August.   https://about.instagram.com/blog/announcements/ introducing-instagram-reels-announcement.

Iqbal, M. (2021). TikTok revenue and usage statistics. Business of Apps. https://www.businessofapps.com/data/tik-tok-statistics.

Isaac, M. (2016). Twitter's 4-year odyssey with the 6-second video app Vine. *New York Times*, 29 October. https://www.nytimes. com/2016/10/29/technology/twitters-4-year-odyssey-with-the-6-second-video-app-vine.html.

IUKB. (2021). Accessibility features supported on TikTok. Indiana University Knowledge Base, University Information Technology Services. https://kb.iu.edu/d/azht.

Janfaza, R. (2020). TikTok serves as hub for #blacklivesmatter activism. CNN, 4 June. https://www.cnn.com/2020/06/04/politics/tik-tok-black-lives-matter/index.html.

Jarvey, N. (2015). Former O2L members form new YouTube channel KianAndJc. *Hollywood Reporter*, 19 January. https://www. hollywoodreporter.com/business/digital/o2l-members-form-new-youtube-764692.

Jenkins, H. (2006). *Convergence Culture: Where Old and New Media Collide*. NYU Press.

Jenkins, H., Ford, S., & Green, J. (2013). *Spreadable Media: Creating Value and Meaning in a Networked Culture*. NYU Press.

Jennings, R. (2018). TikTok, explained. Vox, 10 December. https:// www.vox.com/culture/2018/12/10/18129126/tiktok-app-musically-meme-cringe.

Jennings, R. (2019). VSCO girls and how teen culture goes viral. Vox, 24 September. https://www.vox.com/the-goods/2019/9/24/20881656/vsco-girl-meme-what-is-a-vsco-girl.

Jennings, R. (2020). How a TikTok house destroyed itself. Vox, 1 October. https://www.vox.com/the-goods/21459677/tiktok-house-la-hype-sway-girls-in-the-valley.

Jennings, R. (2021). How a pop-punk girl group became the most hated band on TikTok. Vox, 20 April. https://www.vox.com/ the-goods/2021/4/20/22392694/tramp-stamps-industry-plant-band-tiktok-dr-luke.

Jing, M. (2018). Chinese news app helps reunite missing brother in time for holidays. *South China Morning Post*, 15 February. https://www.scmp.com/tech/social-gadgets/article/2133363/ migrant-worker-lost-his-56-year-old-mentally-ill-sibling-during

Kastrenakes, J. (2020). Charli D'Amelio hits 100 million TikTok followers. The Verge, 22 November. https://www.theverge.

com/2020/11/22/21571189/charli-damelio-100-million-tiktok-followers.

Kastrenakes, J. (2021). TikTok changes text-to-speech voice after voice actor sues. The Verge, 25 May. https://www.theverge.com/2021/5/25/22452815/tiktok-voice-change-text-to-speech-lawsuit.

Katz, Y., & Shifman, L. (2017). Making sense? The structure and meanings of digital memetic nonsense. *Information, Communication & Society, 20*(6), 825–842. https://doi.org/10.108/1369118X.2017.1291702.

Kaye, D. B. V. (2020). Make this go viral: Building musical careers through accidental virality on TikTok. *Flow Journal, 27*(1). https://www.flowjournal.org/2020/09/make-this-go-viral.

Kaye, D. B. V., & Burgess, J. (2021). Algorithmic recommender systems and everyday data cultures: The view from Jazz TikTok. In *Selected Papers of #AoIR2021: The 22nd Annual Conference of the Association of Internet Researchers*, Virtual Event, 13–16 October (pp. 3–6). Selected Papers of Internet Research. https://journals.uic.edu/ojs/index.php/spir/article/view/12088/10224.

Kaye, D. B. V., Chen, X., & Zeng, J. (2021). The co-evolution of two Chinese mobile short video apps: Parallel platformization of Douyin and TikTok. *Mobile Media & Communication, 9*(2), 229–253. https://doi.org/10.1177/2050157920952120.

Kaye, D. B. V., & Gray, J. E. (2020). Copyright gossip: Exploring copyright sentiment and blackbox theories on YouTube. *AoIR Selected Papers of Internet Research*. https://doi.org/10.5210/spir.v2020i0.11247.

Kaye, D. B. V., Rodriguez, A., Langton, K., & Wikström, P. (2021). You made this? I made this: Practices of authorship and (mis)attribution on TikTok. *International Journal of Communication, 15*, 3195–3215.

Keane, M., & Su, C. (2018). The will to power: The BAT in and beyond China. In T. Flew, M. Keane, & B. Yecies (eds.), *Willing Collaborators: Foreign Partners in Chinese Media* (pp. 47–61). Rowman & Littlefield. https://rowman.com/ISBN/9781786604248/Willing-Collaborators-Foreign-Partners-in-Chinese-Media.

Keane, M., & Wu, H. (2018). Lofty ambitions, new territories, and turf battles: China's platforms 'go out'. *Media Industries Journal, 5*(1). https://doi.org/10.3998/mij.15031809.0005.104.

Khamis, S., Ang, L., & Welling, R. (2017). Self-branding, 'micro-celebrity' and the rise of social media influencers. *Celebrity Studies, 8*(2), 191–208. https://doi.org/10.1080/19392397.2016.1218292.

King, A. (2021). *Ratatouille: The TikTok Musical* donates $2MM to struggling stage actors. Digital Music News, 12 January. https://www.digitalmusicnews.com/2021/01/12/ratatouille-tiktok-musical-donation.

Kircher, M. M. (2015). People are completely obsessed with Dubsmash, the lip sync app that's taking over your Instagram feed. Business Insider, 14 July. https://www.businessinsider.com.au/how-to-use-the-dubsmash-lip-sync-app-2015-7?r=US&IR=T.

Kleeman, J. (2019). NL producer and film-maker are latest to accuse YouTube of anti-LGBT bias. *Guardian*, 22 November. https://www.theguardian.com/technology/2019/nov/22/youtube-lgbt-content-lawsuit-discrimination-algorithm.

Knight, W. (2018). The insanely popular Chinese news app that you've never heard of. *MIT Technology Review*, 26 January. https://www.technologyreview.com/2017/01/26/154363/the-insanely-popular-chinese-news-app-that-youve-never-heard-of.

Köver, C., & Reuter, M. (2019). TikTok curbed reach for people with disabilities. Netzpolitic. https://netzpolitik.org/2019/discrimination-tiktok-curbed-reach-for-people-with-disabilities.

Kong, D. (2018). Research report on short video industry [in Chinese]. 36Kr Research Center. http://www.199it. com/archives/672181. html.

Kress, G. R. (2009). *Multimodality: A Social Semiotic Approach to Contemporary Communication*. Routledge. https://doi.org/10.4324/9780203970034

Kress, G. R., & van Leeuwen, T. (2021). *Reading Images: The Grammar of Visual Design* (3rd edn). Routledge.

Kuo, L. (2019). TikTok 'makeup tutorial' goes viral with call to action on China's treatment of Uighurs. *Guardian*, 27 November. https://www.theguardian.com/technology/2019/nov/27/tiktok-makeup-tutorial-conceals-call-to-action-on-chinas-treatment-of-uighurs.

Landes, W. M., & Posner, R. A. (1989). An economic analysis of copyright law. *Journal of Legal Studies*, 18(2), 325–363.

Laurier, C., Grivolla, J., & Herrera, P. (2008). Multimodal music mood classification using audio and lyrics. In *Proceedings of the 7th International Conference on Machine Learning and Applications (ICMLA' 08), December 2008* (pp. 1–6). IEEE.

Leaver, T., Highfield, T., & Abidin, C. (2020). *Instagram: Visual Social Media Cultures*. Polity.

Lebuda, I., & Glăveanu, V. P. (eds.). (2019). *The Palgrave Handbook of Social Creativity Research*. Palgrave Macmillan. https://doi.org/10.1007/978-3-319-95498-1.

Leight, E. (2019). Lil Nas X's 'Old Town Road' was a country hit: Then country changed its mind. *Rolling Stone*, 26 March. https://www.rollingstone.com/music/music-features/lil-nas-x-old-town-road-810844.

Leong, S. (2018). Prophets of mass innovation: The Gospel according to BAT. *Media Industries Journal*, 5(1). https://doi.org/10.3998/mij.15031809.0005.105.

Lessig, L. (2008). *Remix: Making Art and Commerce Thrive in the Hybrid Economy*. Bloomsbury.

Li, A. K. (2019). Papi Jiang and microcelebrity in China: A multilevel analysis. *International Journal of Communication*, 13(0), 3016–34.

Licoppe, C., Rivière, C. A., & Morel, J. (2016). Grindr casual hook-ups as interactional achievements. *New Media & Society*, 18(11), 2540–2558. https://doi.org/10.1177/1461444815589702.

Light, B. (2014). *Disconnecting with Social Networking Sites*. Palgrave Macmillan. https://doi.org/10.1057/9781137022479.

Liikkanen, L. A., & Salovaara, A. (2015). Music on YouTube: User engagement with traditional, user-appropriated and derivative videos. *Computers in Human Behavior*, 50, 108–124. https://doi.org/10.1016/j.chb.2015.01.067.

Lin, J., & de Kloet, J. (2019). Platformization of the unlikely creative class: Kuaishou and Chinese digital cultural production. *Social Media + Society*, 5(4), 205630511988343. https://doi.org/10.1177/2056305119883430.

Ling, R. (2012). *Taken for Grantedness: The Embedding of Mobile Communication into Society*. MIT Press.

Literat, I. (2019). Make, share, review, remix: Unpacking the impact of the internet on contemporary creativity. *Convergence: The International Journal of Research into New Media Technologies*, 25(5–6), 1168–1184. https://doi.org/10.1177/1354856517751391.

Liu, C., Huang, Z., & Turner, G. (2021). TikTok begins testing in-app shopping to challenge Facebook. *Bloomberg*, 11 May. https://www.bloomberg.com/news/articles/2021-05-11/tiktok-begins-testing-in-app-shopping-to-challenge-facebook.

Livingstone, S. (2019). Audiences in an age of datafication: Critical questions for media research. *Television & New Media*, 20(2), 170–183. https://doi.org/10.1177/1527476418811118.

Lorenz, T. (2020a). Hype house and the Los Angeles TikTok mansion gold rush. *New York Times*, 3 January. https://www.nytimes.com/2020/01/03/style/hype-house-los-angeles-tik-tok.html.

Lorenz, T. (2020b). Meet the original renegade dance creator: Jalaiah Harmon. *New York Times*, 13 February. https://www.nytimes.com/2020/02/13/style/the-original-renegade.html.

Lorenz, T. (2020c). What if the US bans TikTok? Gen Z and millennial users have found community on the app, particularly during the coronavirus pandemic: And for some of them, it's their livelihood. *New York Times*, 10 July. https://www.nytimes.com/2020/07/10/style/tiktok-ban-us-users-influencers-taylor-lorenz.html.

Lorenz, T. (2021). Young creators are burning out and breaking down. *New York Times*, 8 June. https://www.nytimes.com/2021/06/08/style/creator-burnout-social-media.html.

Lotz, A. (2014). Building theories of creative industry managers: Challenges, perspectives, and future directions. In A. Santo, D. Johnson, & D. Kompare (eds.), *Making Media Work: Cultures of Management in the Entertainment Industries* (pp. 25–38). NYU Press. https://eprints.qut.edu.au/128881.

Lu, Z., Xia, H., Heo, S., & Wigdor, D. (2018). You watch, you give, and you engage: A study of live streaming practices in China. In *Proceedings of the 2018 CHI Conference on Human Factors in Computing Systems (CHI '18)* (pp. 1–13). ACM. https://doi.org/10.1145/3173574.3174040.

Lyon, D. (2003). Surveillance as social sorting: Computer codes and mobile bodies. In D. Lyon (ed.), *Surveillance as Social Sorting: Privacy, Risk and Automated Discrimination* (pp. 13–30). Routledge.

Lyon, D. (2014). Surveillance, Snowden, and big data: Capacities, consequences, critique. *Big Data & Society*, 1(2). https://doi.org/10.1177/2053951714541861.

Mahrt, M., Weller, K., & Peters, I. (2014). Twitter in scholarly communication. In K. Weller, A. Bruns, J. Burgess, M. Marht, & C. Puschmann (eds.), *Twitter and Society* (pp. 399–410). Peter Lang.

Marris, E. (2019). Why young climate activists have captured the world's attention. *Nature*, 573(7775), 471–473.

Marshall, L. (2004). The effects of piracy upon the music industry: A case study of bootlegging. *Media, Culture & Society*, 26(2), 163–181. https://doi.org/10.1177/0163443704039497.

Martineau, P. (2018). Facebook is tracking you on over 8.4 million websites. *Outline*, 18 May. https://theoutline. com/post/4578/facebook-is-tracking-you-on-over-8-millionwebsites.

Marwick, A. E. (2013). *Status Update: Celebrity, Publicity, and Branding in the Social Media Age*. Yale University Press.

Matamoros-Fernández, A. (2017). Platformed racism: The mediation and circulation of an Australian race-based controversy on Twitter, Facebook and YouTube. *Information, Communication & Society*, 20(6), 930–946. https://doi.org/10.1080/1369118X.2017.1293130.

Matamoros-Fernández, A., & Kaye, D. B. V. (2020). TikTok suicide video: It's time platforms collaborated to limit disturbing content. The Conversation, 8 September. https://theconversation.com/tiktok-suicide-video-its-time-platforms-collaborated-to-limit-disturbing-content-145756.

Matsakis, L. (2020). How TikTok's 'For You' algorithm works. Wired, 10 June. https://www.wired.com/story/tiktok-finally-explains-for-you-algorithm-works.

McLelland, M., Yu, H., & Goggin, G. (2017). Alternative histories of social media in Japan and China. In J. Burgess, A. Marwick, & T. Poell (eds.), The SAGE Handbook of Social Media (pp. 53–68). SAGE.

McRady, R. (2021). Meet Collab Crib: The Atlanta TikTok house that's changing the game. Entertainment Tonight, 25 February. https://www.etonline.com/meet-collab-crib-the-atlanta-tiktok-house-thats-changing-the-game-160953.

McRobbie, A. (2016). Be Creative: Making a Living in the New Culture Industries. Polity.

Meese, J., & Hagedorn, J. (2019). Mundane content on social media: Creation, circulation, and the copyright problem. Social Media + Society, 5(2). https://doi.org/10.1177/2056305119839190.

Meyer, D. (2020). Ratatouille: The TikTok musical streaming concert to benefit the actors fund. Playbill, 9 December. https://www.playbill.com/article/ratatouille-the-tiktok-musical-streaming-concert-to-benefit-the-actors-fund.

Meyer, R. (2016). Why we loved Vine so much. Atlantic, 28 October. https://www.theatlantic.com/technology/archive/2016/10/vine-was-too-good-for-us/505622.

Milner, R. M. (2016). The World Made Meme: Public Conversations and Participatory Media. MIT Press.

Miltner, K. M., & Highfield, T. (2017). Never gonna GIF you up: Analyzing the cultural significance of the animated GIF. Social Media + Society, 3(3), 2056305117725222. https://doi.org/10.1177/2056305117725223.

Minxi, Z. (2020). In the spotlight: Zhang Yiming, the geek who dreams of a big world. China Global Television Network, 8 August. https://news.cgtn.com/news/2020-08-08/In-The-Spotlight-Zhang-Yiming-the-geek-who-dreams-of-a-big-world-SNeUbqi9Og/index.html.

Mitchell, G. (2021). Billboard's Hip-Hop and R&B Rookie of the Month for March: Fousheé. Billboard, 11 March. https://www.billboard.com/pro/foushee-hip-hop-r-b-rookie-of-the-month-march-2021.

Molanphy, C. (2021). Montero is the gayest no. 1 single in Billboard history. Slate. https://slate.com/culture/2021/04/lil-nas-x-montero-call-me-by-your-name-billboard-memes.html.

Monroy-Hernández, A., Hill, B., Gonzalez-Rivero, J., & boyd, d. (2011). Computers can't give credit: How automatic attribution falls short in an online remixing community. In *Proceedings of the International Conference on Human Factors in Computing Systems* (pp. 3421–3430). https://doi.org/10.1145/1978942.1979452.

Montuori, A., & Purser, R. E. (Eds.). (1999). *Social Creativity*. Hampton Press.

Morris, J. W. (2015). Curation by code: Infomediaries and the data mining of taste. *European Journal of Cultural Studies, 18*(4–5), 446–463. https://doi.org/10.1177/1367549415577387.

Murphy, C. (2020). China tech to face even closer scrutiny from global governments. Bloomberg, 1 October. https://www.bloomberg.com/news/articles/2020-10-01/china-tech-to-face-even-closer-scrutiny-from-global-governments.

Murthy, D. (2013). *Twitter: Social Communication in the Twitter Age*. Polity.

Musical.ly. (2017). Bruno Mars invites you to #DanceWithBruno on Musical.ly. Musical.ly, 17 March. https://web.archive.org/web/20170326222856/https:/musicallyapp.tumblr.com/post/158517337564/bruno-mars-invites-you-to-dancewithbruno-on.

Myers West, S. (2018). Censored, suspended, shadowbanned: User interpretations of content moderation on social media platforms. *New Media & Society, 20*(11), 4366–4383. https://doi.org/10.1177/1461444818773059.

Napoli, P., & Caplan, R. (2017). Why media companies insist they're not media companies, why they're wrong, and why it matters. *First Monday.* https://doi.org/10.5210/fm.v22i5.7051.

The Nation. (2018). Tik Tok lets you duet with yourself, a pal, or a celebrity. The Nation, 23 May. Multimedia. www.nationmultimedia.com/detail/lifestyle/30346044.

Newlands, M. (2016). The origin and future of America's hottest new app: Musical.ly. *Forbes*, 10 June. https://www.forbes.com/sites/mnewlands/2016/06/10/the-origin-and-future-of-americas-hottest-new-app-musical-ly.

Newton, C. (2017). Facebook launches stories to complete its all-out assault on Snapchat. The Verge, 28 March. https://www.theverge.com/2017/3/28/15081398/facebook-stories-snapchat-camera-direct.

Nieborg, D. B., & Poell, T. (2018). The platformization of cultural production: Theorizing the contingent cultural commodity. *New Media & Society, 20*(11), 4275–4292. https://doi.org/10.1177/1461444818769694.

Nissenbaum, A., & Shifman, L. (2017). Internet memes as contested cultural capital: The case of 4chan's/b/board. *New Media & Society*, 19(4), 483–501.

Ohlheiser, A. (2020). TikTok has become the soul of the LGBTQ internet. *Washington Post*, 8 January. https://www.washingtonpost.com/technology/2020/01/28/tiktok-has-become-soul-lgbtq-internet.

Ohlheiser, A. (2021). Welcome to TikTok's endless cycle of censorship and mistakes. *MIT Technology Review*, 13 July. https://www.technologyreview.com/2021/07/13/1028401/tiktok-censorship-mistakes-glitches-apologies-endless-cycle.

O'Neill, S., & Nicholson-Cole, S. (2009). Fear won't do it: Promoting positive engagement with climate change through visual and iconic representations. *Science Communication*, 30(3), 355–379.

O'Reilly, C. (2020). Fousheé: 'Black women have been the workhorses of the music industry since time began'. NME, 18 November. https://www.nme.com/blogs/nme-radar/foushee-deep-end-single-af-interview-2020-2818884.

Pappalardo, K., & Messe, J. (2019). In support of tolerated use: Rethinking harms, moral rights and remedies in Australian copyright law. *University of New South Wales Law Journal*, 42, 928–952.

Pappas, V. (2019). Introducing the $200M TikTok Creator Fund. TikTok Newsroom, 16 August. https://newsroom.tiktok.com/en-us/introducing-the-200-million-tiktok-creator-fund.

Pappas, V., & Chikumbu, K. (2020). A message to our black community. TikTok Newsroom, 2 June. https://newsroom.tiktok.com/en-us/a-message-to-our-black-community.

Pariser, E. (2011). *The Filter Bubble: What the Internet Is Hiding from You*. Penguin.

Parker, K., & Igielnik, R. (2020). What we know about gen Z so far. Pew Research Center. https://www.pewresearch.org/social-trends/2020/05/14/on-the-cusp-of-adulthood-and-facing-an-uncertain-future-what-we-know-about-gen-z-so-far-2.

Parker, S. (2015). The evolution of snapchat. *Platform Magazine*, 13 February. https://platformmagazine.org/2015/02/13/the-evolution-of-snapchat.

Pasquale, F. (2015). *The Black Box Society*. Harvard University Press.

Perez, S. (2019). Match Group restructures exec team with focus on Asia. *TechCrunch*, 16 April. https://social.techcrunch.com/2019/04/15/match-group-restructures-exec-team-with-focus-on-asia.

Perez, S. (2021a). TikTok adds auto captions to make videos accessible to hard of hearing and deaf. *TechCrunch*, 6 April. https://social.

techcrunch.com/2021/04/06/tiktok-adds-auto-captions-to-make-videos-accessible-to-hard-of-hearing-and-deaf.

Perez, S. (2021b). Walmart to host a new livestream shopping event on TikTok, following successful pilot. *TechCrunch*, 9 March. https://techcrunch.com/2021/03/09/walmart-to-host-a-new-live-stream-shopping-event-on-tiktok-following-successful-pilot.

Peterschmidt, D. (2015). 7 strategies for engaging your podcast (or show) audience. NPR Training + Diverse Sources Database, 2 October. https://training.npr.org/2015/10/02/7-strategies-for-engaging-your-podcast-or-show-audience.

Petridis, A. (2020). Drake: Dark Lane Demo Tapes review: Rap's whingeing king hits a dead end. *Guardian*, 3 May. http://www.theguardian.com/music/2020/may/03/drake-dark-lane-demo-tapes-review.

Plantin, J. C., & de Seta, G. (2019). WeChat as infrastructure: The techno-nationalist shaping of Chinese digital platforms. *Chinese Journal of Communication*, 12(3), 257–273.

Plantin, J.-C., Lagoze, C., Edwards, P. N., & Sandvig, C. (2018). Infrastructure studies meet platform studies in the age of Google and Facebook. *New Media & Society*, 20(1), 293–310. https://doi.org/10.1177/1461444816661553.

Poniewozik, J., Hess, A., Caramanica, J., Kourias, G., & Morris, W. (2019). 48 hours in the strange and beautiful world of TikTok. *New York Times*, 10 October. https://www.nytimes.com/interactive/2019/10/10/arts/TIK-TOK.html.

Potts, J., Hartley, J., Banks, J., Burgess, J., Cobcroft, R., Cunningham, S., & Montgomery, L. (2008). Consumer co-creation and situated creativity. *Industry & Innovation*, 15(5), 459–474. https://doi.org/10.1080/13662710802373783.

Preece, J., Nonnecke, B., & Andrews, D. (2004). The top five reasons for lurking: Improving community experiences for everyone. *Computers in Human Behavior*, 20(2), 201–223. https://doi.org/10.1016/j.chb.2003.10.015.

Price, E. (2018). Musical.ly and TikTok are joining forces to form a single powerhouse. Fast Company, 2 August. https://www.fastcompany.com/90212600/musical-ly-and-tiktok-are-merging-into-a-short-video-powerhouse.

Qu, T. (2020). Singapore-based TikTok challenger Likee gains ground in short video market. *South China Morning Post*, 18 April. https://www.scmp.com/tech/apps-social/article/3080491/singapore-based-likee-led-former-factory-worker-gaining-ground.

Ravelli, L. J., & van Leeuwen, T. (2018). Modality in the digital age. *Visual Communication, 17*(3), 277–297. https://doi.org/10.1177/1470357218764436.

Reddit. (2021). YouTube Haiku: R/Youtubehaiku. https://www.reddit.com/r/youtubehaiku.

Reser, J. P., & Bradley, G. L. (2017). Fear appeals in climate change communication. In *The Oxford Research Encyclopedia of Climate Science.* https://oxfordre.com/climatescience/view/10.1093/acrefore/9780190228620.001.0001/acrefore-9780190228620-e-386?_prclt=9mz3Yntu.

Rettberg, J. W. (2014). *Blogging.* Polity.

Rettberg, J. W. (2017). Hand signs for lip-syncing: The emergence of a gestural language on Musical.ly as a video-based equivalent to emoji. *Social Media + Society, 3*(4), 2056305117735751. https://doi.org/10.1177/2056305117735751

Rettberg, J. W. (2018). Snapchat: Phatic communication and ephemeral social media. In J. W. Morris & S. Murray (eds.), *Appified: Culture in the Age of Apps* (pp. 188–195). University of Michigan Press.

Ridley, K. (2021). TikTok faces claim for billions in London child privacy lawsuit. Reuters, 21 April. https://www.reuters.com/technology/tiktok-faces-claim-billions-london-child-privacy-lawsuit-2021-04-20.

Robehmed, N. (2017). From Musers to money: Inside video app Musical.ly's coming of age. *Forbes,* 11 May. https://www.forbes.com/sites/natalierobehmed/2017/05/11/from-musers-to-money-inside-video-app-musical-lys-coming-of-age.

Robinson, P. (2016). Musical.ly, the craze turning pop fans into stars. *Guardian,* 4 September. http://www.theguardian.com/technology/2016/sep/04/musical-ly-lip-synch-video-app-turns-pop-fans-into-stars.

Rodriguez, A., & Kaye, D. B. V. (2020). Leave a like if I'm on your #FYP: TikTok's (shared) algorithmically curated content. Paper delivered at the conference 'Digital Intimacies 6: Connection in Crisis', Sydney, Australia. (An abstract can be found at https://digitalintimacies6.wordpress.com/abstracts.)

Rodriguez, S. (2021). Zuckerberg announces new ways for Instagram creators to make money. CNBC, 27 April. https://www.cnbc.com/2021/04/27/zuckerberg-announces-new-ways-for-instagram-creators-to-make-money.html.

Rogers, T. N. (2019). Meet Zhang Yiming, the secretive Chinese billionaire behind TikTok who made over $12 billion in 2018 and called Trump's demands to sell the app 'unreasonable'. Business Insider, 11 November. https://www.businessinsider.com.au/tiktok-billionaire-zhang-yiming-net-worth-lifestyle-2019-11?r=US&IR=T.

Rolli, B. (2020). Drake's chart-topping 'Toosie Slide' could spell disaster for his next album. *Forbes*. https://www.forbes.com/sites/bryanrolli/2020/04/15/drakes-chart-topping-toosie-slide-could-spell-disaster-for-his-next-album/?sh=69fead74430f.

Romero, I. (2020). What's the maximum number of characters for each social network? Metricool, 1 July. https://metricool.com/characters-social-media.

Ross, S. (2016). Flips with no fuss: Flipagram launches in-app 'ephemeral' camera. Business Wire, 21 April. https://www.businesswire.com/news/home/20160421005099/en/Flips-with-No-Fuss---Flipagram-Launches-In-App-%E2%80%9CEphemeral%E2%80%9D-Camera.

Sakariassen, H., & Meijer, I. C. (2021). Why so quiet? Exploring inhibition in digital public spaces. *European Journal of Communication, 36*(5), 494–510. https://doi.org/10.1177/0267323121011017346.

Sandvig, C., Hamilton, K., Karahalios, K., & Langbort, C. (2016). When the algorithm itself is a racist: Diagnosing ethical harm in the basic components of software. *International Journal of Communication, 10*, 4972–4990.

Savic, M. (2021). From Musical.ly to TikTok: Social construction of 2020's most downloaded short-video app. *International Journal of Communication, 15*, 1–21.

Sawyer, K., & DeZutter, S. (2009). Distributed creativity: How collective creations emerge from collaboration. *Psychology of Aesthetics, Creativity, and the Arts, 3*, 81–92. https://doi.org/10.1037/a0013282

Sawyer, R. K. (2003). *Improvised Dialogues: Emergence and Creativity in Conversation*. Greenwood.

Schellewald, A. (2021). Communicative forms on TikTok: Perspectives from digital ethnography. *International Journal of Communication, 15*, 1437–1457.

Schroeder, A. (2021). Olivia Rodrigo's 'SoUR' has the internet in its feelings. Daily Dot, 21 May. https://www.dailydot.com/unclick/olivia-rodrigo-sour-reactions.

Schwarz, J. A. (2017). Platform logic: An interdisciplinary approach to the platform-based economy. *Policy & Internet, 9*(4), 374–394. https://doi.org/10.1002/poi3.159.

Seaver, N. (2017). Algorithms as culture: Some tactics for the ethnography of algorithmic systems. *Big Data & Society, 4*(2), 205395171773810. https://doi.org/10.1177/2053951717738104.

Segaetsho, B. (2020). Straight TikTok? All the signs & how to avoid. ScreenRant, 6 July. https://screenrant.com/straight-tiktok-alt-explained-avoid-tips.

Sehl, K. (2020). How to use YouTube live to engage your audience: A step-by-step guide. Hootsuite: Social Media Marketing & Management Dashboard, 1 April. https://blog.hootsuite.com/youtube-live.

Senft, T. (2008). *Camgirls: Celebrity and Community in the Age of Social Networks*. Peter Lang. https://www.academia.edu/205283/Camgirls_Celebrity_and_Community_in_the_Age_of_Social_Networks.

Seoane, M. F. V. (2020). Alibaba's discourse for the Digital Silk Road: The electronic World Trade Platform and 'inclusive globalization'. *Chinese Journal of Communication, 13*(1), 68–83. https://doi.org/10.1080/17544750.2019.1606838.

Shifman, L. (2013). Memes in a digital world: Reconciling with a conceptual troublemaker. *Journal of Computer-Mediated Communication, 18*(3), 362–377. https://doi.org/10.1111/jcc4.12013

Shu, C. (2020). Reddit acquires Dubsmash. *TechCrunch*, 14 December. https://techcrunch.com/2020/12/13/reddit-acquires-dubsmash/?guccounter=1.

Siddiqui, A. (2020). TikTok finally rolls out 'Reply with Video' feature! Digital Information World, 31 March. https://www.digitalinformationworld.com/2020/03/tiktok-finally-rolls-out-reply-with-video-feature.html.

Singh, M. (2020). Trump bans US transactions with Chinese-owned TikTok and WeChat. *Guardian*, 7 August. https://www.theguardian.com/technology/2020/aug/06/us-senate-tiktok-ban.

Singh, R. (2020). List of TikTok-like Chinese short video apps that are NOT banned in India. Gadgets to Use, 5 September. https://gadgetstouse.com/blog/2020/09/05/list-of-tiktok-like-chinese-short-video-apps-that-are-not-banned-in-india.

Sinnreich, A. (2010). *Mashed Up: Music, Technology, and the Rise of Configurable Culture*. University of Massachusetts Press.

Smolentceva, N. (2019). TikTok: World's most successful video app faces security concerns. Deutsche Welle, 27 March. https://www.dw.com/en/tiktok-worlds-most-successful-video-app-faces-security-concerns/a-48063869.

Smule. (2015). The solo duet: Creating harmonies when you're all by yourself. *Smule*, 13 July. https://devblog.smule.com/the-solo-duet-creating-harmonies-when-youre-all.

Sobrinho, A., & Glăveanu, V. P. (2017). Creativity, communicability and organizational culture: An introduction to the study of hierarchy as both a facilitator and constraint in organizational change. *Creativity: Theories, Research, Applications, 4*(2). https://doi.org/10.1515/ctra-2017-0010.

Soha, M., & McDowell, Z. J. (2016). Monetizing a meme: YouTube, content ID, and the Harlem Shake. *Social Media + Society*, 2(1). https://doi.org/10.1177/2056305115623801.

Southerton, C. (in press). Lip-syncing and saving lives: Healthcare workers on TikTok. *International Journal of Communication*.

Spangler, T. (2016). Musical.ly Live.ly stars earning thousands from adoring fans. Variety, 31 October. https://variety.com/2016/digital/news/musical-ly-live-ly-streaming-stars-earning-1201904864.

Spangler, T. (2018). Musical.ly is shutting down, users moved to TikTok video app. Variety, 2 August. https://variety.com/2018/digital/news/musically-shutdown-tiktok-bytedance-1202893205.

Spanos, B., Dickson, E. J., & Garber-Paul, E. (2020). The viral videos that built YouTube. *Rolling Stone*, 4 February. https://www.rollingstone.com/culture/culture-features/youtube-viral-videos-953263.

Squires, C. R. (2002). Rethinking the black public sphere: An alternative vocabulary for multiple public spheres. *Communication Theory*, 12(4), 446–468.

Stevens, W. E. (2021). Blackfishing on Instagram: Influencing and the commodification of black urban aesthetics. *Social Media + Society*, 7(3). https://doi.org/10.1177/20563051211038236.

Stokel-Walker, C. (2020a). How TikTok responds to controversy: With more educational videos. Protocol: The People, Power and Politics of Tech, 15 June. https://www.protocol.com/tiktok-education-north-america.

Stokel-Walker, C. (2020b). TikTok sweeps Britain but Norwegians watch more videos. Bloomberg, 30 September. https://www.bloomberg.com/news/articles/2020-09-30/tiktok-users-in-uk-germany-france-italy-norway-ages-screentime-open-rates.

Su, C. (2019). *Changing Dynamics of Digital Entertainment Media in China*. PhD thesis, Queensland University of Technology. https://eprints.qut.edu.au/130744.

Sunder, M. (2012). *From Goods to a Good Life: Intellectual Property and Global Justice*. Yale University Press.

Sunder, M. (2021). TikTok's bad dance moves: It's about time black creators of pop culture are paid for their art. *Los Angeles Times*, 7 July. https://www.latimes.com/opinion/story/2021-07-07/tiktok-black-creators-strike-dance-copyright.

Sweney, M. (2020). They built it, but people did not come: The cautionary tale of Quibi. *Guardian*, 23 October. http://www.theguardian.com/tv-and-radio/2020/oct/23/why-quibi-is-a-cautionary-tale-shortform-netflix.

Tabeta, S. (2018). How young Chinese are reshaping their society with virtual gifts. *Nikkei Asian Review*, 30 June. https://asia.nikkei.com/Business/Companies/How-young-Chinese-are-reshaping-their-society-with-virtual-gifts.

Tavares, G. (2019). As Chinese short video apps invade Brazil, TikTok and Kwai do battle. EqualOcean, 17 November. https://equalocean.com/analysis/2019111712212.

Taylor, M. (2019). Schoolchildren go on strike across world over climate crisis. *Guardian*, 24 May. https://www.theguardian.com/environment/2019/may/24/schoolchildren-go-on-strike-across-world-over-climate-crisis.

Thew, H., Middlemiss, L., & Paavola, J. (2020). 'Youth is not a political position': Exploring justice claims-making in the UN climate change negotiations. *Global Environmental Change, 61*, 1–10. https://doi.org/10.1016/j.gloenvcha.2020.102036.

Thomala, L. (2021). China: Number of short video users 2020. Statista, 15 February. https://www.statista.com/statistics/1005629/china-short-video-user-number.

TikTok. (2019a). TikTok democratizes eLearning with the launch of the #EduTok Program. TikTok Newsroom, 18 October. https://newsroom.tiktok.com/en-in/tik-tok-democratizes-e-learning-with-the-launch-of-the-edu-tok-program.

TikTok. (2019b). Virtual items policy. TikTok Legal, February. https://www.tiktok.com/legal/virtual-items?lang=en.

TikTok. (2019c). DIY: Duets & Reactions on TikTok. TikTok Newsroom, 22 March. https://newsroom.tiktok.com/en-gb/diy-duets-reactions-on-tiktok.

TikTok. (2019d). Introducing the TikTok for Black Creatives incubator program. TikTok Newsroom, 16 August. https://newsroom.tiktok.com/en-us/tiktok-for-black-creatives-incubator-program.

TikTok. (2019e). TikTok Creator Fund: Your questions answered. TikTok Newsroom, 16 August. https://newsroom.tiktok.com/en-gb/tiktok-creator-fund-your-questions-answered.

TikTok. (2020a). Investing to help our community #LearnOnTikTok. TikTok Newsroom. https://newsroom.tiktok.com/en-us/investing-to-help-our-community-learn-on-tiktok

TikTok. (2020b). TikTok hosts first-ever global culture LIVE marathon with iconic institutions from around the world. TikTok Newsroom. https://newsroom.tiktok.com/en-au/tiktok-hosts-first-ever-global-culture-live-marathon-with-iconic-institutions-from-around-the-world-an.

TikTok. (2020c). Adding clarity to our community guidelines.

TikTok Newsroom, 8 January. https://newsroom.tiktok.com/en-us/adding-clarity-to-our-community-guidelines.

TikTok. (2020d). Product tutorial: Reply to comments with video. TikTok Newsroom, 18 June. https://newsroom.tiktok.com/en-us/product-tutorial-reply-to-comments-with-video.

TikTok. (2020e). How TikTok recommends videos #foryou. TikTok Newsroom, 19 June. https://newsroom.tiktok.com/en-us/how-tiktok-recommends-videos-for-you.

TikTok. (2020f). New on TikTok: Introducing Stitch. TikTok Newsroom, 4 September. https://newsroom.tiktok.com/en-us/new-on-tiktok-introducing-stitch

TikTok. (2020g). Introducing TikTok for business. TikTok Newsroom, 26 October. https://newsroom.tiktok.com/en-ie/tiktok-business.

TikTok. (2020h). Year on TikTok: Music 2020. TikTok Newsroom, 16 December. https://newsroom.tiktok.com/en-us/year-on-tiktok-music-2020.

TikTok. (2021a). Creator Playlist. TikTok Help Center. https://support.tiktok.com/en/using-tiktok/creating-videos/creator-playlist.

TikTok. (2021b). *TikTok Transparency Report*. TikTok Safety, 24 February. https://www.tiktok.com/safety/resources/transparency-report-2020-2?lang=en&appLaunch=.

TikTok. (2021c). Introducing TikTok Video Editor: Easily create native video ads in your browser. TikTok Business, 2 April. https://www.tiktok.com/business/en-AU/blog/introducing-tiktok-video-editor-easily-create-native-video-ads-in-your-browser.

TikTok. (2021d). Introducing Immersive Music Creative Effects. TikTok Newsroom, 8 April. https://newsroom.tiktok.com/en-us/immersive-music-creative-effects.

TikTok. (2021e). DMA geo-targeting enabled for businesses on TikTok. TikTok Business, 4 May. https://www.tiktok.com/business/en/blog/dma-targeting-enabled-for-businesses-on-tiktok.

TikTok. (2021f). Congratulations Khaby Lame for 100M followers, bringing joy to our global community. TikTok Newsroom, 11 August. https://newsroom.tiktok.com/en-us/congratulations-khaby-lame-for-100-m-followers-bringing-joy-to-our-global-community

Tönnies, F. (1965 [1887]). Gemeinschaft und Gesellschaft. In T. Parsons, E. Shils, K.D. Naegele, & J.R. Pitts (eds.), *Theories of Society* (pp. 191–201). Free Press.

Transsnet About. (2021). Boomplay (Transsnet Music Limited) [in Chinese]. www://transsnet.com/about.

Trust, G. (2019). Lil Nas X's 'Old Town Road' leads Billboard Hot

100 for 19th week; Ariana Grande & Social House's 'Boyfriend' debuts in top 10. *Billboard*, 12 August. https://www.billboard.com/articles/business/chart-beat/8527171/lil-nas-x-old-town-road-number-one-hot-100-19-weeks.

Trust, G. (2021). Olivia Rodrigo's 'drivers license' continues record reign with 8th week atop global charts. *Billboard*. https://www.reuters.com/business/tiktok-owner-bytedances-2020-revenue-soars-net-loss-45-bln-memo-2021-06-17.

Twitter. (2021). Vine FAQs. Help Center. https://help.twitter.com/en/using-twitter/vine-faqs.

Upson, J. W., Ketchen, D. J., Connelly, B. L., & Ranft, A. L. (2012). Competitor analysis and foothold moves. *Academy of Management Journal, 55*(1), 93–110.

van Dijck, J. (2013). *The Culture of Connectivity: A Critical History of Social Media*. Oxford University Press.

van Dijck, J. (2020). Seeing the forest for the trees: Visualizing platformization and its governance. *New Media & Society*. https://doi.org/10.1177/1461444820940293.

van Dijck, J., Poell, T., & de Waal, M. (2018). *The Platform Society: Public Values in a Connective World*. Oxford University Press.

van Doorn, N. (2017). Platform labor: On the gendered and racialized exploitation of low-income service work in the 'on-demand' economy. *Information, Communication & Society, 20*(6), 898–914. https://doi.org/10.1080/1369118X.2017.1294194.

Velasquez, A., Wash, R., Lampe, C., & Bjornrud, T. (2014). Latent users in an online user-generated content community. *Computer Supported Cooperative Work (CSCW), 23*(1), 21–50. https://doi.org/10.1007/s10606-013-9188-4.

Vie, S. (2014). In defence of 'slacktivism': The Human Rights Campaign Facebook logo as digital activism. *First Monday*. https://firstmonday.org/ojs/index.php/fm/article/download/4961/3868.

Wagner, K. (2017). Flipagram, once considered a serious threat to Instagram, has been acquired by Chinese news aggregator Toutiao. Vox, 31 January. https://www.vox.com/2017/1/31/14459116/flipagram-acquisition-toutiao.

Wagner, K. (2018). 'Stories' was Instagram's smartest move yet. Vox, 8 August. https://www.vox.com/2018/8/8/17641256/instagram-stories-kevin-systrom-facebook-snapchat.

Wakabayashi, D. (2017). Inside the Hollywood home of social media's stars (don't be shy). *New York Times*, 30 December. https://www.nytimes.com/2017/12/30/business/hollywood-apartment-social-media.html.

Waldron, J. (2012). Conceptual frameworks, theoretical models and the role of YouTube: Investigating informal music learning and teaching in online music community. *Journal of Music, Technology and Education, 4*(2), 189–200. https://doi.org/10.1386/jmte.4.2-3.189_1.

Walmart. (2021). Walmart doubles down on TikTok shopping, hosts all-new live stream shopping event. Walmart. https://corporate.walmart.com/newsroom/2021/03/09/walmart-doubles-down-on-tiktok-shopping-hosts-all-new-live-stream-shopping-event.

Wang, E., Wu, K., & Zhu, J. (2020). Exclusive: ByteDance investors value TikTok at $50 billion in takeover bid: Sources. Reuters, 29 July. https://www.reuters.com/article/us-bytedance-tiktok-exclusive-idUSKCN24U1M9.

Wang, F. (2016). 揭秘网络直播平台监管小组: 女主播穿吊带就算违规 [The secret moderation team for live-streaming platforms: Wearing camisole is considered a violation]. *People's Daily Online*, 5 May. media.people.com.cn/n1/2016/0505/c40606-28325930.html.

Wang, W. (2021). 接到举报线索 900 余条! 全国"扫黄打非"办通报"抖音"平台被行政处罚 [More than 900 reports received: The Office of the National Work Group for Combating Pornography and Illegal Publications informed that Douyin received administrative punishment]. Xinhua News, 8 January. http://www.xinhuanet.com/legal/2021-01/08/c_1126960251.htm.

Wang, W., & Wu, J. (2021). Short video platforms and local community building in China. *International Journal of Communication, 15*, 1–32.

Wang, W. Y., & Lobato, R. (2019). Chinese video streaming services in the context of global platform studies. *Chinese Journal of Communication, 12*(3), 356–371. https://doi.org/10.1080/17544750.2019.1584119.

Ward, T. (2020). The Hype House is changing the face of TikTok. *Forbes*, 24 February. https://www.forbes.com/sites/tomward/2020/02/24/the-hype-house-is-changing-the-face-of-tiktok.

Weir, M. (2020). How to duet on TikTok and record a video alongside someone else's. Business Insider, 29 December. https://www.businessinsider.com/how-to-duet-on-tiktok.

Weiss, G. (2021). TikTok test will let creators pay to promote their own videos on the 'For You page'. Tubefilter, 11 May. https://www.tubefilter.com/2021/05/11/tiktok-test-creators-pay-to-promote-on-fyp.

Wells, G., Li, S., & Lin, L. (2020). TikTok, once an oasis of inoffensive fun, ventures warily into politics. *Wall Street Journal*, 8 July. https://www.wsj.com/articles/tiktok-ventures-warily-into-politicsand-finds-complications-11594224268.

Wen, M. (2020). 短视频、 直播带货已成新经济形态 [Short videos and live commerce have become the new economy]. *National Business Daily*, 11 September. http://www.nbd.com.cn/ articles/2020-09-11/1503212.html.

Whateley, D. (2020). How much money brands will pay for a TikTok sponsored video compared to YouTube, according to an influencer agency. *Business Insider*. https://www.businessinsider. com/influencer-marketing-cost-per-view-on-tiktok-compared-to-youtube-2020-1.

Whateley, D. (2021). Snapchat won't pay $1 million per day to creators anymore but says it will still dish out 'millions per week'. *Business Insider*, 22 May. https://www.businessinsider.com/snapchat-ends-spotlight-paydays-still-paying-creators-millions-2021-5.

Wikström, P. (2012). A typology of music distribution models. *International Journal of Music Business Research, 1*(1), 7–20.

Wikström, P. (2013). The music industry in an age of digital distribution. In C. Gandarias & L. Estévez (eds.), *Change: 19 Key Essays on How the Internet is Changing Our Lives* (pp. 423–444). Turner.

Wikström, P. (2020). *The Music Industry: Music in the Cloud* (3rd edn). Polity.

Wilken, R. (2018). Social media app economies. In J. Burgess, A. Marwick, & T. Poell (eds.), *The SAGE Handbook of Social Media* (pp. 279–296). SAGE. https://doi.org/10.4135/9781473984066.n16.

Willson, M. (2016). Algorithms (and the) everyday. *Information, Communication & Society, 20*(1), 137–150. https://doi.org/10.1080/1 369118X.2016.1200645.

Winkie, L. (2015). The life and death of the flash cartoon. *Vice*, 17 October. https://www.vice.com/en/article/ppxm3b/the-life-and-death-of-the-flash-cartoon-456.

Wongkitrungrueng, A., & Assarut, N. (2018). The role of live streaming in building consumer trust and engagement with social commerce sellers. *Journal of Business Research, 17*, 543–556. https:// doi.org/10.1016/j.jbusres.2018.08.032.

Xin, Z., & Feng, C. (2021). ByteDance value approaches US$400 billion as it explores Douyin IPO. *South China Morning Post*, 1 April. https://www.scmp.com/tech/big-tech/article/3128002/value-tiktok-maker-bytedance-approaches-us400-billion-new-investors.

Xin, Z., & Qu, T. (2020). TikTok's algorithm not for sale, ByteDance tells US: Source. *South China Morning Post*, 13 September. https:// www.scmp.com/economy/china-economy/article/3101362/ tiktoks-algorithm-not-sale-bytedance-tells-us-source.

Xinhua. (2018). 抖音推出"政务媒体号成长计划" 联手政府媒体机构

打造正能量传播爆款 [Partnering with government media organizations, Douyin launches Growth Plan for Governmental Accounts to promote trends of positive energy]. Xinhua News, 31 August. www.xinhuanet.com/2018-08/31/c_1123362189.htm.

Xinhua. (2020). China focus: China tightens regulations on livestreaming e-commerce. Xinhua, 16 December. http://www.xinhuanet.com/english/2020-12/16/c_139594812.htm.

Yang, J., & Wang, T. (2020). ByteDance, an algorithm-backed firm with globalization ambitions. China Global Television Network, 8 August. https://news.cgtn.com/news/2020-08-08/ByteDance-an-algorithm-backed-firm-with-globalization-ambitions--SNbGeeFopq/index.html.

Yang, Y. (2020). 农民直播带货大有可为 [Farmers' live commerce holds great promise]. Xinhua News, 23 September. http://www.xinhuanet.com/comments/2020-09/23/c_1126528328.htm.

Yang, Y., & Goh, B. (2020). TikTok owner ByteDance shuts down overseas news aggregator TopBuzz. Reuters, 5 June. https://www.reuters.com/article/us-china-bytedance-idUSKBN23C0SC.

Yeung, E. (2019). China internet report 2019. *South China Morning Post.* https://research.scmp.com/products/china-internet-report-2020.

Young, J. O. (2008). *Cultural Appropriation and the Arts.* Blackwell.

YouTube. (2021). Overview of copyright management tools. YouTube Help. https://support.google.com/youtube/answer/9245819?hl=en&ref_topic=9282364.

Yu, P. (2006). TRIPS and its discontents. *Marquette Intellectual Property Law Review, 10*(2), 369–410. https://scholarship.law.marquette.edu/iplr/vol10/iss2/7.

Zarsky, T. (2016). The trouble with algorithmic decisions: An analytic road map to examine efficiency and fairness in automated and opaque decision making. *Science, Technology and Human Values, 41*(1), 118–132.

Zellner, X. (2020). Fleetwood Mac's 'Dreams' charts on Hot 100 for first time since 1977, thanks to TikTok revival. *Billboard,* 13 October. https://www.billboard.com/articles/business/chart-beat/9464533/fleetwood-mac-dreams-returns-hot-100.

Zellner, X. (2021). Olivia Rodrigo charts all *Sour* songs in Hot 100's top 30. *Billboard,* 1 June. https://www.billboard.com/articles/business/chart-beat/9580721/olivia-rodrigo-all-sour-songs-hot-100-top-30.

Zeng, J. (2020). 'Smart is the nü (boshi) sexy': How China's PhD women are fighting stereotypes using social media. In K. Warfield,

C. Abidin, & C. Cambre (eds.), *Mediated Interfaces: The Body on Social Media* (pp. 157–174). Bloomsbury.

Zeng, J., & Abidin, C. (2021). '#OkBoomer, time to meet the Zoomers': Studying the memefication of intergenerational politics on TikTok. *Information Communication and Society*, 24(16), 2459–2481.

Zeng, J., Abidin, C., & Schäfer, M. S. (2021). Research perspectives on TikTok and its legacy apps. *International Journal of Communication*, 15, 3161–3172.

Zhang, X., Wu, Y., & Liu, S. (2019). Exploring short-form video application addiction: Socio-technical and attachment perspectives. *Telematics and Informatics*, 42, 101243. https://doi.org/10.1016/j.tele.2019.101243.

Zhang, Z. (2021). Infrastructuralization of Tik Tok: Transformation, power relationships, and platformization of video entertainment in China. *Media, Culture & Society*, 43(2), 219–236. https://doi.org/10.1177/0163443720939452.

Zhao, Y. (2021). 短视频平台竞相开拓消费新场景 [Short video platforms compete to develop new consumption scenarios]. *Beijing Daily*, 9 April http://finance.people.com.cn/n1/2021/0409/c1004-32073629.html.

Zhong, R., & Frenkel, S. (2020). Third of TikTok's US users may be 14 or under, raising safety questions. *New York Times*, 19 September. https://www.nytimes.com/2020/08/14/technology/tiktok-underage-users-ftc.html.

Zhou, X. (2020). 抖音电商：撑起字节千亿营收的第二曲线 [Douyin e-commerce: Crucial contributor to ByteDance's 100-billion revenue]. The Paper, 28 April. https://www.thepaper.cn/newsDetail_forward_7177479.

Zhu, J. Y., & Yang, Y. (2020). Exclusive: TikTok-owner ByteDance to rake in $27 billion ad revenue by year-end: Sources. Reuters. https://www.reuters.com/article/china-bytedance-revenue-idUSKBN27R191.

Zulli, D., & Zulli, D. J. (2020). Extending the internet meme: Conceptualizing technological mimesis and imitation publics on the TikTok platform. *New Media & Society*, 146144482098360. https://doi.org/10.1177/1461444820983603.

Index